Guitar Towns

Guitar Towns

A Journey to the Crossroads of Rock 'n' Roll

Randy McNutt

INDIANA

University Press

Bloomington & Indianapolis

This book is a publication of

Indiana University Press
601 North Morton Street
Bloomington, IN 47404-3797 USA

http://iupress.indiana.edu

Telephone orders 800-842-6796
Fax orders 812-855-7931
Orders by e-mail iuporder@indiana.edu

Library of Congress Cataloging-in-Publication Data

McNutt, Randy.
    Guitar towns : a journey to the crossroads of rock 'n' roll / Randy
McNutt.
        p. cm.
    "Selected hits from regional music towns": p.
    Includes bibliographical references (p.   ) and index.
    ISBN 0-253-34058-6 (alk. paper)
    1. Popular music—United States—History and criticism.   I. Title.
ML3477 .M42 2002
781.64'0973—dc21
                                    2001005663

1 2 3 4 5   07 06 05 04 03 02

To Robyn McNutt Beck
my sister and original singing partner

The door to the past is a strange door. It swings open and things pass through it, but they pass in one direction only. No man can return across that threshold, though he can look down still and see the green light waver in the water weeds.

—Loren Eiseley

CONTENTS

ACKNOWLEDGMENTS

Without the patience and help of many good people, this book would not exist. Foremost is Susan Havlish, the sales and marketing chief at Indiana University Press. She believed in the idea of an offbeat music travel narrative and made it come to life. Thank you, Sue, for your efforts and encouragement.

I also thank my editor, Jane Lyle, for her good work on my manuscript, former editor Jeff Ankrom for his, and Rick Kennedy for his advice.

Many other people contributed in different ways, and I owe them all my gratitude. Unfortunately, some of the music people have died, including Johnny Vincent of Jackson, Mississippi, and Marcus Van Story of Memphis. Both were American music icons in their own ways, and they are missed.

During the years that I traveled and talked about writing this book, I received wise counsel and encouragement from others. They include: Jim Wilson, my professor and friend, who first interested me in the travel narrative at the University of Cincinnati in 1990; Allen Reynolds, the Nashville producer and songwriter who supported the concept of this book; Rusty York, the Cincinnati studio owner and guitarist who has been a part of the regional music scene for decades; producer Shad O'Shea, who has placed two hundred masters and lived the regional dream; Cosimo Matassa, the New Orleans recording wizard who so graciously allowed me to pester him about the old days; writer and editor John Baskin, who for some reason took the time to show me the way in 1981 and has never stopped helping me; and John Eckberg and Dick Swaim, who read parts of the manuscript and urged me to tell them more. Their support came at a good time.

Also I thank my wife, writer Cheryl Bauer, for her patience. She edited the book as I was writing it over the years, traveled with me often, and never complained (well, except for the time in Muscle Shoals when the temperature was 100 degrees and she was hungry and tired). And then there's my friend Wayne Perry, the busy songwriter who went along sometimes and always remained fascinated with reliving the day of America's regional music system.

Guitar Towns

Hamilton, Ohio: Driving the Blues

One sleepless night, I turned on the radio and heard "Cry Like a Baby" by the Box Tops. It was like hearing the song for the first time. I couldn't get it out of my mind over the next few weeks, and I grew hungry for other songs from my past. They reminded me of the years when I produced records in Cincinnati with Wayne Perry, now a writer for the Backstreet Boys, Tim McGraw, Lorrie Morgan, and other major acts, and the late Herman Griffin, a singer who once recorded with Berry Gordy Jr. and married Mary Wells.

Wayne and I grew up in Hamilton, Ohio, twenty-five miles northwest of Cincinnati, once an important recording capital. I met him at the Mosler Safe Company in our factory town, home to 60,000 people and a musical melting pot of southwestern Ohio. We landed at Mosler briefly after high school, but our hearts were in music. While he sang blue-eyed soul four nights a week at a place called the Half Way Inn, I searched other clubs for rock groups to produce. When they turned me down, I turned to Wayne. We'd escape from dreary factory-office jobs by daydreaming about songs. When the boss was away, Wayne would burst into my little office to write a melody to my lyric. He didn't even have a guitar. Tough factory workers walked by and shook their heads as Wayne sang, "Come on baby, give me the green light, turnin' me on and on." After work, we'd go to his parents' house to write songs on a dilapidated upright piano that his father had dragged home. Musically, we were soul mates; physically, polar opposites. He stood no taller than five feet, six inches, compared with my six feet, and unlike me, he exuded the confidence of a hungry lion. He did everything in a hurry. We worked for a lovable curmudgeon who addressed us both as "young man" and disliked our obsession with records. We looked sixteen. I wore button-down shirts and chinos, Wayne hip white nylon shirts with navy blue polka dots and tight-fitting jeans with gold embroidery on the cuffs. As we worked, he'd suddenly sing the hook line of a current hit, or inexplicably shout, "Hey, all right!" as he walked around the office, his arms swaying like a tin windup toy's.

At lunch we'd rush to Hyde's Drive-In for some Big Bob burgers and the latest sounds on WSAI, Cincinnati's 50,000-watt Top 40 station (AM, of course). For an hour we'd exhaust our ideas and my Karmann Ghia's weak battery, until we had to sneak back into the factory through a side door. But the risk was worth the trouble, for we now had exciting possibilities—writing and recording. We hero-worshipped guys like songwriter Dan Penn and producer Chips Moman from Memphis, and any other independents who earned a living by making records and writing songs in towns like ours. We were fascinated by regional studios that had built reputations for their cities and created many hits.

As I played our old tapes on that restless night, I realized that Wayne and I were once tiny pieces in a large mosaic called the regional music system. From the 1940s to the 1970s, its music centers employed thousands of people, nurtured top studio bands, and became the hometowns of America's greatest hits. As post-war good times began to roll, self-contained music cities accommodated the growing demand for blues, hillbilly, and rock 'n' roll discs. From Chicago to Philadelphia to Atlanta, the hits rang out. The unorganized system operated like a loose coalition of independent countries fighting the superpowers. They also developed their own arrangers, recording engineers, songwriters, music publishers, distributors, jukebox operators, pressing plants, and cooperative radio stations that played pop, rock, country, jazz, and R&B. In retrospect, it is amazing that so many regional cities could capture parts of the national market, but they were like stubborn brush fires breaking out spontaneously. When one cooled, another took its place, until eventually they burned themselves out. Although nowadays a hit might emerge from a regional city, the music is usually made with electronic instruments and a homogeneous production.

Still sleepless at dawn, I decided to find our roots and celebrate the era when hometown labels could launch national hits and compete with the major companies. It would be a journey to celebrate America as well as its music. Regardless of racial and cultural origins, a good song was always appreciated in the heyday of the regional center. Black singers recorded songs by white writers, and white singers cut songs by black writers. Country acts recorded R&B songs, and R&B acts picked up country songs. Everyone drew from the well of great American talent.

I went looking for our musical past in all the right places. Of course, I hit the mega-icons: New Orleans, Memphis, Muscle Shoals. But I also found some small, overlooked music centers and their pioneers as I roamed the back roads. Soon I was staying out two days to two weeks on musical vacations. Over the years, I saw studios turn into flower shops and temporary-job agencies, and nightclubs become pet stores and flea markets. I felt like an archaeologist digging into layers of vinyl and shellac as I rediscovered the nation's lost songs and, perhaps, my youth. At the newspaper where I worked, co-workers joked about my mission. Each summer they discussed vacations in exotic places. I said, "You should try Muscle Shoals, Alabama." They thought I was joking. My destinations matched personal tastes in America's roots music, history, popular culture, and rural and Southern heritage. When I told friends I had driven fifty miles out of my way just to see the studio where Elvis Presley recorded "Good Rockin' Tonight," they looked at me strangely but admitted that they'd like to see it too. So I traveled far to find the people who made the music, before time flooded them out. I didn't always seek the most famous names. I met journeymen performers whose collective efforts built reputations for their communities and musical styles.

Each spring my itch for sonic Americana worsened with the tree pollen. I navigated with two dozen old and new state and local maps, which I stored in a nylon briefcase on my back seat. Right away, I realized that I couldn't visit every music center. So I limited my journeys to areas with strong roots-music ties. I preferred the Soul Zone, a musical hothouse stretching from Cincinnati to the Gulf of Mexico, and an area that wielded a disproportionate influence on American music for decades. Amazingly, Southern music teams, often consisting of blacks and whites, made high-quality records as their cities churned with racial conflict. Preferring Dixie roadhouses that still echoed with Jerry Lee Lewis' thumping piano, I headed into the spiritual home of rock 'n' roll and my favorite Civil War battle sites. Torrid heat and humidity became my seasonal releases. Wherever I went, I found seminal record companies and studios, forgotten songwriters and producers, and performers whose better records remind me of ancient monuments— vaguely familiar to millions, yet created by a long-dead race.

As a teenager in the mid-1960s, I'd sit in a worn and overstuffed orange rocker and endlessly play the new 45s that I bought at Imfeld Record Shop, a small independent not far from home. Soon columns of sleeveless 45s grew in my bedroom, forming black pillars halfway to the ceiling. My mother cringed. In college, I'd run to a newsstand to buy the latest *Billboard* for two brief columns: "Action Records," featuring the regional breakouts, and "From the Music Capitals of the World." A regional breakout was an unheralded disc discovered by a metropolitan radio market where programmers dared to take chances on new records. Bored out of my mind in accounting, I'd imagine those cities. Imagine I could play guitar. Discreetly I'd turn to the news from the music capitals—from Madrid to Cincinnati. Only in this newsy column could I read that Penn, the enigmatic white soul singer who co-wrote James and Bobby Purify's "I'm Your Puppet" and Aretha Franklin's "Do Right Woman—Do Right Man," had turned to producing records in Memphis with "The Letter" by the Box Tops. Months later, in August 1967, I watched the charts each week as the record climbed to No. 1. Someday, I vowed, I'd see my name in that column, visit Memphis, and maybe even meet Dan Penn.

By then, I had been hanging around recording studios, learning the tricks of the console from a few scruffy independent producers who befriended me. Today their kind has been decimated by the good gray bureaucrats of the corporate record industry. I recall Herman Griffin most vividly. The short, wiry black man—in his mid-thirties by then, but looking a decade older—started performing songs and acrobatics in Detroit clubs, where Berry Gordy Jr. discovered him. Herman became Gordy's first artist, before Motown Records was formed. Despite his stature, Herman spoke in a surprisingly deep voice (probably because he smoked so often) and punctuated every other sentence with the word "dig." "You dig, my man?" Once he arrived at a session with two women draped in fur boas, carrying a portable television and a bottle of gin. When I asked what the TV was for, he replied, "Dig, my man, the World Series is on tonight!" He turned on the TV in the control room—during our session.

What I liked most about my producer friends was the romantic uncertainty of their lives. They were always on the verge of something—a big hit, earning the big money, buying a Cadillac, getting a divorce. They discovered all kinds of local talent, recorded and leased master tapes to independent and major labels, and used their precious up-front money (advances from larger labels ran from $500 to $2,000 for a single then) to pay for their next session. They advised me freely: "Kid, always mix a song with tiny speakers so you'll know how it will sound on a car radio"; "Hide your money inside your socks when you're on the road"; "*Never* trust a record distributor." Good advice, but what impressed me most was my new friends' clout. A producer from Podunk, Ohio, could discover a ragtag band, record it in a tinny studio for a few hundred dollars, then haggle personally with a New York City record mogul.

Wayne and I did it. In 1970, we assembled our own studio rhythm band in Cincinnati and started traveling to Nashville, New York, and other cities to mix tapes, pitch our songs, and search for some elusive dream.

Years later, our adventures played in my mind as I followed roads once taken by our musical ancestors. I traced them, genealogically and geographically, until I felt I knew them. Usually I bypassed the interstates in favor of local roads. Once marked in blue on highway maps, they became known as blue highways. I call them the Blues. In the 1950s they supported thousands of privately owned restaurants, roller rinks, juke joints, dance halls, small-town theaters, and roadhouses. When performers could find no larger places to play, they traveled to small establishments on America's back roads. Musicians often drove hundreds of miles a day, performed for a few hours, then resumed traveling the next day. They were locked in a perpetual excursion.

At times I felt their hot riffs jangle faintly across my front bumper. I glimpsed the past, present, and future of American music from a used four-wheel-drive Eagle, made by American Motors, another defunct independent. I preferred to travel in a red civilian Hummer until I saw its $80,000 sticker price. So on many trips I settled for the old hatchback Eagle, which provided the traction of a Jeep and the comfort of a car. My mechanic retrofitted it with some high-tech parts and bolstered its suspension to meet the rigors of the lonesome highway. Eight years later, Red Eagle sported a dented rusty fender, a flame-spewing carburetor, and 160,000 miles on the odometer. By then it looked like a tank that had just emerged from battle. But it carried me unfailingly from the Ohio to the Mississippi and into small back-river country.

Sometimes I arrived to find that the local record industry had vanished decades ago, so I looked for the place where country meets the blues. Sometimes I found the legends still making music, and young performers trying to find a national voice. Often I traveled alone, sometimes with my wife, Cheryl, or with Wayne Perry. I didn't mind driving fifty miles to see historical markers and museums, or to search for old 45s. Hours shot past like bullets as I defined music with a strong sense of place. My writing froze each man, woman, and town in their own times, like snapshots saved in a memory box.

If on the road I found a rare soul or rockabilly band in a roadhouse, I would yell, "That's all right, mama!" If I found no bands and nothing interesting on the radio, I would play an audio cassette that I'd made from old records and remember my father, Bill McNutt, and the songs he sang on our front-porch swing. An instrumental, "Driving the Blues" by King saxophonist Tab Smith, blared in the hollows and bayous as I searched for musical artifacts. Wind at my back and volume turned loud, I set out to enjoy the glory of the American groove.

New Orleans: Sea Cruise

With the stereo blaring "Sea Cruise" and our hair blowing wildly, I drove toward New Orleans, the epicenter of early R&B. The gulf air felt damp and balmy, mingling the scents of crepe myrtle and fish. Suddenly Fort Pike appeared on a lowland, twenty-three miles east of the city. The nineteenth-century outpost, shaped like home plate and made of crusty brick, was part of the nation's early coastal defense system. Cheryl, my navigator, suggested that we stop to rest and see the state commemorative park. But after walking around the grounds for no more than ten minutes, I noticed red spots breaking out all over my bare legs—blood. "We do have a little mosquito problem," a ranger confided. "They always choose one person to attack." Fifteen minutes later, I was itching uncontrollably. We checked into the nearest motel, an attractive but musty place with a roach smashed on a bathroom wall. I turned the rickety air-conditioner on high, watched too many *I Love Lucy* episodes, and stayed in for the night. Every two hours, Cheryl placed an ice pack on my welts; at 2 A.M. she counted 102 bites on my raw legs.

Thanks to a handy tube of hydrocortisone cream, we set out later that morning to find the *old* New Orleans. It has intrigued me since childhood, when I watched the detective series *Bourbon Street Beat*. A few televised seconds of Mardi Gras, unusual architecture, lush gardens, and unfamiliar music convinced me that the city existed in some other time and country. To an Ohio boy, New Orleans looked downright otherworldly.

I wasn't disappointed in the real thing. Old Spanish colonial buildings looked like something carved from white and gray bone, and the skyline glistened in the early-morning fog like tiny Christmas lights. I tried to imagine the day when urban New Orleans meant party-time clubs—hundreds of them—from the French Quarter to the parishes. Some people come here to drink, eat, and unwind. I came looking for the time when Chris Kenner recorded the original "Land of 1000 Dances" and musicians worked day and night.

From 1948 to 1963, the city was a musical boom town. Independent labels allied themselves with radio stations to launch records that are still played today. Colorful performers used to wander into the city's only good

Minit Records of New Orleans took Ernie K-Doe's "Mother-in-Law" to No. 1 on the *Billboard* pop charts in 1961.

Robert Parker's "Barefootin'," another New Orleans creation, became a No. 7 *Billboard* pop record on the NOLA (New Orleans, Louisiana) label in 1966.

In 1959, Frankie Ford's "Sea Cruise" entered the Top 15 on the national pop charts and helped solidify Ace Records as a hot independent.

Singer-musician Dr. John—Mac Rebennack—is a New Orleans institution.

Fats Domino, a New Orleans pianist and vocalist, recorded the title track to *The Big Beat*, a 1959 teenage film.

Clarence "Frogman" Henry's first hit, "Ain't Got No Home," was introduced to a new generation of listeners in the 1990s by an unlikely source—conservative radio voice Rush Limbaugh. The record, made in New Orleans, originally hit in late 1956.

Disc jockey Shad O'Shea worked at WNOE in New Orleans in the late 1950s and eventually settled in Cincinnati, where he became a DJ and record producer. He is still active there as the owner of Fraternity Records.

Pioneer recording engineer Cosimo Matassa personally recorded most of New Orleans' hits. Photo by Randy McNutt.

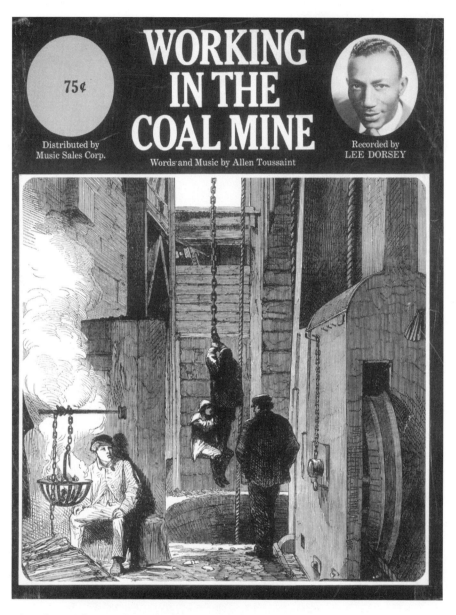

Talented New Orleans producer Allen Toussaint produced and wrote
Lee Dorsey's 1966 pop hit "Working in the Coal Mine."

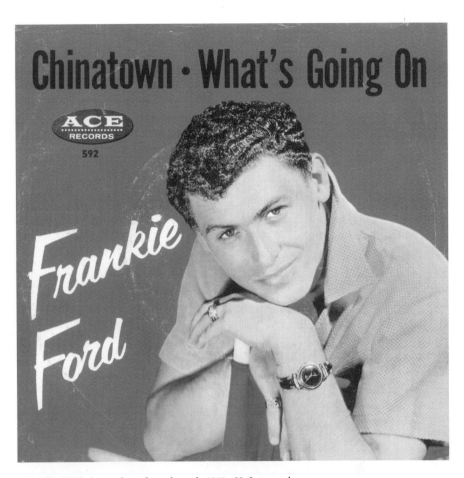

A Frankie Ford picture sleeve from the early 1960s. Unfortunately, none of his other single releases could match the popularity of "Sea Cruise."

Fats Domino recorded his early hits in New Orleans, his hometown.

recording studio and ask engineer Cosimo Matassa to make a record. Months later, with some luck, their names would burst across the Gulf Coast like flash floods.

"Radio airwaves practically exploded in New Orleans in the 1950s," recalled Shad O'Shea, a disc jockey at WNOE from 1958 to 1960. "Man, we'd draw unbelievable ratings of thirty-six to forty-five percent, and give away $10,000 in one contest—enough to buy a house. Memorable characters on the local music scene hung out at our station, but we didn't treat them like stars. To us, they were just a bunch of guys who'd gotten lucky."

People of various races and cultures appreciated the records made in New Orleans, because studio musicians provided original, evocative licks. This broadened interest in R&B and helped accelerate its fast evolution into rock 'n' roll. By the mid-1950s, New Orleans musicians had already played on dozens of national hits, including Little Richard's "Tutti-Frutti," Lloyd Price's "Lawdy Miss Clawdy," and Antoine "Fats" Domino's "I'm in Love Again."

Then, as easily as they'd come, the hits stopped, and the industry's boom times moved elsewhere. Even the number of gigs declined. Musicians still feel the effects. Though a couple of small independent labels turn out good music, they can't reach a wide audience the way local independents did in the early 1960s. Radio no longer cooperates. Yet New Orleans will always be known as an incubator of American music—jazz in the early 1900s, R&B in the 1950s, funk in the 1970s, rap in the 1990s.

Early that night we went looking for a club—a cool one. We drove out Tulane Avenue, drifted around, and found the Fountain Bay Club Hotel. A sign in front read: "In the Racquets Club Tonight—Mr. Frankie Ford." I told Cheryl that he had to be *the* Frankie Ford, the one who sang "Sea Cruise" in 1959, but all she could remember was Johnny Rivers' minor hit in 1971. Ford's version is definitive, and my favorite New Orleans record. In 1958 he joined another seventeen-year-old singer, Jimmy Clanton, as a label mate on Ace Records in Jackson, Mississippi. The handsome boys combed their hair straight back and recorded at Cosimo's, but the similarities ended there. Clanton, a Baton Rouge native, became Ace's major artist, while Ford battled to be heard. The young singer enjoyed a brief, wild ride, and then it was over. Of Ford's three chart records on Ace, only "Sea Cruise" was a national hit, peaking at No. 14 on the *Billboard* pop chart. But back home in New Orleans, he has remained a nightclub king for years.

We saw him on a Monday night, a big green ring on his finger and every brown hair in place. Contemporary pop songs for a dozen preoccupied people in the bar—just Frankie Ford and a grand piano. After he finished a set, including his hit, I mentioned to him that "Sea Cruise" was a memorable record of my childhood because of its foghorn and bell. (Actually, the horn came from a transcription disc.) Every time I hear his record, I'm amazed by its booming, clear sound. To me it represents the good-time ambience of New Orleans, soulful music, and the wonders of electronic-tube recording.

To Ford, born Frank Guzzo in suburban Gretna, Louisiana, the record will always mean a job. He started singing professionally as a child, when liquor laws weren't enforced stringently, and he refined his act in local clubs by observing black performers. "I wanted to sing so badly that I graduated from high school at sixteen," he said. "One night in a club, a record distributor named Joe Caronna came up to me and said, 'Want to make a record?' I said, 'Sure, who doesn't?' He said he'd call me. About a month later, he did. He wanted me to come down to Cosimo's that day because the owner of Ace Records was in town. Joe asked if I had any material to record. So I went over and cut a song I'd written called 'Cheatin' Woman.' All in one day I got a new record and a new name—Frankie Ford."

At seventeen, he joined Huey "Piano" Smith and the Clowns as a vocalist. The veteran black band had already cut Smith's original "Sea Cruise," using the group's vocalist, Bobby Marchan. Vincent overdubbed Ford's voice, and Ace released the disc under his name in late 1958. "It laid around for seven months before it hit the national charts in 1959," Ford said. "Dick Clark picked up on it, and that was all my record needed. You can't label it anything but rock 'n' roll. It was not the bubblegum music of its era, yet it entertained. As it received more airplay, I went on the road. I was one of the more polished acts. Some performers could sing only two songs during the transition between early rock and the Beatles. Everything was turned inside out, and nobody knew where the business was going. This actually helped me slip in on a small, independent label. Most disc jockeys assumed I was black. Of course, I was no stranger to playing with black musicians. When I showed up in Philadelphia to sing at a theater, the promoter said, 'Oh, man, you're white!' I said, 'Yeah, well, nobody's perfect.' Fortunately he let me rehearse, and he liked me enough to let me go on stage. I was a hit with the audience, who didn't care if I was white. It's incredible that one song has made such an impact on my life, but it has helped me work all this time. Obviously I can do other things, but the hit is what a lot of people come to hear, and that's what is important. Today my act is middle of the road; my crowd is an older crowd. A lot of artists have recorded 'Sea Cruise' since my record came out, including Johnny Rivers, but nobody has taken it away from me yet."

Ford impressed me as a friendly, dedicated musician who long ago exchanged the demands of the road for the thrill of singing in a hotel in his hometown. He can't see himself retiring, but he will reduce his workload as he ages. "I'll take life as it comes," he said. "I can do what I'm doing and feel good about picking up my pay at the end of the week. I'm in a position where I can pick and choose. I know I'll be performing, health permitting, as long as I want. A lot of people who I knew back then have had to enter other ends of the music industry to earn a living, but I've been able to perform steadily. I don't tire of singing. In the late 1970s I even appeared in a movie, *American Hot Wax*. A producer called me and asked, 'Do you still have your teeth?' I said yes. 'What about your hair?' Yes. So he cast me as myself. When the movie came out, *Time* wrote something like: 'Frankie Ford singing "'Sea Cruise,'" Chuck Berry singing "'Maybellene,'" and Jerry Lee Lewis doing "'Great Balls of Fire'" couldn't save *American Hot Wax*.' On the next page, the magazine panned Elizabeth Taylor in *A Little Night Music*. I never thought I'd have anything in common with Elizabeth Taylor."

Old New Orleans reminds me of an art film—quirky characters, exotic locations, twisting plots. My favorite story involves Lee Dorsey, who later sang "Working in the Coal Mine." Before his hits in the 1960s, he worked in a body shop owned by disc jockey Ernie the Whip. One day, while Dorsey was singing under a car, independent producer Reynauld Richard arrived to pick up his car. He heard Dorsey and yelled, "Hey, you wanna make a record?"

The whole city operated with flair and nonchalance. Legendary pianists Professor Longhair and James Booker played in small clubs, and R&B disc jockeys Poppa Stoppa (Clarence Hayman), Dr. Daddy-O (Vernon Winslow), and Jack the Cat (Ken Elliot) played new records hot off the presses. Jack the Cat appeared at hundreds of record hops with his wife, Jacqueline, who called herself Jackie the Kitten. Promoters remember the days when Hayman, in the ultimate test of regional loyalty, would take a new disc out of their hands and slap it onto a turntable—many times without first auditioning it. He wasn't guessing completely, for he knew all the local performers. He even nicknamed Clarence Henry the "Frogman" (because of his deep voice) and was the first to play Frogman's first hit, "Ain't Got No Home," on Argo Records.

In those days, Specialty, Imperial, DeLuxe, and other independents either maintained offices in New Orleans or hired local talent scouts, long before the majors caught on to the action. Imperial, of Los Angeles, turned pianist Fats Domino into an international star. Unlike Little Richard, Fats was sexually benign. Whites loved his laid-back style, a mixture of Dixieland, pop, and blues. I played "Blueberry Hill" so often as a boy that the disc wore smooth. My father sang it at home. Fats recorded under the direction of Dave Bartholomew, an urbane bandleader and trumpeter who grew up in Edgard, Louisiana. In 1949, Bartholomew, adapting music straight from the streets, become the first producer to turn out national hits from New Orleans, using simple, catchy arrangements that sold millions of records. The hits continued with Tommy Ridgley, Jewel King ("3 x 7 = 21"), and Shirley and Lee.

Bartholomew and later Allen Toussaint introduced their city's rich music to the pop world and defined the roles of record producer and arranger. As a result, both men have been inducted into the Rock 'n' Roll Hall of Fame. I respect their loyalty as much as their music. They could have become major music figures in Los Angeles and New York, but chose to live and work in New Orleans.

Toussaint started playing in local nightclubs at age thirteen and soon became a session musician at Matassa's J&M Recording Studio. Because I grew up on Toussaint's records, I had to see where he worked. This turned out to be a middle-class neighborhood called Gentilly, home of his Sea-Saint Recording Studios. Toussaint's reputation, not the studio, attracted the Meters, Paul McCartney, and the Rolling Stones in the early 1970s. Toussaint's eclectic material ranged from the instrumental "Java" by Al Hirt to "Ooh Poo Pah Doo" by Jesse Hill, "I Like It Like That" by Chris Kenner, and "Fortune Teller" by Benny Spellman. As the years passed, Toussaint became the remake king. Somebody recorded his songs again every few years, reintroducing him to a younger audience. Glen Campbell recorded "Southern Nights." Devo did "Working in the Coal Mine." The Stones tried "Fortune Teller."

Obviously, my interest in New Orleans music runs exclusively to the R&B side—records with that loose and funky party sound in their grooves. Though few musicians and singers got rich in New Orleans back then, they lived the way they wanted. They could work constantly: nightclubs lined the streets, and musicians played in shifts. The whole city was one big party. "When the strippers went off stage at 3:30 A.M.," Freddy Fender told a writer for *Blue Suede News*, "we went on. We played until noon. Sometimes we'd get a gig at night, sixty miles from New Orleans. We'd drive for hours, and play for forty-five minutes."

Local music evolved from the songs of *La Nouvelle Orleans*, founded in 1718 on a bog between the Mississippi and massive Lake Pontchartrain. The town was no place to sing about then. Two hundred settlers lived in little bug-infested houses and cypress huts. They say that life was so tough that settlers had to make music to keep from crying. When they asked the king of France for wives, he sent prostitutes from Salpetriere prison. As it grew slowly, the city brimmed with French, Spanish, blacks, a variety of white Americans, and people of mixed ancestry. Musically, they influenced and annoyed one another for years. When Louisiana entered the Union in 1812, city officials enacted new laws to stop citizens from banging on drums, blowing horns, and singing in coffeehouses after 10 P.M. Legislation didn't help much. "It is a noticeable fact," a local newspaper editor observed, "that whenever the organ grinder vanishes away an epidemic is pretty sure to fill his place."

By the 1890s, two epidemics had hit New Orleans: yellow fever and ragtime. Local pianists—called *professors* because they willingly tutored young players—added Latin rhythms to the music. Jazz began in the early 1900s when cornetist Joe "King" Oliver played in Storyville, the infamous neighborhood that attracted sailors like a bare thigh. By then, jazz had erupted all over New Orleans. Musicians armed themselves with kettles, horns, cigarbox fiddles, and cheese-box banjos. They blended black folk music, funeral marches, Mardi Gras tunes, and French songs. From Storyville's brothels and corner bars to the city streets, the music played until the city's respectable people accepted it.

In 1917, Navy secretary Josephus "Tea Totaling" Daniels threatened to close the local naval base if the city didn't shut down its infamous red-light district, a den of predictable infections. Officials complied, thus forcing Storyville's prostitutes and gamblers to relocate. Until then, quiet Bourbon, named for the royal family of France, was known principally for its intricate ironwork. Its rise—or fall, depending on your predilections—began just after World War I. By the 1940s, Bourbon Street had become synonymous with sin, a steaming gumbo of sex, liquor, and traditional jazz. In those days, segregation restricted Bourbon Street to whites.

All over New Orleans, gambling and strip clubs operated twenty-four hours and hired bands that combined jazz licks with blues songs to create the New Orleans Sound. The sound reverberated particularly from the Dew

Drop Inn, originally a black lunch stand and barbershop at 2836 LaSalle Street. Owner Frank Painia hired jazz orchestras led by Duke Ellington and Lionel Hampton, top blues performers, and drag-queen revues with seven-piece bands. Rhythm and blues took root in Painia's dance hall, nicknamed the Groove Room, which booked popular local performers and national acts—James Brown, Little Richard, Guitar Slim, Gatemouth Brown, Ivory Joe Hunter, and Bobby "Blue" Bland. Dozens of other blues clubs operated in New Orleans then, including the Blue Eagle, the Cadillac Club, the Dream Room, the House of Blue Lights, and the Club Tiajuana.

With their freewheeling R&B style, New Orleans' players appealed to rock 'n' roll radio. Often the two genres converged perfectly. For the local record labels, small didn't necessary mean weak, as distributor Joe Banashak demonstrated with his Minit label. In March 1963, while pushing Ernie K-Doe's "Mother-in-Law" to No. 1 on the national pop charts, the tiny New Orleans company outflanked Columbia, Capitol, RCA, and other majors. In a musical coup, Minit managed to hire Toussaint, the song's composer, as staff producer. As K-Doe (born Ernest Kadore Jr., and pronounced Kay Dough) tells the story, Toussaint wrote "Mother-in-Law" but didn't like it, so he threw it in the studio's trash can. K-Doe identified with it, though, so he rummaged through the can until he found it. He asked Toussaint to cut it with him because it was universal. Forty years later, K-Doe is still singing the song in New Orleans. "Everybody will have a mother-in-law, a common-law, or some type of law," he told writer Bill Griggs. "Do you dig where I'm comin' from? Someone is gettin' married every second of every day."

By equal serendipity, New Orleans created a well-oiled music machine, propelled by nightclubs, radio stations, Cosimo Matassa's little studio, and, of course, the weather. I arrived in summer, because my imagination knows the city as a steamy, decadent place. I was not disappointed. Natives explained that humidity is an intangible part of their music, somehow adding a loose feeling. I could think only of the days before air-conditioning, when sweaty throngs packed smoky nightclubs. "New Orleans was so hot, so funky, that when you walked down the street, you'd hear this 'squish, squish, squish' under your feet—silverfish," O'Shea said. "I still think there's something about the weather that contributes to the funky sound. When I worked there, a bunch of little labels operated all across town. They didn't have a lot of money, but they had talent and desire. As I recall, Cosimo's studio was in an old avocado-packing plant. As soon as Cosimo would finish recording, he'd pull out a little lathe and cut a lacquer master on the spot and run it down to the pressing plant. The whole process didn't take three hours. But some of the greatest records of all time came out of his studio. Of course, radio backed local record companies then. We played a lot of records that we knew were only regional hits. But that didn't matter. Those regional records became secrets known to only the people on the Gulf Coast. New Orleans probably produced more regional hits than any other city. They were a part of the culture.

"At the time, music was changing from R&B to rock. We were up on the mezzanine of the elegant Sheraton Charles Hotel on Canal Street. Earl Long, the Kingfish's brother, used to hang out at the station all the time because James A. Noe, Jr., the governor's son, owned it. Earl was a disheveled guy who had B.O. and a lot of women. To me, he represented the craziness of the city. Down the street, you could hear any kind of music you wanted. Within a block or so you could hear trumpeter Al Hirt, clarinetist Pete Fountain, and the R&B singer 'Frogman' Henry. He used to play in a little restaurant called the Court of Two Sisters. This was before the big money took over. Frogman had a large tip jar, like a pickle jar, sitting on top of his piano. It was usually full. I'm sure he depended on the additional income. And this was *after* his hit 'Ain't Got No Home.'

"But man, what a town! We did about anything, on and off the air. I remember a news guy at our station who'd read the news doing his Huckleberry Hound impersonation. At Christmastime in 1958, some sleazy local label owner came up to the station with bottles of booze and a hot blonde call girl. We used to play his records. I think the guy was involved with the mob. While seven or eight of us sat around, the record guy said, 'Merry Christmas, boys! Whoever wants Marie can have her.' Of course, all he cared about was getting his records played. Now, that was old-time rock 'n' roll."

In the early 1960s, New Orleans' good times began to end. District Attorney Jim Garrison vowed to clean up the bars. Though loved by local musicians, the bars had a bad reputation nationally, and Garrison was determined to change the city's image. Few entertainers took him seriously at first. Then reality struck. As Mac Rebennack (Dr. John) explained in his autobiography, *Under a Hoodoo Moon,* "A twenty-four-hours-a-day happening city was being closed. . . . the clubs were out of biz, the record industry running to Memphis, to Muscle Shoals, to anywhere else it could, carrying squabbling record execs and leaving a panicked musicians' union." To make things worse, urban renewal and highway construction claimed many older nightclubs on Canal Street. Meanwhile, the union fined musicians for playing on sessions at Matassa's new three-track studio, wrongly assuming that additional tracks would mean fewer sessions. Rebennack believes that the union's decision contributed heavily to the demise of New Orleans as a major recording center.

But the city faced another threat—competition. Motown Records had changed the nation's tastes to smooth soul. (Some Motown executives actually came to New Orleans to recruit studio sidemen.) Compared with the hits emerging from Detroit, not to mention England's rock records with roots in the blues and pop, New Orleans' R&B sounded old-fashioned. Independent record companies that had depended on New Orleans went bankrupt or merged with larger companies. When the Groove Room closed in the late 1960s, the city lost a powerful symbol of local musical identity; and when Painia died in 1972, so did the soul of the Dew Drop. By the time I saw it, the club had become just another vinyl-sided building—a little hotel. Other old clubs had turned into Pizza Huts and Taco Bells and parking lots.

⌒

Near the Mississippi, I met an elderly bluesman who offered to talk about the old clubs for a hundred dollars. I thought he was joking, so I kept talking: Did Joe "Mr. Google Eyes" August, a fifteen-year-old blues singer who earned his name by ogling the women, really drive a 1949 purple Mercury with leopard-skin upholstery? Did Larry Williams drive a new Cadillac with "Short Fat Fannie" painted in gold on the doors? Did musicians emerge from the ladies' room with bras dangling from their guitar necks? Did players back drag-queen shows like Black Beauty and Her Powder Puff Revue? The old man snapped, "Where's my hundred?" We walked away.

Oddly enough, the end of segregation helped cripple the Dew Drop and other black clubs. When blacks were allowed to go anywhere, they wanted to see Bourbon Street. Segregation in New Orleans always seemed a contradiction. Though the city was a happy-go-lucky place that defied society's rules, it could be as staunchly segregationist as Selma or Bogalusa. The Citizens' Council of Greater New Orleans once distributed circulars that read: "NOTICE! STOP—Help Save The Youth of America. Don't Buy Negro Records. (If you don't want to serve Negroes in your place of business, then do not have Negro records on your jukebox or listen to Negro records on the radio.) The screaming, idiotic words and savage music of these records are undermining the morals of our white youth in America. Call the advertisers of the radio stations that play this type of music and complain to them! Don't Let Your Children Buy, or Listen to, These Negro Records."

The next day I walked down LaSalle Street and tried to imagine all the flashy cats who had once strutted there. Their faces moved through my mind like so many ghosts. Suddenly Cheryl ducked into an antiques shop. We saw a fancy chair that sold for $3,000. I bought a green city map, "Where to Find It in New Orleans, 1952," for $4. Its advertisements offered dining and dancing at places called the Blue Room, in the Roosevelt Hotel; the Swan Room, in the Monteleone Hotel; and the Rumpus Room, on Charles Avenue. All offered big bands. To me, this was a magic map to a lost world.

Awed by so much history, I walked around town for fifteen minutes or so, looking for the old buildings. On a whim I called Cosimo Matassa. He said, "Come on over to the Quarter and I'll talk to you."

We had to drive through the narrow streets of the French Quarter, passing pink and turquoise shuttered houses and guides driving horse-drawn carriages. We found Matassa's Market, a neighborhood grocery at Dauphine and Philip streets, and parked a block away. A barefooted customer, wearing a black leather jacket despite the summer heat, purchased a quart of milk while a clerk called upstairs for Matassa. "Wait here," she said sternly. A few minutes later he popped out of the pineapples. He was a strikingly elegant and forceful man, tan and round. A border of white hair around his bald head matched a fancy white sport shirt. His large Roman nose protruded noticeably, giving him the distinctive look of a character from a Dickens novel. He led us along the narrow aisles, past a deli preparation area, and through a large metal door as thick as one on a submarine. We took a few steps outside and then walked up narrow wooden steps to a dark room where two computer screens glowed dimly in green. The surroundings reminded me of an accountant's office. I saw no music memorabilia anywhere. Matassa pointed to an adjacent room and said, "This was my bedroom when I was a boy. We lived here above the store. Now my sons own it." He helps keep the grocery's books. Before we could talk, the telephone rang three times. He answered "Cosmo" really fast, dropping the *i* from his name. "Yeah. Sure. Got it." Click.

He started talking fast: "I never did have anything past eight-tracks, and most of the hits were cut on one- and two-tracks. When you make records by multi-track, you're hearing a performance that never took place. Musicians go in and put down a rhythm track, then add and subtract things. It's truly a synthesized process. By the time I got something new in equipment, everybody else had passed that point. Today there are dozens of studios in New Orleans. Bands own a lot of gear now, a lot of it digital. I don't do production work anymore. I call myself a consultant. I've been involved with people who have legal problems. I know the technology. I'm an expert witness."

Despite his unsophisticated studios, Matassa helped create 21 gold records and about 250 national-chart hits—not to mention dozens of regional records. He watched the New Orleans Sound evolve inside his first studio, J&M Recording, like a scientist observing a culture sprouting in a laboratory dish. Musicians crammed into the ten-by-twelve-foot room, sometimes elbow to elbow, in an old building with wires strung all along the walls. The place had only three electrical outlets and three microphones. The sound was muddy, but the studio turned out hits because of the talented session musicians. Matassa kept up with technological advances as best he could. When he couldn't afford a new piece of studio gear, he'd build something similar. On any night, Matassa could be found sitting behind a tiny console, wearing a crisp white T-shirt and dark chinos. He spoke of those days with total recall, polite but businesslike, seemingly unaware of his musical cult status. Perhaps that's because he didn't become rich from the music. But one thing is certain: as the studio engineer, he personally recorded most of New Orleans' hits through the mid-1960s.

His musical leanings came by chance. Cosimo Matassa was born April 13, 1926, in New Orleans to an Italian father who operated several small businesses, including the grocery and a jukebox outlet. "I was going to Tulane University to be a chemist when the war in Europe ended in 1945," Matassa said. "When I didn't get drafted, my father said, 'Go back to school or go to work.' I didn't want to continue with chemistry, so I started working in the jukebox business. I backed into the record business; it wasn't a deliberate career move. In those times, a popular record was worn out—we used 78s—in a couple of weeks, and we'd put new ones on the jukeboxes and sell the old ones, which was a big thing then. We moved next door, to the corner of Rampart and Dumaine, and remodeled the building into an appliance and record shop. In the late '40s I decided to open a recording studio in the back room. It was an afterthought; I wanted only to give amateurs and semi-professionals a place to record direct-to-disc."

Matassa's first big R&B hit was "Good Rockin' Tonight" by Roy Brown, a New Orleans native who had been singing in Galveston. He combined his roots, gospel and blues, in a shouting style. In 1947 Brown wrote the song on a paper bag. He took it to Wynonie Harris, a popular blues singer who was appearing at the Dew Drop. Brown asked Harris to record it. Brown needed the money at the time; he thought Harris could bring home a hit. When Harris refused to listen to the song that night, Brown visited another club to pitch the song to pianist Cecil Grant, who suggested that Brown record the song himself. At 4 A.M., Grant called Julius Braun, an owner of the independent DeLuxe Records in Linden, New Jersey, to suggest a session. The call woke Braun, but, being a good businessman, he asked Brown to sing the song on the telephone. Sufficiently impressed, Braun agreed to book recording time at Matassa's studio. In early 1948, DeLuxe finally released "Good Rockin' Tonight." Disc jockey Poppa Stoppa jumped on it, and suddenly all of black New Orleans knew the line: "Weeeell, I heard the news, there's good rockin' tonight!" (I assume Poppa knew the term *rockin'* was slang for sexual intercourse.)

Meanwhile, Harris went to Cincinnati to record some songs—including "Good Rockin'"—for King Records. King hurriedly pressed his version and rushed it onto the market. His cover record became the bigger hit, a No. 1 record that spring, although Brown's version did well, too, reaching the teens. Today, Harris' version is considered a forerunner of rock 'n' roll. The song has been recorded many times, most importantly in 1954 by a young Elvis Presley for Sun Records. Few people realized it then, but Presley's version totally merged black and white music.

In the mid-1950s, Matassa worked with mostly black singers: Smiley Lewis, Oscar "Papa" Celestin, Jewel King, Chubby Newsome, and other performers discovered by DeLuxe. "The Braun brothers, David and Julius, got here early, looking for local talent," Matassa said. "They had a local guy, band leader Paul Gayten, and he'd find things for them to record. They let him take care of it. I recorded one of the best female vocalists I ever heard, Annie Laurie, who did an early version of the now-familiar 'Since I Fell for You,' but today few people remember her. She sang in Gayten's band. Under different circumstances she would have been a diva—an operatic soprano—because she had a lot of emotional carryover in her voice. But living in her times and in her social environment, that wasn't going to happen. We cut some hits on her, but her records didn't do her justice."

Gayten and other producers brought into Matassa's studio some of New Orleans' finest players, who supplemented their gig money by playing on sessions. The 1950s studio band included Earl Palmer and Charles "Hungry" Williams, drums; Frank Fields, bass; Ernest McLean, guitar; Salvador Doucette and Edward Franks, piano; and Lee Allen and Alvin "Red" Tyler, saxophone. Tyler, a gifted musician, helped organize and arrange hundreds of sessions. The musicians hung around the studio, informally picking up tips and making friends. That's one reason why their music was so loose. Nobody knew what a "session musician" was; they knew only how to play, regardless of location. The only pressure they felt was playing as flawlessly as possible, for one mistake could ruin a session done on a one-track recorder.

"By 1950 the hits started flying out of the studio—it was about the only one in town," Matassa recalled. "I'm surprised it stayed that way for so many years. We did a lot of national hits, but also a lot of regional hits. The independent record people really cared for the music they were making. It's not like they came into some Third World situation and mined it. They enjoyed the music; they thought it was worthwhile to record. That's not to say they did it to help the artist, because in many cases they didn't. But the label people were sincere. Business continued to grow, and about 1950 I bought a mono Ampex 300 tape recorder, a great leap forward from direct-to-disc because now I could intercut takes, using a good intro from one and a good chorus or ending from another.

"The strange thing is, the songs we recorded talked about the same subjects that are discussed today, but in a far better fashion. After all, the prime movers for lyrics are money, drink, and sex. The old lyrics talked about these things, but generally speaking, even those that were violent were violent in a bit more cerebral fashion. In 1960 we did a thing for Aaron Neville called 'Over You,' about a guy telling his girlfriend, 'Listen, if you leave me, they'll be low talking and slow walking over you'—he'd kill her. It showed the personal rage, but it didn't recommend that everybody do it. You didn't get the impression that you should get a gun and spray bullets around. In that sense, almost illiterate people composed words that were better, politically and socially, than they are these days, even though they talked about the same subjects. Of course, we had our problems then. Radio stations that would play Fats Domino wouldn't play Little Richard. The difference was the perception. I'm not sure I understand it. I do know it was no small concern to us down here that Pat Boone had the biggest-selling versions of Little Richard's records. I say it all the time: it's enough to make you hate white buck shoes."

Yet white bucks had little impact on social reality: Richard—and his music—was too wild for such conservative times. In fact, considering segregation and "Little Richard" Penniman's homosexual flamboyance, it's a wonder that he was allowed to stand within ten feet of a microphone and recording machine. But for the young Georgian who performed around the South in the early 1950s, destiny could not be contained. In 1955 he sent a demo tape to Specialty Records in California. At first, label executives didn't know what to think of Richard. But at the urging of staff producer Robert

"Bumps" Blackwell, Specialty owner Art Rupe agreed to record this new gospel-style singer—Little Richard. Rupe insisted that Blackwell do it at J&M Recording, where Specialty had recorded hits for Lloyd Price and Guitar Slim.

On the day of the session, Blackwell arrived to find a boisterous, lewd performer whose material didn't flatter his frantic singing style. Blackwell worried that Rupe would explode over the futile session. The morning had not gone well. Blackwell had a feeling that he would leave without a good master take. But during lunch at the Dew Drop, Richard jumped up on the stage, pounded the piano, and sang a nonsensical dirty song he performed in the clubs: "Awop-bop-a-loo-mop . . . !" Blackwell liked the piano licks and rhythm, so he told Richard to return to the studio. They faced a formidable job, for by then Richard's voice had weakened, and they still lacked a suitable song. In desperation, Blackwell called Dorothy LaBostrie, a local cook who had been pestering him to record her material. This time, Blackwell didn't care about her lack of experience; he was desperate for a rewrite. According to a popular version of the sketchy story, she went to work on the spot and an hour later returned with a sanitized version of the song. (She changed "Tutti-frutti, good booty" to "Tutti-frutti, aw rooty.") Richard blasted the piano and vocal mike for fifteen more minutes, and on the third take sang "Tutti-Frutti" right.

When his hits started, they came furiously, like an outburst from a child: "Long Tall Sally," "Rip It Up," "Lucille," "Good Golly Miss Molly." Spreading a musical contagion, he traveled across the country with his band, the Upsetters. Richard exuded energy; he was a walking generator. He'd drink five cups of coffee before each show, and consume another five during intermission. He insisted that his band members also wear heavy makeup and dress in clothing as loud as their music. Despite Richard's effeminate ways, "Thousands of women took off their panties and threw them at us," recalled New Orleans drummer Charles Connor, who started playing for Richard at seventeen. "We'd be playing and dodging panties. Sometimes they'd land on one of my cymbals. I'd pick 'em up with a drumstick and wave 'em in the air, and that would just make the women crazier."

Little Richard's heavy backbeat and wild ways called more attention to Matassa's studio, which in 1956 he moved to 521–523 Governor Nicholls Street and renamed Cosimo's. Nobody cared about the name change; most people called his studio Cosimo's anyway. The new place included two recording studios but lacked air-conditioning. This was tantamount to suicide in humid New Orleans. Matassa pondered the problem for months.

Then he bought a couple of tons of ice, placed it in a box outside, near a big fan, and blew cool air into the building through an open window. He finally gave up the idea because it was too much trouble. Nobody complained, though. Regardless of temperature, singers showed up and sang their lungs out. Local performers followed to him to his new white building like children following the piper.

Just when the city and studio were poised to define the growing American R&B market, the times—and Matassa's luck—changed. Earl Palmer left to become an A-team drummer on the West Coast, and another important New Orleans musician, Harold Battiste, left to arrange West Coast sessions, including a number of Sonny and Cher hits. As the local recording scene declined, Matassa fought back. He formed Dover Records, a recording, distribution, and pressing company aimed at a national audience. He used Dover to distribute other local labels. It was a good idea, but Matassa lacked money and time. Dover's first hit, Robert Parker's "Barefootin'," came on NOLA (New Orleans, Louisiana) Records in 1966. Later that year Dover hit again, with Aaron Neville's Top 5 hit "Tell It Like It Is," on the Parlo label. The burly black singer admired Hank Williams and worked as a longshoreman when he wasn't painting houses. Most people don't realize that he's the same Aaron Neville who became famous again in the 1990s by singing adult contemporary songs such as "Don't Know Much" with Linda Ronstadt. He earned so little money from his 1966 hit that all he had to show for it was a 45 single, spray-painted gold, that hung on a wall of his shotgun house.

The hit couldn't save Dover from its creditors, and soon the company crashed. The banks refused to lend Matassa money, and the Internal Revenue Service wanted its share of everything, including his studio. Stubbornly refusing to declare bankruptcy, Matassa started the long process of paying off his debts. As he watched the IRS sell his studio equipment—assorted pieces of his life—he knew he had lost his tenuous grip on the national record market. Yet he persisted. In the early 1970s he opened a little eight-track studio on Camp Street and named it Jazz City Recording. But it came too late. Studio competition had arrived. Then came disco. Nobody wanted the old New Orleans Sound. Things got so bad that musicians fled again, and distributor Joe Banashak placed thousands of discs—the stock from his Instant and Minit labels—out on the street for the trash collectors. "The whole scene collapsed," Banashak told me years ago. "We couldn't do anything to stop it."

Nowadays, Cosimo Matassa wonders what would have happened if he had found more cash when he needed it, but it's not a subject that he ponders often. The music business has changed too much. Not even the annual New Orleans Jazz and Heritage Festival and its 450,000 visitors can compensate for the loss of local hits that once charmed the world. Not even a high-quality label named Black Top, with artists such as Earl King and Snooks Eaglin, or Allen Toussaint's new NYNO (New York/New Orleans) Records, can bring back the days of regional hits and $10,000 radio contests.

"There's a lot of great stuff that still sounds local in New Orleans," Matassa said, "but it doesn't get put on the national market as much as it should. Some of it's really good. We have a lot going on here. But the big record companies are bottom-line-oriented. It amazes me that a record company can look at an artist and say, 'Well, we can sell only 200,000 albums by this guy, so we won't record him.' It's staggering, but it says something about the times. Fortunately, I never knew that kind of attitude. I was able to enjoy the music, all kinds of music, while earning my living. Isn't that a marvelous life?"

Jackson, Mississippi: Just a Dream

New Orleans and Jackson are linked by Interstate 55 and a trail of hot record deals. Geographically, the cities are about 180 miles apart; culturally, 180 degrees. Jackson is tidy streets, straight arrows, and Eudora Welty. New Orleans is benders, Bourbon Street, and Tennessee Williams. On Saturday night, Jackson's Wal-Mart attracts good old boys from Tougaloo and Little Yazoo, while New Orleans greets wide-eyed tourists at Tipitina's.

In the 1950s, New Orleans and Jackson used musicians interchangeably. Their happy songs—more music from my youth—boomed from my car's cassette player as I drove south one magical summer, but by then I no longer naively believed that New Orleans existed independently of the world—or even of the South. New Orleans does, in fact, owe a small part of its musical success to Jackson, the capital of Mississippi, and to John Vincent, a loyal Mississippian whose erratic career parallels the rise and fall of New Orleans as a regional music center.

Jackson was nothing like I had expected, perhaps because I didn't know what to expect. A lot of concrete and glass, yet still the Old South. I drove around the downtown and concluded that Jackson was the cleanest city I had ever seen. No candy wrappers or trash anywhere. (That's another difference between Jackson and New Orleans.) On the edge of town, I parked the Eagle, reclined in my bucket seat, and stared at white clouds blowing across wide Southern skies. For a moment I imagined I was living in 1955, a time of social change but also of great opportunity. Here in Jackson, a small town by urban standards, the music mattered more than the money. When radio stations played a local record, the hair stood up on the back of the singer's neck, and the whole town buzzed with expectation. A nobody was suddenly somebody, the talk of his town—maybe even his country.

Songs ruled in Jackson and New Orleans then. Despite their differences, the cities still share a common regional heritage, a passion for the blues, and the everlasting spirit of Johnny Vincent. I couldn't visit New Orleans without stopping in Jackson to meet the epitome of flamboyant producers, a key figure in New Orleans and Jackson music circles for a half-century. On the nights when I was probably watching *Bourbon Street Beat*, Vincent was roaming the French Quarter in search of talented blues singers who worked in clubs that few white people dared enter. He was a human yo-yo. He'd visit New Orleans, drive back to Jackson to sell some records, then return to New Orleans on back-country roads where he knew every juke joint and hamburger stand worth a visit. Then he'd go back to Jackson. When his breed vanished like five-cent coffee, Johnny persisted in a business ruled by computers, world markets, and corporate slaves. He became their antithesis, a businessman who used *his* ears, not a focus group's.

What I liked most about him was his enthusiasm. He loved the music, the thrill of hearing a melodic hook line for the first time. For him, the act of making a record was almost a religious experience—and a simple one. Not that he was perfect. Like his independent contemporaries, he has been accused on occasion of not making royalty payments, but then he was also known to pay "advances" to struggling older artists whom he had known for years. In truth, Johnny was neither the most knowledgeable producer nor the richest, but he had a convincing, cocky style that was undeniably Johnny V. A blend of used-car salesman and record producer, he must have been an

Producer Johnny Vincent, founder of Ace Records, sits in his office in Jackson, Mississippi, in 1995. He died in 2000. Photo by Randy McNutt.

Jackson, Mississippi

Jimmy Clanton's first hit, "Just a Dream," rose to No. 4 on *Billboard*'s pop chart in 1958.

Jimmy Clanton became Ace Records' first white teenage pop star in the late 1950s.

Pop singer Jimmy Clanton recorded for Johnny Vincent's Ace label in Jackson, Mississippi.

impressive man to encounter during his prime. He smoked long cigars and waved them like batons; hyped 45s by hiring teenage girls to write thousands of postcards to radio stations across the country; changed young Frankie Guzzo's last name to Ford because he—Johnny, of course—liked Ford cars; smiled agreeably during recording sessions and periodically yelled, "Put some *sheeet* into it!"; gambled next month's rent on another record pressing; and talked in a down-home accent that made him sound like part slick producer, part Huey Long.

As his career expectations multiplied, Johnny's reputation grew like bayou moss. He needed hits like some men need new lovers. Stories circulated about Johnny's eccentricities. According to legend, one day he agreed to pick up a new artist, singer Bobby Marchan, at the New Orleans bus station. Johnny didn't know that Marchan often dressed in women's clothes. In vain Johnny paced around the terminal, searching for a young man, until he finally approached a woman sitting on a bench. Before he could speak, Marchan's male voice boomed, "Mr. John Vincent?" Johnny's jaw dropped. But even at their recording session, he continued to address Marchan as a woman. When musicians finally explained Marchan's situation, Johnny V nearly fainted.

Meeting Johnny was a priority on this trip. I knew the time had come. His health was going bad, I had heard, and I wanted to discuss recording with one of the few producers to achieve commercial success in the old and new record industries. Sadly, as I was writing this chapter in the winter of 2000, Johnny died. When I heard the news from Wolf Stephenson, vice president of Jackson's Malaco Records, I thought that a part of the music had died with Johnny. Stephenson described him as a mentor and supporter. At Johnny's funeral, Stephenson realized that death had claimed more than a record-industry veteran. It ended Jackson's old record business and the musical thread that had stretched from the 1940s to the present. Nothing would be the same.

Johnny's Ace label broke hit records when I was a kid and resumed its work four decades later by repackaging the old songs and releasing new R&B albums. By the 1990s, Ace had metamorphosed into a modern niche label, like many others that now cater to collectors and serious music fans. But this time, for a change, Johnny made some money. When I visited him on his label's fortieth anniversary and his seventieth birthday, the happiest man in the record business was directing Ace from a nondescript office park in Pearl, a Jackson suburb. The area is still a busy little soul center. Malaco, a modern R&B independent, is so firmly established in its field that it bought the Muscle Shoals Sound Studios in 1985 and the Select-O-Hits distributor-ship in Memphis a decade later. Reconciled with the loss of Top 40 airplay, Malaco has continued making funky music for a devoted audience. At Ace the story was similar, but Johnny conceded no ground to the major labels. He still believed he could reach No. 1. Somewhere out there lurked the right song and the right performer. All Johnny had to do was find them.

On arrival at the Pearl Office Park, I wasn't sure I had found the right place. No Ace sign—no sign at all—hung outside the modern brick com-plex. I watched several guys enter one of the offices, between the Pearl Medi-cal Lab and Janet's Hair Gallery, so I followed them. I saw them tripping over boxes of compact discs, heard soul music blaring from a back room, and felt Johnny's drawl echoing all over. Framed album covers, music-pub-lishing awards, and gold records covered the walls. Heavy tan carpet covered the floor. In the middle of the office, a receptionist in her late twenties di-rected foot traffic. Johnny's small office was anchored by a brown metal desk and matching chair that squeaked every time he fidgeted. Cassettes and contracts cluttered the top of his desk. He greeted me warmly, and after I assured him that I wasn't related to a Jackson lawyer with my last name, he laughed and radiated the aplomb of a carnival barker. He was bald and tan with a smooth face, and he smiled a lot, like a politician at a fund-raiser. His accent revealed an authentic wheeler-dealer and old-time Mississippian, born John Vincent Imbragulio on October 3, 1925, in Laurel, ninety miles southeast of Jackson. His parents, Phillip and Tina Imbragulio, reared four children and owned a restaurant. Johnny would sit in front of the jukebox for hours, listening to records by Guy Lombardo and other big bands. When he returned home from the service in late 1945, he followed his instincts and started a jukebox business and later a record shop, catering to black customers. He enjoyed selling and listening to the blues, and besides, he didn't face much competition. Few whites cared about selling blues records.

"Black records were hard to find then," Johnny said. "The independent labels—Specialty, DeLuxe, Aladdin, King, and others—made eighty percent of black records. I started likin' the business so good that I decided to catch the bus to New Orleans to see if I could find a distributor to hire me. I didn't have a quarter, and I had just gotten married. But I loved records. I found myself a job as a record salesman, with Jackson and Mississippi as my terri-tories. It was a dream come to life."

About this time, Johnny learned that a lot of blues singers lived within seventy-five miles of his home, so he started a small label, Champion, to record them. He walked right up to Big Boy Crudup, composer of "That's

All Right Mama," and asked him to cut a record. "In those days you didn't have many studios," Johnny said. "I cut Big Boy at WRBC Radio in Jackson. I gave him $25 for the session, and he was satisfied. Now, that was *my* kind of money. All I had to do was change his name around a bit on the record to avoid any contractual problem with another label. I picked him up at his place, a little shotgun house with holes all over it. A pitiful place, with an outhouse in back. You really could shoot a shotgun off in it and not even hit a plank. Big Boy never did have no money. None of them old blues singers ever had any money if they stayed down here in Mississippi."

Johnny didn't earn much money from the Champion discs himself, but he loved the thrill of recording. All the while, the music of New Orleans stayed with him like an itch. About 1950, he noticed that something was happening in the city's black nightclubs—barrelhouse piano, parade beat, blues, and jazz had combined to create what would come to be called the New Orleans Sound. It also fascinated Art Rupe, the owner of Specialty Records in Los Angeles. In 1952 he bought Champion and hired Johnny as Specialty's New Orleans talent scout and producer at $587 a month.

Although it was exciting, the new job placed Johnny in danger. Recording blacks in rural Mississippi—even in New Orleans—was not the best way to make white friends and influence people. The region was still a stronghold of the Ku Klux Klan and other segregationists. Johnny didn't mind risking his reputation to talk to black singers, but he did worry about threats of violence. An angry farm foreman once chased him away with a shotgun when Johnny stopped to talk to a worker about making a record. Unflinching Johnny did not care; he left for the Dew Drop Inn and other black clubs that booked blues stars. "At the time," he said, "everybody wanted that old New Orleans sound. It was early rock 'n' roll. A lot of good artists came out of the town, so naturally I went lookin' for them. I'd also go on the road for five or six weeks at a time to promote records. I'd sleep in YMCAs and bus stations. See, old Rupe didn't want me to stay in hotels. He said, 'Don't ever have dinner with nobody at night. Always take him to lunch. It's cheaper.' Old Rupe was the greatest motivator in the world. He used to say, 'Johnny, if I had a brother, I'd like him to be just like you.' Then he fired me."

Rupe told Johnny that the firing was an austerity move; Johnny maintained that it was because Rupe owed him royalties. But by then, the issue didn't matter. Johnny had already decided to start another label. It never occurred to him to go to New York or Los Angeles. After all, Jackson, population 100,000 then, and New Orleans, about 550,000, were all he knew.

Both cities had long ago overcome the destruction of ninety years earlier, when the Union navy captured New Orleans (a leading maker of sheet music) and General William Sherman rode into Jackson and burned parts of it. Typically, Johnny didn't care much about business or history. He opened an office in Jackson for one reason—he lived there. Unlike most local entrepreneurs, he thought of raw materials in terms of piano players and singers, of blues clubs and microphones. He wouldn't be a candidate for president of the chamber of commerce.

In 1955, Johnny's new Ace label became New Orleans' first commercial national record company, the forerunner of Minit, Ric, Seven B, Dover, NOLA, and others. Johnny said that the company name came casually enough. While walking with his friend Les Birhari, owner of the Meteor label in Memphis, Johnny bought an Ace comb and said, "Lester, I'll call my label Ace. It'll be the first one listed in the telephone book." Appropriately, Johnny formed the label in the same year that *Billboard* started its Top 100 chart, RCA Victor agreed to sign Elvis Presley, and rock 'n' roll began to grow across the country and in the Deep South.

Meanwhile, over at 309 North Farish Street, a Hattiesburg native named Lillian McMurry had the same idea—to make records at home in Jackson. She operated the Record Mart, which sold black records and sponsored a popular radio show. Though distasteful to many Southern whites, the idea of selling and making black records wasn't new. It dated to the 1920s, when white talent scouts for Paramount and Gennett—both northern labels—searched Mississippi for blues players. But McMurry put a new spin on it. She was a white *woman* selling black records.

Through the 1950s, blacks and whites seldom mixed socially, even in much of the North, but sometimes the music brought them together. That's what happened in Jackson. Black musicians stopped at McMurry's shop, a brick building painted yellow with a big black record on the front and old-fashioned listening booths inside. An unlikely blues fan, McMurry never heard a black record until she was thirty. But when she finally heard Wynonie Harris wail, she liked the music well enough to invest in it. While her husband ran a furniture store in the other half of the building, she operated the record shop and its mail-order business. Like Johnny Vincent, she wasn't satisfied with merely selling records. She wanted to make her own, so she founded the Diamond Record Company and a subsidiary, Trumpet Records, and even opened a crude little studio. Although Trumpet never became a national commercial force, as Ace eventually did, it became an important label to blues fans. McMurry advertised her record store on Woodson "Woody" Walls' *Ole Hep Cat* show on WRBC and signed to Trumpet more black gospel groups, blues singers, and a few white hillbilly bands. Armed with singles by seminal artists such as electric bluesman Sonny Boy Williamson, the gospel Southern Sons Quartette, and blues singer Elmore James, McMurry obtained radio airplay in a number of cities across the South. But Trumpet was too black, too nonconformist, to cross over to pop radio. Trumpet operated more like a modern roots-music independent— Jackson's own Malaco, for example—in that it sold smaller quantities to a narrow audience and depended on word-of-mouth testimonials.

In recent times, Malaco has put Jackson's name in the music trade magazines for its national hits and R&B Grammy nominations. Malaco is a growing but no-frills operation that still operates out of an industrial warehouse at 3023 West Northside Drive, where the company first rented space from Johnny Vincent in 1966. But now, after repeated expansions, the company is called the Malaco Music Group. (The past is not forgotten. The firm's logo substitutes a black LP for the o in Malaco.)

The seeds of the company were planted in the early 1960s, when Tommy Couch, a native of Tuscumbia, Alabama, arrived at the University of Mississippi in Oxford to major in pharmacology. On a lark, he started booking bands for dances held by Pi Kappa Alpha. Many were black and white soul bands (in the usual Southern irony, Ole Miss had been a major bastion of segregation). Joining Couch in this sideline was another pharmacy major named Gerald "Wolf" Stephenson, a Columbia, Mississippi, native and the fraternity's social chairman. (The nickname comes from his college days, when he portrayed the Wolfman in a fraternity play.) After college, Couch headed to Jackson, his wife's hometown, to work in a drugstore. When he couldn't get music out of his mind, he formed a little booking agency, Malaco Attractions, with his brother-in-law, Mitchell Malouf, an Ole Miss accounting major. By 1965, a line of Ole Miss associates—from musicians to alumni—had shown up in Jackson to work for Malaco, which soon expanded with a franchise from the Hullabaloo nightclub chain. Stephenson, who was filling prescriptions in a Jackson pharmacy, soon joined the agency, in Johnny's office building downtown.

"The city was surprisingly active for a smaller music market," Stephenson said. "There wasn't much happening with recording here. Bob McRee had a little studio, where later he cut 'Lover's Holiday' by Peggy Scott and Jo Jo Benson. Back then, studios were not sophisticated, at least by today's standards. In 1967 we picked up a four-track Ampex recorder and naively thought we'd cut some hits. We didn't know much about the machine, but there were plenty of good musicians around to make things exciting. The atmosphere was vibrant. When I quit working part-time to join Tommy in the business, we starved to death for a year. Then one day some folks came into the studio to record a blues singer. I didn't think much of their album. So I told Tommy, 'Hey, if they can get a deal with *that* guy, then we should record something for old "Mississippi" Fred McDowell. He's much better.' Of course, we knew he traveled across the world playing his bottleneck blues. We had known Fred for years. He used to play at our fraternity dances. So we cut an album for him, *I Do Not Play No Rock 'n' Roll.* Capitol bought it, and it was nominated for a Grammy in 1969. All of a sudden we'd made a classic, and we were off and running. We did anything to earn a nickel: jingles, educational programs, records—the whole shootin' match."

Malaco's commercial heyday began in 1970, when producer Wardell Quezergue came up from New Orleans to make some records. The partner from the broke NOLA label needed a place to start over, and Jackson's little Malaco Studio seemed a refuge. Stephenson said that Malaco agreed to provide studio time if Quezergue would supply the artists and produce their sessions. Quezergue was a human machine in the studio, more like a benevolent drill sergeant than a producer. The veteran trumpet player knew the value of rehearsal. Nothing was left to chance. When he spoke, people listened. He wore Barry Goldwater glasses and held his cigarette at a jaunty angle that reflected an air of authority. The first thing he leased to Atlantic's Cotillion label in New York was "Funky Thing" by the Unemployed. It wasn't a huge hit, but everyone was pleased to finally have accomplished something. Later that spring, Quezergue gathered a number of singers and musicians, brought them up to Jackson on a junker of an old school bus, and recorded rhythm tracks until everyone collapsed. The sessions yielded a number of hits, including Jean Knight's "Mr. Big Stuff," a funky little Stax novelty put-down of an inflated male ego, and King Floyd's "Groove Me," on Malaco's Chimneyville label. Both singles reached the Top 10 on the pop charts and enhanced Jackson's growing reputation as a city where black and white musicians grooved together.

"The '70s improved things for us," Stephenson said. "We bought an eight-track recorder. Other hits came out of our studio: 'Misty Blue' with Dorothy Moore, and 'Ring My Bell' with Anita Ward. Even in those days, if you had something worth a flip, you could get it played on the radio at least a few times. An artist could still go into his local station and be treated with respect. But that changed in the late '70s, when the public lost input. That is the number one thing that killed the independents—consolidation of local radio programming. Now somebody from out of town decides what the local stations will play. There are few real local DJs left. But in the past, they would play new stuff, and a lot of times something would come of it, too. As business worsened, the independent distributors collapsed. They went fast. In the early 1970s we must have had twenty-some distributors, and by the end of the decade the list had shrunk to six. Most of them went bankrupt. We knew we had to do something. Later we bought half-interest in Select-O-Hits of Memphis because it was always our most stable distributor and an admirable company. It was a good fit for us. We always were heavily influenced by what the labels and studios were doing in Memphis anyway."

Malaco's studio musicians weren't all from Memphis. Mostly white males, they came from throughout the South: James Stroud and Steve Featherston, drums; Carson Whitsett, Paul Davis, and George Soule, piano and organ; Ray Griffin and Don Barrett, bass; and Jerry Puckett and Michael Toles, guitar. Stroud would become a major Nashville producer, and Davis a popular vocalist, of "Cool Night" fame.

When the hits stopped in the early 1980s, the studio musicians scattered, and Malaco adjusted to a new market. By then, many black artists insisted on working with black musicians. But Malaco rolled on, and became one of the few independents to adapt to changes in the business—a lack of radio support, disintegration of distributors, and high operating costs. These days Malaco persists, recording older R&B singers Johnny Taylor and Little Milton, and even blues master Bobby "Blue" Bland. But Stephenson insists that Malaco is *not* a blues label. It makes rhythm and blues. "It's hard to find somebody who knows what R&B is anymore," he said. "The jocks think we're totally blues. The national rhythm and blues charts don't even reflect true R&B—at least by my old standards. It's difficult to sell enough old-time blues; we can't exist on it. Now, R&B is another matter. It's what we love. We push it on TV, radio, the Internet. With it we went from two employees to two hundred. I didn't fully realize that I've been doing this thing for thirty-three years until we put out a boxed set. Suddenly, there it was right in front of me: my whole career. Now every day I get up and say, 'What am I still doin' in this business?'"

Shortly after forming Ace in 1955, Johnny Vincent stopped at McMurry's recording studio with blues singer Earl King to cut "Those Lonely, Lonely Nights." It became Ace's first hit. Johnny used his modest profits to head back to New Orleans, where he knew exactly where to find the best performers. He recalled, "I took Huey Smith over to the studio and said, 'Cosimo, I ain't got no money.' He said, 'Don't worry about it. Pay me when you get it.'"

Matassa's faith—or indifference—paid off, for in a few years Ace arrived with Smith's double-sided hit "Don't You Just Know It" and "High Blood Pressure," Frankie Ford's "Sea Cruise," and Jimmy Clanton's "Just a Dream," "Go, Jimmy, Go," "Another Sleepless Night," and "Venus in Blue Jeans." Ace released a number of now-obscure R&B records that turned into Gulf Coast hits. (In those times, coastal radio supported local acts like a patriotic war bond buyer, even when the records had little chance of cracking the national charts.)

When "Don't You Just Know It" started moving across the South like a heat wave in late 1957, ABC-Paramount Records summoned Johnny to Philadelphia to discuss leasing the master tape. President Sam Clark offered $50,000; Johnny's pulse quickened. "Clark said, 'If you don't lease it, we'll cut the song with Lloyd Price and beat you on it.' I said, 'Can I have a minute to think it over?' I went to the telephone and called Buster Williams, who had a pressing plant in Memphis. . . . He said, 'Do you want to be in the record business, son?' I said, 'Yes, suh!' He said, 'Then I'll press all the records you want and give you unlimited credit.'" As a precaution, later Johnny went to see Dick Clark, host of *American Bandstand*. "There were a bunch of guys there waiting to see Dick," Johnny said. "They'd come in and sit in his lobby. Each time one guy would go into Dick's office, all the others would move up one chair. Man, I was so scared, I kept moving *back*. I didn't know what to do. I'd never made more than $100 a week in my life. Finally, when everybody left, Dick came out and said, 'Why do you keep moving back? Come on in and we'll talk.' I told him, 'Mr. Clark, if Lloyd Price covers our record, we won't have a chance.' He said, 'Now, don't you worry about a thing. If you got it in the grooves and I like your record, I'm going to play it. I don't care if they fire me.' And he played our record, too. He'd get on television and say, 'The record's breakin' in Texas! Breakin' in Louisiana! Breakin' in Virginia!' And boy, I ain't lyin' to you, that record just took off. We sold about 800,000 copies real quick. It was a great feeling, knowing a little old record I'd cut in New Orleans was being heard all over the country."

By early 1958, Ace was rolling. The year turned out to be the apex of Johnny's career. In March, "Don't You Just Know It" went to No. 9 on the Top 100, and in July Jimmy Clanton's ballad "Just a Dream" hit No. 4 on the *Billboard* Top 100 chart. Other hits arrived that year, too, and Johnny started playing the role. Ace flourished into the Kennedy administration. By 1962, Jimmy Clanton had appeared on *American Bandstand* a number of times, further enhancing his status as a teen idol. Riding the Clanton wave, Ace turned to a more commercial approach, and in the process began to sound like every other pop label. The gutsy New Orleans Sound—a rough-edged, black party sound—gave way to slick New York–style arrangements with strings.

Johnny could not have known that life was about to change for the worse. A tornado called the Beatles was ready to strike America in late 1963. The band would bring the so-called British Invasion and start an obsession with long-haired rock bands. All Ace had to offer were R&B singers and a fading teen king. As records failed for Ace and other independents, New Orleans and Jackson declined as a recording region. Johnny knew that Ace needed better distribution. In desperation, he merged with a larger independent, Vee-Jay Records of Chicago, but their honeymoon soon ended. Vee-Jay developed financial problems, and Ace lost everything. In 1965, Johnny closed the doors. He needed work.

"I hit hard times," he said. "My wife divorced me. I had four kids to support. I started all kinds of businesses. None of them did any good. I sold the publishing rights to four big songs for $20,000. I blowed it all. Years later, I pressed up a World's Fair record. It laid an egg. I ate the whole pressing—60,000 copies. Then about 1990, a shirt-maker in Jackson wanted to reactivate Ace with me. We ended up going into debt, and he had to leave, so all I could do was take over. We started putting out some new soul material and many other things, and business turned around. Suddenly, everything I did was right. I lived out my dream, man—making records. Now Ace does $2 million, $3 million a year. But I'm older. I just wanna play with the label. I'm gonna sell, and try to stay on in some capacity. I guess it's time. I'm a diabetic. I've had triple bypass surgery. I've got cataracts tremendously, to where I can't see good. I wobble when I walk, but I still love the record business. It's all I have left."

Suddenly the telephone rang. Johnny motioned for me to turn over a CD, and I saw a colorful song title: "Love Is So Good When You're Stealing It." It was matched only by "You Left a Gold Mine for a Gold Digger."

"It's *soul*, man," Johnny said, finally off the phone. "It's old but it sells."

He rotated in the squeaky chair and pushed an audio cassette into a black tape deck behind his desk. "Now, this is a rap record," he said. "I think I got the beat the kids will go for." He turned the volume up so loud that the bass shook the frames on the walls. As the performers rapped and sang about looking for their honey, Johnny shifted in his seat, tapped his pen, and sang along: "He's a-lookin' for his hawn-eee, a-lookin' for his hawn-eee." Squeak, squeak. He turned the sound down abruptly and said, "Yeah, well, you get the idea. I'm doin' a deal right now with Willie Clayton, the R&B singer, for a live album. Willie wasn't nothin' when we picked him up. Now he's *big*. Man, we've got rockabilly, soul, rap, gospel. I'll try anything. I've even got an album on Frankie Ford, *Hot and Lonely*. Hey, ain't that a great title? Oh, Frankie sings better than ever; he's still a big boy. He's still got the old New Orleans Sound."

Exactly.

Thibodaux, Louisiana: When There's No Way Out

On the evening of the summer solstice, I poked around a little black cemetery in Thibodaux, Louisiana, looking for the grave of bluesman Eddie Jones, better known as Guitar Slim. At first glance I thought I had come to the wrong place, for the unnamed cemetery was surrounded by old frame houses that put the living and the dead in an eerie juxtaposition. Across the street, somebody had spray-painted "Black is back!" on the yellow walls of a closed nightclub. I wondered if Slim, who is buried about two hundred feet away, ever sings there on thick summer nights, and if his uneasy spirit sways with the tall grass. I imagined him as the blues version of Marley's ghost, dragging a red electric guitar, leaping across the smooth white sarcophagi, and wailing about the crazy things he used to do.

Slim lived hard and died young, like a character in a blues song. In 1954, his single "The Things That I Used to Do" hit No. 1 on *Billboard*'s R&B charts and became the best-selling record of the year. Like Slim, the song was Delta blues, electric division. His vocal style, a blend of blues and gospel, now seems as natural to the region as bayous and jambalaya, but these days you seldom hear his records played on the radio. When I told a friend that I was going to Thibodaux (pronounced TIB-a-doe) to find Guitar Slim's grave, he looked at me blankly and said, "Slim who?" The next day he ran up to me at the office and said, "Hey, I heard Guitar Slim's record on the radio last night!" He proclaimed the coincidence mystical.

When Slim started singing in the late 1940s, Cajun, zydeco, Dixieland, and modern jazz ruled the night. In the region's tough rural clubs, where soft hands and hard liquor flowed freely, some bar owners strung curtains across the stage to screen white customers from black musicians. Slim graduated to a store in New Orleans that sold herbs, records, and voodoo dolls. He played as if in a trance. One night he struck his head while on stage, but he refused to quit, even as blood gushed onto his white suit.

By 1950, *Louisiana Weekly* proclaimed Slim "the New Orleans blues sensation," and he shot across the South as briefly and brilliantly as a meteor. His few recordings went on to influence Frank Zappa, Stevie Ray Vaughan, and Billy Gibbons of ZZ Top, and to affect legions of unknown rock guitarists. By turning up the volume on his public-address system, us-

The grave of blues singer Eddie "Guitar Slim" Jones in Thibodaux, La.,
1995. Photo by Randy McNutt.

ing only treble, Slim created a distorted fuzz-tone sound that would be imitated by 1960s rock bands. (Slim didn't use amplifiers; the public address system was louder.) Because he handled the electric guitar aggressively, yet sensually, Slim was a prehistoric rock guitarist. He sang differently, too, sounding more like an early soul singer in New Orleans' Moonlight Inn and the Club Tiajuana. His performances influenced Earl King, the noted blues singer and guitarist, and possibly even a young Ray Charles, who played on local recording sessions. All the performers knew Slim, for he did more than entertain. He captivated.

Sadly, Guitar Slim is only vaguely familiar now. He died before the 1950s ended, an eon ago in music history. Young musicians don't remember him. Not many of Thibodaux's 14,000 people are likely to know his name, either, although he lived and performed in the southern Louisiana city and helped develop its reputation as a rural music center. These days, Thibodaux is too busy growing, too busy forging better racial relations, to remember the 1950s. Same city, different world. Occasionally, strangers like me will take a blues pilgrimage to Slim's grave and call Aaron Caillouet, a former city councilman and record collector whose 1994 mayoral campaign included a promise to proclaim a Guitar Slim Day and erect a graveside monument to the singer. Caillouet (pronounced KUY-u-wet) lost that election, but not his love for the blues.

I called him early from Baton Rouge, seventy-five miles northwest of Thibodaux, and he agreed to meet me in the cemetery after a parish commission meeting. I drove south on Louisiana Highway 1, which accommodates mostly small towns and runs parallel to Bayou LaFourche, a navigable waterway that empties into the Mississippi. For miles I passed rice and cotton fields so flat that they appeared to go on forever. The drive seemed to last for days. Cars traveled thirty miles an hour. At times the road zigzagged into swamps and plantation country, revealing new brick and vinyl-sided houses sitting next to dented mobile homes with Spanish moss hanging from the trees. I went through small French towns named Belle Rose, Napoleonville, and Labadieville, and past stands of blooming crepe myrtle. Rural Napoleonville, population 800, looked anything but grand, although it was named for the emperor himself by a follower who had moved to the Louisiana country at the beginning of the nineteenth century. During the Civil War, Union troops boarded their horses in Napoleonville's Christ Episcopal Church and used its stained-glass windows for target practice. Such Yankee arrogance must have angered Braxton Bragg, the Confederate general who owned a Labadieville sugar plantation, and Edward Douglass

White, a local Confederate officer who would one day become a United States Supreme Court justice.

Farther south on Highway 1, I saw a number of weathered roadhouses with so much atmosphere that I could hear pianos tinkling and shotglasses clanging upon scarred oaken bars. The faded sign for boarded-up Tu-Lu's offered "Adult Dancing," and I pictured sweaty couples wrapped tighter than Twinkies. Driving through the lush countryside, in humid 95 degree weather, I saw green fields superimposed over my teenage vacation memories. I recalled newly integrated downtowns across the South, all dark-brick Victorian places with white linen napkins folded neatly on cafeteria tables, and seas of black faces moving everywhere. My family had never seen so many black people back in Ohio. It was like going to another country. Although I attended an integrated school at the time in Hamilton, I knew little of black culture. It seemed as different to me as the cultures of India or China. Now I realize that our town was not much different from Southern towns in those days. Both were segregated in their own ways. No blacks (at least none I can remember) lived in our older, working-class neighborhood, and nobody mentioned them. They lived in an even older neighborhood called the Second Ward, about three miles north of my house. They rarely entered our neighborhood, not even to buy a loaf of bread. Nevertheless, I did know something about black music because I heard it on the radio every day. I didn't think of it as black. If it had a beat and a good melody, I liked it. In those days I knew nothing of Guitar Slim or his small role in shaping the music that I enjoyed.

When I finally arrived in Thibodaux, the rural landscape immediately shifted to suburban. Fast-food restaurants appeared like mirages on one end of the city, old neighborhoods on the other. On my maps, Thibodaux was a black dot surrounded by blue lakes and thin blue lines—rural roads that ran through vast sugarcane fields. What I thought was a precisely carved canal ran through town and into the fields, but I soon learned that it is Bayou LaFourche. A city clerk told me, "It's one hundred miles long—the longest street in the world." In tourism advertisements, Thibodaux promotes itself as "Bayou LaFourche country's best-kept secret," because the city, the seat of LaFourche Parish, is still hidden in the country. It features a Holiday Inn, a Howard Johnson Lodge, more than twenty buildings (mostly Queen Anne Revival homes) on the National Register of Historic Places, and Laurel Valley, the largest surviving nineteenth-century sugar plantation.

Around Thibodaux, lush green seas and bumpy gray roads have changed little since the early 1950s, when bluesmen and Klansmen passed each other on their divergent nightly rounds. I could almost see Guitar Slim driving so fast that the forty-five-mile ride west from New Orleans seemed to last only fifteen minutes. In my mind I saw kids in dusty bib overalls running to the gate to watch Slim's Cadillac fly past their shacks and the antebellum homes. On those Saturday nights, Thibodaux surged with eager black faces from backwater towns and farms. They packed into a popular nightclub called the Sugar Bowl, owned by a black entrepreneur named Hosea Hill. (Locals called him "Hosey.") He knew talent and how to promote it, and in later years he managed Slim. When Slim performed at the Bowl, crowds came early and stayed late.

By the time I arrived in town, the Sugar Bowl was gone. Somebody told me that the building burned in the 1980s, so I stopped in the library for information. A reference librarian said she had never heard of the Sugar Bowl or Guitar Slim, but he sounded interesting. It was as though his wild nights had never happened; the only evidence of his life was in the cemetery. For twenty minutes I searched for Slim's grave while an old black man watched me. Assuming I was looking for a relative, he informed me that the white cemetery—a fancier place filled with larger tombs—was on the south side of town. He said that in Thibodaux, white and black still prefer their own cemeteries, despite the official demise of segregation in the 1950s. I continued to search for the large monument that I expected to mark Slim's grave, but I found instead a small limestone cross with worn letters: Eddie Jones. Born Dec. 10, 1925. Died Feb. 7, 1959. (Even the tombstone added mystery to his life, for his record company biography listed his birth year as 1926.) The cross looked a century old; beneath it lay a star without an epitaph. I noticed that Slim and a few other people were buried, but most rested above ground, in sarcophagi. In this lowland region, the old man said, only the indigent are buried. Most bodies are placed in surface vaults to prevent caskets from popping out of the wet ground. He directed me to a section between the Baptists and Methodists, sort of a Protestant no-man's land where Slim's casket appeared ready to spring forth upon an unsuspecting world.

Slim probably would not mind the location. He lived for the moment, not eternity. Immediately after his discharge from the army in 1946, Edward Jones returned to his hometown, Greenwood, Mississippi, to perform in local taverns. A year later, he went on the road. He improved his guitar style by listening to the blues of Gatemouth Brown and Aaron T-Bone Walker, but somehow Slim retained his musical independence. He sounded—and looked—unusual. People started calling him Guitar Slim because at six feet and 160 pounds, he appeared taller and thinner to the eye. The public associated Slim with his first love, the electric guitar. He always carried it. Appropriately, he called it the Devil, and spoke of it as though it were alive. Early in his career, he performed with a drummer named Willie Nettles and fifteen-year-old pianist Huey Smith, who would one day write and record "Don't You Just Know It," "Rockin' Pneumonia and the Boogie Woogie Flu," and other songs for Ace Records. Slim always hired talented musicians and performed in the best clubs. His group became one of the South's tighter bands, entertaining thousands of people every weekend.

Unfortunately, his working environment was not agreeable to a man who loved strong whiskey, gin, and wine, fast women, faster cars, and hundred-dollar bills in his pocket. His flamboyance attracted women, and their beauty attracted him. While in Las Vegas, he hired a "shake dancer" to accompany his band back home. He didn't need additional female company. In his room above the Dew Drop Inn in New Orleans, he partied all night. When most people his age were rising to dress for work, Slim was relaxing by blasting the hallway with hot licks and turning up the volume until it shattered nerves and glass. Slim didn't care. He liked to practice. When the police arrived, they usually found him surrounded by young women. Sheets of song lyrics written in eyebrow pencil were tacked to his walls. He composed songs about loving women ("Later for You Baby"), leaving them ("Well I Done Got Over It"), and celebrating them ("I Want to Love-a You"). A female entourage followed him everywhere. Jerry Wexler, the Atlantic Records executive, recalled waiting for Slim at rehearsal in the late 1950s: "The next thing we saw was a tidal wave of humanity pouring down the street, children and grownups, couriers announcing to the world, 'Here come Slim! Slim on the way!' A fleet of Cadillacs pulled up, and [Slim] himself emerged in a mobile bower of chicks in red dresses—matching the Cadillacs—and a retinue of courtiers, seneschals, janissaries, mountebanks, and tumblers."

Despite Slim's ostentation, fellow singers liked him and respected his talent. They thought he was funny, too. Strangers misunderstood. They laughed when he made faces and talked fast in a mumbling, thick rural accent, often in rhyme. On stage, he looked equally odd. His legs bowed like rubber bands, and he danced, contorted, and uncoiled to the crowd's delight. This human Slinky was loud in every way. He loved red suits and white shoes. In other moods, he wore blue, green, purple, and orange suits with matching shoes and hair. When he smiled, a gold tooth shone prominently. "Nobody could outdo Slim," producer Johnny Vincent said. "He was a dude. Every time he came out on stage, you'd see a new Slim."

His outrageous appearance would be imitated by modern rock performers. Unfortunately, so would his excesses—a pint of gin and a fifth of port a day. (Despite his prodigious drinking abilities, Slim was once defeated in a drinking contest by James Davis, who joined Slim's band at seventeen. Slim nicknamed Davis "Thunderbird," reportedly after they had been drinking Thunderbird wine. The T-Bird went on to record with many blues stars—and to die on stage at age fifty-three.) Another band member, Lloyd Lambert, once told writer Jeff Hannusch that he had warned Slim to slow down, but Slim replied, "Lloyd, I live three days to y'all's one. The world won't owe me a thing when I'm gone."

When "The Things That I Used to Do" hit No. 1 (and reportedly sold a million copies) in January 1954, Slim received a new Cadillac as a "gift" from Specialty Records. He promptly got drunk and hit a bulldozer. Somehow, in an alcoholic stupor he managed to work regularly, compose music on deadline (in the studio, when necessary), and write such darkly prophetic titles as "Bad Luck Blues," "Trouble Don't Last," "Reap What You Sow (Bad Woman Blues)," "Sufferin' Mind," and "It Hurts to Love Someone." His songs, with well-crafted melodies and intelligent lyrics, reflected his joy and pain and modern music's early evolution.

Slim recorded his better songs for Specialty, for a royalty of one-half cent per record. At first he hesitated to join the label, because competitor Atlantic, which finally did sign him toward the end of his life, originally offered him three cents per record. But Vincent, Specialty's New Orleans producer, possessed a personality slicker than shellac. He told Slim, "Man, they won't pay you; we will. Nobody can pay you three cents a record!" So in October 1953, Slim and his band entered Cosimo Matassa's J&M Recording in the French Quarter to cut "The Things That I Used to Do" and three other original songs. Slim told friends that a devil and an angel had appeared to him in a dream, offering songs. He chose the devil's. Pianist Ray Charles arranged the session, which Vincent said lasted ten hours because Slim demanded a string of retakes and played too loud. (Matassa remembers him as a tube-blower, but Slim also had trouble keeping time.) The next day, label owner Art Rupe heard the songs over the telephone. He hated them and threatened to fire Vincent if the first record did not sell.

From its headquarters in Los Angeles, Specialty released many black records that few white people ever heard—boogie-woogie piano, straightforward blues, R&B, and gospel. Specialty became a musical mining company. It identified New Orleans as a rich vein, came in and tapped it, then moved on to other areas. Rupe, a successful white businessman, is remembered today mainly by collectors, but in the mid-1950s he sold millions of records for the pioneer rockers Little Richard, Lloyd Price, and Larry Williams. Apparently Rupe did not appreciate Slim's darker blues, but he didn't mind releasing records that he had no personal interest in, so long as they made money. To Rupe's surprise, "The Things That I Used to Do" received heavy airplay and turned Slim into a national star.

He attracted thousands of customers to the Dew Drop Inn in New Orleans. Like Slim, it never shut down. When he climbed up on its stage, he became a Crescent City happening through which customers vicariously fulfilled their fantasies—the women, the adulation, the money, the cars, the no-cares lifestyle. For a few hours, at least, they could forget the kids and the bills. With the hit, Slim finally gained the national audience he needed. He sang at Gleason's and the Ebony Club in Cleveland, the Club Walahiye in Atlanta, and the Palms Club in Hallandale, Florida. At the Apollo in New York, Slim once became so excited that he wouldn't stop playing. Stagehands had to drop the curtain, but Slim continued. In Louisiana, his act became a legend. Before battles of the bands, Slim would tell the other performers— Fats Domino, Bobby Bland, and anybody else with enough nerve to share the stage with him—that he would win. In clubs, he'd often walk off the stage and into the street, playing guitar with an electrical cord that stretched, according to varying estimates, from 200 to 350 feet. Sometimes he stood on the shoulders of a muscular valet. Traffic stopped. Drivers honked. Woman ran up and touched him. He walked on the tops of cars, picking his guitar and somehow not missing a beat. (Today Guitar Slim Jr. performs a more sedate version of the blues in New Orleans.)

When Slim's hit fell off the charts, Rupe released "The Story of My Life," also recorded at the Vincent session. It was a good record, but not a national hit. Slim could not understand. He asked how a great blues singer could go from No. 1 to nothing. The record men said he just wasn't lucky this time. Trying again, Specialty recorded Slim in Chicago and Los Angeles, but those recordings also failed to sell, despite the work of talented producer Robert "Bumps" Blackwell. Through it all, Slim remained popular in the South, where crowds knew his colorful ways. He would still show up for work, even though by 1958 the alcohol had compromised his health. To make things worse, Slim ruptured himself while riding his guitar on stage. Nevertheless, in February 1959 he embarked on an East Coast tour. He looked tired but seemed enthusiastic and ready to play. He didn't last long. Slim collapsed after performing in Newark, New Jersey. A few hours later, on February 7, he died of pneumonia in New York City. He was only thirty-four years old.

Like many blues singers before and after him, Slim left this world with nothing. But he left on his terms. The news of Slim's passing was overshadowed by the deaths a few days earlier of rock stars Buddy Holly, J.P. "The Big Bopper" Richardson, and Ritchie Valens, in a plane crash. Back in Louisiana, people did not hear of Slim's death for a week. Hosea Hill flew Slim's body to Thibodaux, arranged a large funeral at the Mount Zion Baptist Church, and reportedly buried the singer in an unmarked grave with his favorite gold-top Gibson Les Paul. Later, out of guilt or friendship, Hill erected the small cross. When Hill died in 1973, he was interred—above ground—next to Slim.

At Hill's vault I met Caillouet, a white man in his early fifties. The setting sun cast a deep red glow over the graves. Caillouet had not eaten dinner yet; he had been campaigning for parish president. He wore the politician's summer uniform: dark pants and a white short-sleeved shirt, open at the neck. As we talked, a black man named Henry Young, Caillouet's boyhood friend and a Thibodaux concrete contractor, stopped to say hello. He had brought his mother to the cemetery, and while she visited other graves we talked about Slim's. Young, a quiet man with a kind face, said, "When Slim was living in Thibodaux and going at it, things were exciting. Thibodaux was a big stop on the nightlife rounds. Every artist knew Thibodaux, even James Brown and all the big-city bands. As a kid, I remember seeing Slim at Hosey's. Hosey brought in all the black artists from New Orleans. Man, what a sound!"

"Remember sneaking in under the fence at Slim's show at the minor-league ballpark?" Caillouet said.

"Yeah, Slim would go out into the audience with his guitar, and the crowd would go crazy. Back then, all the musicians wanted to do was play. They didn't think too much about money and the future. They played for the thrill. I heard that Hosey locked up Slim in some contract for life, but Slim's real downfall was his drinkin'. When you're drinkin' and throwin' away your money, you're only livin' from week to week. He was a poorly man.'"

"In those days," Caillouet said, "we had segregation in town, so the white kids who liked black music had to sneak into the ballpark to watch the performers. We looked at segregation as something we had to live with. We didn't think about it. Blacks had their theaters, whites had theirs. Blacks had their lounges, whites had theirs. But people got along as neighbors. As a white kid in the '50s, I had a hard time describing the appeal of rhythm and blues. It just took over. Back then, white adults liked to see Little Richard and Fats Domino and other black singers perform in white clubs and VFW halls. I always thought that black people believed the whites were trying to steal their music. Most white audiences didn't care for the bluesmen like Guitar Slim and Bobby Bland. Those guys pulled mostly black audiences."

Caillouet grew up in a mixed neighborhood near the cemetery. He and the black kids had one thing in common—the music. "I didn't think there was anything wrong with watching black performers," he said. "On all these streets, promoters used to staple posters on telephone poles to announce the coming of black bands. People would yell, 'Fats is back!' I remember how easily Domino's fingers—rings and all—glided over the keys. You just knew that Fats was a star. But Slim, now, he was something more. He was the flashiest performer I ever saw."

"He wore T-shirts with suits and a wide fedora before they were the style," Young said. "He played a big hollow-body electric guitar then, and it seemed to move with him like it was a natural part of his body. After Slim died, Hosey kept bringing in plenty of talent. He didn't miss a beat. He'd book artists during the week so he didn't have to pay them as much. When Hosey died, we lost that live entertainment. The town changed. It's a shame, too. You don't see it no more."

Young stared at Slim's grave. "Think you can put up a monument for him, Aaron?"

"I'll keep trying, Henry, but nowadays hardly anyone in Thibodaux knows who he was."

They shook hands and left for their families and dinner. Caillouet said he would play a Guitar Slim album and relax. For a few minutes I stayed around to watch the sunset and contemplate Slim's kaleidoscopic life—the bars, the liquor, the women, the songs. Searching for my car keys, I randomly pulled a scrap of paper from my pocket. On it I had scribbled "Guitar Slim's last songs were 'If I Had My Life to Live Over' and 'When There's No Way Out.'"

The stories of his life.

Shreveport: Susie-Q

State Route 120 in western Louisiana cuts through vast woods and tiny rural towns named Pelican, Many, and Grand Encore. Town signs include the word *community,* perhaps to assure travelers that the countryside has ended. Near Marthaville, population 200, I passed a portable yellow church sign that read: "If you're looking for a sign from God, this is it." I saw a couple of stores, a few houses, a Pentecostal church, and a sign for the Rebel State Commemorative Area. At first I thought the Rebel State referred to Louisiana, but then I learned the park was named for a Confederate soldier who was separated from his unit during a skirmish at Crump's Corner, near Marthaville. Three Union soldiers killed him as he looked for water. A local family named Barnhill buried the unidentified soldier, and their relatives cared for his grave for a century. In 1961, newspapers wrote about him, and in 1962, at a time of heated civil-rights demonstrations, the state erected a black wrought-iron fence and historical marker at the grave of the Unknown Confederate Soldier. He became the focus of the new Rebel State Commemorative Area. Today they'd probably name it something else.

Even a century after the soldier's death, Civil War wounds had not healed. Animosity festered in the late 1950s and early 1960s when Northerners arrived to help organize blacks to vote. But gradually the times improved, and the focus of the park shifted from war to music. The main attraction, the Louisiana Country Music Museum, features an amphitheater where George Jones, the Oak Ridge Boys, Bill Monroe, Roy Acuff, Jimmie Davis, and Slim Whitman have performed.

As I pulled into the museum's empty parking lot on a comfortable summer afternoon, I noticed a ranger—dressed in green uniform shorts—riding a lawn mower. He waved as I parked next to the modern one-story brick building. The museum, built to honor native country and gospel performers (and any others who have performed in the state or contributed to country music), starts with a curving entryway and a narrowing walkway that suggests the shape of a fiddle.

Inside, the silence hurt my ears. I waited for ten minutes, then finally laid my $1 admission on the counter and walked around. Suddenly a deep

Nat Stuckey's first big hit was labeled "Sweet Thing" by Paula Records of Shreveport, but was pronounced "Sweet Thang." It was a No. 4 hit in 1966. Stuckey called his band the Sweet Thangs.

Jimmie Davis, the singing Mississippi governor, in a 1940s publicity photo.

Jim Quayhagen makes a point in the Louisiana Country Music Museum, where he was curator in 1995. Photo by Randy McNutt.

Stan "The Record Man" Lewis in his Jewel/Paula Records office in Shreveport in 1995. Photo by Randy McNutt.

voice echoed throughout the museum: "Well, hellooo there!" The ranger who had waved to me, a tall man in his fifties, walked up and shook hands. Sporting a dark handlebar mustache and a bald head, he resembled a slender G. Gordon Liddy. His business card, featuring his caricature with a pipe, identified him as Jim Quayhagen, "interpretative ranger and country music fan." He said his assignment is like working in hillbilly heaven, even though the museum attracts too few visitors. "We don't have the money to promote the place," he said. "It's an obscure treasure. Somehow we have to keep our music's heritage alive. I've been to England three times, and there the kids know what happened at Hastings. Now, if you go up the road here to Marthaville and ask the kids when the Civil War was fought, they'll look at you blankly and say, 'Huh? What Civil War?' We can't let that happen to our music."

Glass cases held hundreds of artifacts, including Dick Hart's tan cowboy hat and a fan magazine featuring Hart's Rangers from 1945; photographs of Louisiana fiddlers (black and white) who played for minstrel shows, house parties, fish fries, political rallies, harvest festivals, camp meetings, revivals, and military musters; first pressings of some 45s; sheet music for Nat Stuckey's hit "Sweet Thang"; singer Jimmy "C" Newman's shirt and cap (the "C" stands for "Cajun"; he hails from a town named Big Mamou, Louisiana); a fiddle owned by Roy Acuff; Wayne Raney's harmonica; Edison records made by country music pioneer Vernon Dalhart under a whole list of aliases; Grandpa Jones' cowbell; Charlie Louvin's cowboy suit; and a photograph of Huddie Ledbetter, the black Louisianian known as Leadbelly, who sang hillbilly, folk, and blues.

Quayhagen loves his Louisiana because its music is varied and deeply ingrained in the culture. In the early to mid-twentieth century, jazz and ragtime were big in New Orleans, zydeco in Louisiana's southwest, the blues in the Delta, country string bands in the northwest, and Spanish and western swing in the west. Having been in ultra-commercial Nashville only a few days earlier, where most of the recordings sounded the same, I saw some irony in the music's roots.

As we passed more exhibits, Quayhagen never stopped talking. Music triggered memories of his Southern youth, when in Shreveport he attended shows at the *Louisiana Hayride* in the 1950s. "So much in life is happenstance," he said. "We end up where we are for various reasons, some of them pretty flimsy. Luckily I found this job, in my home region. It's the same way with performers. Before Ernest Tubb became a star, he had a bout with tonsillitis. Doctors removed his tonsils, and his voice changed. What would he have been without that operation? Jim Reeves first got a job on the *Hay-ride* as a guitarist. He wanted to sing. One night Hank Williams came in drunk. In desperation, the *Hayride* people turned to Jim and said, 'Can you go on?' What if Hank had been sober that night? I remember seeing Slim Whitman, a Shreveport postman, sing on the show every Saturday night. He had to keep the postal job to support his family. What if he never left the post office? And, of course, Elvis Presley sang 'Blue Moon of Kentucky' on the *Grand Ole Opry,* but he wasn't well received. *Opry* managers didn't tolerate flops, so they didn't ask him back. He came over to the *Hayride.* One night he asked the crowd, 'If you like my music, will y'all please buy my new record?' I turned to a buddy and yelled, 'No!' We considered Elvis a competitor for the girls. He was good-looking, and he had *hair.*"

We turned a corner and stepped into a life-size recreation of a country church, complete with pews and pulpit recovered from a local nineteenth-century Baptist sanctuary. Quayhagen stood behind the pulpit, cleared his throat, and motioned for me to sit. "I was born a Belgian Catholic," he said in a resonant voice, "but I know all the old Baptist hymns. I listened to songs written by an itinerant black songwriter and evangelist named Thomas A. Dorsey, not to be confused with bandleader Tommy Dorsey. He was a sinful man, he said, but the Lord would help him overcome his sins and get to heaven. Dorsey had a great impact on modern gospel music. His music is listed under a number of songs in the Baptist hymnal. In the 1940s, Mahalia Jackson recorded his 'Take My Hand, Precious Lord.' In the 1950s, the song was resurrected by Tennessee Ernie Ford and Red Foley. Elvis made it popular again in the 1960s. In 1951, Foley recorded another Dorsey song, '(There'll Be) Peace in the Valley (for Me),' and it reportedly became the first gospel song to sell a million copies. Now, if he had had an angel looking after him, or at the least a lawyer, maybe he could have gotten some royalties."

At a wall display of Jimmie Davis memorabilia, Quayhagen bowed his head. Davis, governor of Louisiana from 1944 to 1948 and from 1956 to 1960, sang on the *Hayride.* Quayhagen touched a button to start a recording of Davis' "You Are My Sunshine" and said, "In the fall of 1943, Jimmie Davis campaigned in Many, Louisiana, on a semi truck and flatbed trailer. My mother and dad, both liberal knee-jerk yellow-dog Democrats, were right there with little Jimmy Quayhagen, who looked like a Bangladesh orphan: skinny legs, snotty nose. We were so poor, we couldn't afford a cat; we had a possum. Our family picked cotton. It weighs as much as concrete. I think picking cotton gives you soul. A lot of country and blues singers picked cotton, especially ones from families like ours. Well, naturally, my folks went to see Jimmie Davis. The people loved him. He stood up on the trailer and said, 'I'm Jimmie Davis and I'm running for governor. I've got a great political speech prepared for y'all today, but would you rather hear a song?' The crowd screamed, 'Sing, Jimmie, sing!' Jimmie had a strange policy: he didn't kiss babies. But he reached down and grabbed me and pulled me up on the stage. We sang a song together: 'Promise me that you will never be nobody's darlin' but mine. . . .' I never got a royalty; he got elected. On that day, he must have locked up about every vote in Sabine Parish simply by singing. He became the only governor—nay, the only politician I have ever heard of—who did not break a single campaign promise. That's because he didn't make any. He sang his way right into the governor's mansion that fall and became a non-controversial governor in a controversial time." Quayhagen played the tape one more time. "Do you hear me singing in the background? If so, you have a vivid imagination."

Driving through Marthaville a few minutes later, I couldn't stop thinking of Jim Quayhagen's face—and his beloved music. He showed me its evolution and its ghosts. Inside the museum, all songs blended: black and white; rural and urban; gospel and hillbilly; everything and rock 'n' roll. Someday, five thousand years from now, the museum might be uncovered from under a lava sea by perplexed archaeologists and anthropologists, who will examine the remains and conclude that Louisiana's old-time country was truly the people's music.

The next morning, I ended up on the commercial strip in Bossier City, which looked like any other until I found a red ranch complex that was a former home of the *Hayride*. As I pulled into the driveway, construction workers were carrying away *Hayride* signs and memorabilia as they converted the building into a Christian teen center. Suddenly reality struck me: in the day of rocking country, the *Hayride* is like a 1958 Rambler—a woeful anachronism that won't come back in style.

Jeff Hall, the proud tenant and a twenty-year-old minister, saw some irony in the building's new role. "This place will be a refuge from drugs, alcohol, and tobacco," he explained. "The kids need a place to go to have fun. Our vision for the Winning Way complex is to see thousands of souls saved and families come together like never before. I'll even make a miniature golf course out front that spells out 'Praise Jesus.'"

A half-century earlier, Hank Williams appeared on a *Hayride* stage in a drunken daze. Nevertheless, the live show, broadcast by KWKH, attracted

3,000 people to the Municipal Auditorium on Saturday nights. The show started as the *Saturday Night Roundup* in 1936. In 1948, station owner John Ewing decided to expand and rename it. When the *Grand Ole Opry* told a young Elvis Presley not to return (he'd be better off driving a truck), he joined the *Hayride*. Presley's voice boomed into twenty-eight states, and KWKH's clear-channel signal covered the "Ark-La-Tex" region—southwest Arkansas, northwest Louisiana, and northeast Texas—like a tarpaulin. By the time Presley left the show eighteen months later, RCA Victor—and the famous Elvis wiggle—had created the biggest name in America. At his fare-well *Hayride* concert, on December 15, 1956, 13,000 people crammed into Hirsch Coliseum. To calm the kids, emcee Horace Logan grabbed a micro-phone and uttered some famous first words: "Ladies and gentlemen, Elvis has left the building."

The *Hayride* replaced Presley with Bob Luman, a rockabilly singer straight out of high school in Texas. He balanced the show with country stars such as Slim Whitman, a postal worker who recorded for Imperial Records in Los Angeles. In the KWKH studio in 1952, Whitman and his band recorded his first three hits: "Indian Love Call," "Rose-Marie," and "Love Song of the Waterfall."

When Williams left to go on tour, Logan replaced him with Jim Reeves and other new singers. The *Hayride* became the second-largest country music show in the nation and promoted the Browns, Webb Pierce, Sonny James, Kitty Wells, Patsy Montana, Red Sovine—hundreds of country per-formers. At its peak, the show amassed a network of about seventy local radio stations out of about nine hundred in the country.

But by 1958, times had changed. The *Hayride* faded, and Logan left town. Television viewing, personnel changes, and cultural upheaval finally overcame the show. Late that year, it switched from weekly to monthly per-formances, and later to occasional ones—then to none. In the late 1980s, a revived *Hayride* reopened, but it didn't last. When I arrived in 1995, its final venue was the ranch complex in neighboring Bossier City. By then the building had been used most recently for a restaurant called the Hayride Kitchen. Eventually the building just sat there—18,000 square feet of emp-tiness.

At the ranch, Hall showed me a wall covered with the signatures of per-formers who had signed while waiting to go on stage. I stepped onto that stage and tried to imagine an enthusiastic crowd, but all I could see was a pile of junk—broken tables, tarnished kitchen appliances, and a podium with the *Hayride* name inscribed on the front. History moved on before my eyes. "Hey, there!" Hall yelled to me as he pulled a rusty horseshoe from a wall. "You want a souvenir of the *Louisiana Hayride*?"

I drove away in a daze and ended up on the strip in neighboring Bossier City. In the lobby of Ralph and Kacoo's restaurant, I stared at a 12½-foot stuffed ("harvested") alligator named Jumbeaux. An old man in a red flannel shirt walked up to me and said, "Now, ain't he some little gator?" At lunch, I passed on the gator meat and took the whitefish. Later I looked down the busy highway, which once rocked with strip clubs, dive bars, and sexy hot attractions. I saw gadget-rental stores, more bars, and Taco Bell. The scene—Any Highway, U.S.A.—did not meet my expectations of Louisiana's roots-music capital, a community that once nurtured R&B, gospel, zydeco, country, rockabilly—even musical politics.

In Bossier City and Shreveport in the 1940s, music and politics intersected like two old highways. During a gubernatorial campaign, Doc Guidry, the King of the Cajun Fiddlers, joined boogie-woogie pianist Moon Mullican and guitarist Joe Shelton to introduce candidate Jimmie Davis, the singer and composer of "You Are My Sunshine." Their blatant partisanship angered Congressman Jimmy Morrison, who bought full-page advertisements in the Shreveport newspaper to announce a speech—for adults only. A large crowd of curious people attended, and Morrison cranked up a Victrola and played Davis' "Red Nightgown Blues." Morrison hoped that the record would expose Davis as a phony, but the crowd paid no attention to the message. They were too busy dancing. An angry Morrison grabbed the disc, broke it into pieces, and yelled, "Elect him if you want!" They did.

Politically and financially, Shreveport has always been important to northern Louisiana. The seat of Caddo Parish, on the Red River near the Texas border, has been prosperous since its founding in 1837. During the Civil War, the city served as a temporary capital of the Confederacy. In 1906, somebody struck oil, unleashing gushers and entrepreneurial drilling. By the 1940s, the city bustled with oil firms, refineries, and cotton producers. In 1950, the year the *Hayride*'s popularity leaped beyond the borders of Louisiana, 127,206 people called Shreveport home.

In those days, XERF radio also became another major influence on Shreveport musicians. Its transmitter, based across the Rio Grande in Mexico, boomed with from 250,000 to 500,000 watts. The signal rolled across Texas and Louisiana like a tornado, bringing the latest sounds of Faron Young and Johnny Cash—and sometimes the new music. Disc jockeys sold mail-order items: baby chicks, holy oil, ballpoint pens, D-Con mouse and rat killer, Last Supper tablecloths, and "autographed" pictures of Jesus.

Although KWKH grew in the 1950s, a local music industry didn't. It went to Nashville. Because Shreveport lacked studios and record companies, the city didn't develop a special sound, as New Orleans did with black party music. Instead, Shreveport absorbed pieces of the blues, country, gospel, and rock 'n' roll, and adapted them to northwest Louisiana culture and geography. The city's most famous song, Dale Hawkins' "Susie-Q," reflected all of these sounds until it became something original in itself. The rockabilly classic, powered by an understated melody and James Burton's repetitive, haunting guitar lick, foreshadowed rockabilly's evolution into generic rock 'n' roll. But bigger things would follow. In the 1960s, Shreveport would become a record distribution hub and the home of three independent labels that would dominate the "Ark-La-Tex" region for the next two decades and turn vinyl into gold.

As I walked around the modern downtown, the musical past came to life. I felt it everywhere. A life-size sculpture of Huddie Ledbetter, the black singer-songwriter better known as Leadbelly, stood on a street corner with his guitar. When I glanced at him, he looked alive. (I did not see the noticeable scar that some people claimed ran around his thick neck.) Leadbelly reportedly could sing five hundred original songs. In the mid-1920s he performed for Texas governor Pat Neff, who pardoned him of a murder charge. But the early days of the Depression found him back in prison again, this time in the infamous Louisiana State Penitentiary. On travels for the Library of Congress, folklorist John Lomax discovered Leadbelly at the prison, where he worked in the laundry. Lomax liked his voice, his vast repertoire, and his bravado. Leadbelly called himself the King of the Twelve-String Guitar Players of the World. Lomax cut some songs with Leadbelly on a portable recorder. Leadbelly liked to yell "Huh!" while singing. Later he moved to Shreveport and accepted a job as Lomax's personal driver. "Lomax was a wee bit wary of the barrel of a man, soon to be known in the national press as the murdering minstrel," said Keith Abel, a Shreveport music historian. "Even so, the two set off on a recording spree of street musicians, hoedown pickers, and prisoners in the American Southland." Along the way, Leadbelly cut his share of songs and became a folk-song hero among liberal Northerners. (His most famous song, "Good Night, Irene," was later recorded by the Weavers.) When he appeared in New York, a newspaper headline read: "SWEET SINGER OF THE SWAMPLANDS HERE TO DO A

FEW TUNES BETWEEN HOMICIDES." He wore bib overalls and a red bandanna. Despite his following, Leadbelly wasn't able to change his violent ways; he returned to prison for stabbing a man sixteen times.

I wondered if Leadbelly had ever walked along the streets in Shreveport's nineteenth-century cotton district. Driving slowly, one eye observing the crusty architecture, I found a renovated neighborhood on Commerce Street. A giant guitar hung from the front of a red brick building, above the words "James Burton's Rock 'n' Roll Cafe." Although Burton's name means nothing to most people, his music is another matter. They've heard it on dozens of hit records. By 1960 he was a major rock guitarist, backing Ricky Nelson, Hawkins, and Luman. In the 1970s, he joined Elvis Presley's musicians, the Taking Care of Business Band.

Something in Shreveport's water must spawn good musicians. Famed studio bassist Joe Osborn also grew up there and played music in high school. After learning from the records of Scotty Moore and Chet Atkins, he left for Las Vegas, then moved on to Los Angeles, where he became one of the city's top session musicians. With drummer Hal Blaine and pianist Larry Knechtel, Osborn played on hundreds of hits by artists such as the Fifth Dimension, Frank Sinatra, the Grass Roots, Richard Harris, Johnny Rivers, Petula Clark, and the Mamas and the Papas. Osborn estimates that he has played on at least 125 Top 10 hits, including "This Diamond Ring" by Gary Lewis and the Playboys, "Bridge over Troubled Water" by Simon and Garfunkel, and "We've Only Just Begun" by the Carpenters. In the 1990s he moved back to Louisiana. Another Shreveport native, drummer D.J. Fontana, has also played on dozens of hit rock and country records, and served in Presley's band for years. Fontana started on the *Hayride* at fifteen. When asked one night if he'd accompany an unknown kid named Presley, Fontana replied, "Well, sure, that's what I'm here for. I'll just keep it simple."

At noon I walked inside the Rock 'n' Roll Cafe, unaware that it didn't open until later in the afternoon. The place was empty. Just as I turned to walk out, I noticed a man working in the back. In the dim light I recognized Burton's angular face and the mop of brown hair that flowed down his neck. He stood on a ladder, changing lightbulbs. I asked if we could talk, and he politely agreed—after he finished his job. As he twisted the bulbs, I wondered why talented hands bothered with such a routine task.

"Shreveport is my home, personally and musically," he said. "I lived in California for years, but it didn't feel like home. Shreveport is the cradle of music in this part of the country. For hundreds of miles around us, all the way to the Carolinas, people listened to the *Hayride* on the radio. It influenced me and many other musicians. When I was young, I also listened to Frank 'Gatemouth' Page's R&B show here in town. So I had both the country and the R&B thing happening. By the time I was a teenager, I was mixing country and old blues licks. I played on the *Hayride* at fourteen. We had dozens of clubs then out in Bossier City. I played in my share of them. So by the time I started playing with Dale Hawkins, I had already backed some of the biggest names in country music. With rock 'n' roll coming on strong in 1957, our band went over to KWKH to make 'Susie-Q.' We just sat around and played. Back then, you just couldn't walk into a recording studio. We didn't even have one. The station was our studio. After the record got popular, things moved fast for me. The next thing I knew, I was sixteen years old and playing for Ricky Nelson out in L.A."

At the offices of Imperial Records in Los Angeles, Nelson overheard Luman's group (Burton and bassist James Kirkland) auditioning for owner Lew Chudd. Curious, Nelson walked down the hall to investigate. He liked their sparse rockabilly sound, so he invited the musicians to watch a recording session at Master Recorders. Soon Burton joined Nelson's band; he played on his records, toured with him, and even appeared on *The Ozzie and Harriet Show.* The work led Burton into a long career as a Los Angeles session musician. As his reputation grew, he toured with other performers and played on sessions for artists as diverse as Presley, the Monkees, the Supremes, Johnny Mathis, Buffalo Springfield, Frank Sinatra, the Beach Boys, Judy Collins, and Joni Mitchell. They all received a little piece of Shreveport in Burton's tasteful licks. In the 1970s, he played on thirty sessions a week—sometimes more—for Buck Owens, Emmylou Harris, John Denver, and other stars. "I had to be versatile to play on so many sessions for so many years," Burton said. But when the Los Angeles session business tightened in the 1980s, he longed for his native Louisiana. Eventually he returned to Shreveport, and a few years later he opened the rock cafe. "A musician has to play," he said, as he climbed the ladder to change another lightbulb. "I'm not giving up music. I'm just expanding my base."

When Burton was appearing on the *Hayride* in the late 1950s, Stan Lewis was selling records across town and starting to build an empire of discs. He turned his record store into one of the South's more prosperous music operations, then turned to releasing R&B, rock, and country hits on his own Jewel, Paula, and Ronn labels. Lewis also built one of the South's larger independent distributors, which helped promote independent labels and regional sounds.

The producer, publisher, label owner, and distributor was born near Shreveport on July 5, 1927, to hard-working Italian parents, Frank and Lucille Lewis. His father worked in a meat-packing house during the Depression, and in 1941 opened a family grocery. Young Stan helped. Even then, he preferred music—big-band jazz by Duke Ellington, Glenn Miller, and others, and the blues and gospel songs that people sang in his racially mixed neighborhood. He also played clarinet in the high school band. In the late 1940s he started buying jukeboxes, pinball machines, and records. The discs came from a little R&B store at 728 Texas Street. In 1948, Lewis bought the store and renamed it Stan's Record Shop. At eight by twelve feet, the one-story shop was smaller inside than some people's living rooms, but Lewis crammed it with R&B and a few country records. He continued to work in his father's grocery while his wife, Paula, worked in the shop. They came up with a catchy slogan ("728—Don't Be Late!") and advertised on KWKH, trying to reach a simmering youth market. They even held autograph parties for recording artists, including Presley. Lewis worked twelve hours a day and became the first local businessman to hire blacks in retail sales.

"I grew up selling newspapers and milk bottles and shining shoes," he said. "I made nickels and dimes. Today, people step over coins and don't bother to pick them up. But they were big money when I grew up. During World War II, I played drums a little to make extra money. The real drummers were off to war. I was too young to go. I saved all my money—$2,500. And that's what I went into the record business with."

His timing was perfect. All across the country, dozens of entrepreneurs were forming independent record companies, including King in Cincinnati, Specialty and Imperial in Los Angeles, and Chess in Chicago. Their owners sought out Lewis when they came into Shreveport with big dreams and little cash. They stored discs in their trunks next to tape recorders on which they sometimes recorded singers on the road. "I met all these guys when they first put out their records," Lewis said. "As their companies grew into great monsters, my shop grew with them. We did mail-order and retail. I picked up the distribution thing on my own, and grew into it. It wasn't planned. I didn't have board meetings. I just *did* it." By 1954, Lewis did more than sell and distribute records. He produced several Top 10 national country and R&B hits for independent labels. They included blues singer Lowell Fulsom's "Reconsider Baby" for Checker, Jimmy and Johnny's "If You Don't, Somebody Else Will" for Chess, and Jimmy "C" Newman's "Cry, Cry Darling" for Dot. By then, Lewis had already forged strong friendships with independents Art Rupe of Specialty and Leonard Chess of Chess Records. When Chess traveled around the South, promoting new releases, he'd always stop in Shreveport to eat dinner with Stan and Paula and give them all of the records he had left in his car—often hundreds of 78s—at no charge.

Lewis stood out among distributors because he was honest and aggressive. He viewed the relationship between record label and distributor as a partnership. Distributors' contributions to popular music are often overlooked, because people prefer the more glamorous work of record labels. But powerful distributors like Lewis—and few were as influential—helped make independent labels a success in the early 1950s. Label owners courted him. Lewis opened new retail stores and provided one-stop and distribution services for far-flung record shops. By the late 1950s, his company ruled western Louisiana and eastern Texas.

I found Lewis, a distinguished-looking man with a soft voice, at his office in a 1950s building at 1700 Centenary Street. Young men and women rushed past me in the halls. Keith Abel, the company's foreign representative, took me into Lewis' small office, where awards and photographs of music stars hung on the walls, and his desk overflowed with papers and audio cassettes. The telephone rang every five minutes—an unusual ring, like the English telephones on a PBS show. Lewis ignored it. He sighed and apologized for delaying me that morning. Problems with distributors, artists—even a missed dental appointment. More succinctly, a problem with time.

For a man of average size, Lewis is distinctive. His wavy gray hair contrasts with olive skin and large, dark eyes that spoke to me. They looked tired at 11 A.M. I thought Lewis was a sincere and friendly man, reserved but forthright and candid. He wore a loud jacket and tie, which gave him the look of a used car salesman. Clearly he understated his company's role in local music history, but he knew that he had achieved something important.

"I was close to our people," he said. "Shreveport was not a distribution center. It was a 'half-percent market,' meaning it wasn't no market, really. So I created a market with mail order, advertising with Wolfman Jack on XERF in Del Rio, Texas; Hoss Allen on WLAC in Nashville; and other early R&B disc jockeys. I sponsored a show called *Stan's Record Review*. We helped the manufacturers break records, and in turn, they stayed with me. Other people like me got out when they were successful and went to New York or Los Angeles. But my roots were here. I had a good thing going. Why should I move? If I went to Chicago or L.A., I couldn't dominate the market the way

I did here. I was the big fish in the little pond. Up north, I'd have been a little bitty fish in a great big pond, and I'd have been sliced up ten different ways."

The *Hayride* helped him, too, at least in the early days. It operated in a different world then. "People didn't have a lot of money," Lewis said. "We had no air-conditioning, no television yet. Our town had only one radio station company, which picked up three networks to speak of—ABC, CBS, Mutual. Life was simple. What do you do for entertainment? You go to a drive-in movie, get a hamburger, or go window-shopping downtown (this was when there was a downtown). In those times, the *Hayride* was a big, big thing. KWKH owned the local newspaper and other ones. When they used to play country records in the mornin', there was no such thing as ratings. Disc jockeys played whatever they wanted. You had no other station competing in the same market, so you could build a Jim Reeves, Webb Pierce, Nat Stuckey, and others, and play their records. Unfortunately, things didn't work out for the show on television. When television came along, KWKH applied for a license with the intention of televising the *Hayride* on Channel 12, but then one of the owners—they were from an upper-crust family—died, and some interest was lost. That was it.

"If I would have had good sense, I'd have started my own labels back then, in the early '50s. But I was young and lacked the necessary foresight. Shreveport had the potential to become another Nashville. Remember, Nashville didn't have all the studios and labels back then, either. Some people in Shreveport think they can bring it all back here today, but we're living in a computer world with a lot of entertainment options. When I was selling tickets to the *Hayride* in my record shop, people used to come in from New Mexico, all over Texas, Missouri, Arizona, Kansas. They were on vacation, and they came here just like they come to Branson, Missouri, today. I'd like to think it could be that way again, but you can't buy enough advertising to build up an artist today who you built up for nothing in the old days."

Preoccupied by his distribution business, Lewis didn't think seriously about establishing his own labels because he feared he might compete with the labels that he distributed. But he continued to produce records independently for other companies. In 1957 he took Hawkins, a record shop employee, into KWKH to cut "Susie-Q" after the station signed off the air late one night. It was rock 'n' roll at its most intimate and primitive: bass, drums, guitar, vocal. They used only three microphones. Although it became a bigger R&B hit than pop, the record showed an early musical fusion that represented Shreveport. The record's opening guitar lick is one of rock's most enduring and identifiable. Hawkins and Lewis talked about writing a song while they worked together in the record shop. Lewis said the title came to him easy enough: he and Leonard Chess both had daughters named Susan. When Lewis mentioned this to Hawkins, they wrote the song. Naturally, Lewis found a sympathetic ear at Chess Records, which released the song on its Checker subsidiary. When "Susie-Q" rose to No. 27 on the *Billboard* charts in June 1957, Hawkins quit the record shop and toured America. The native of Mangham, Louisiana, who also played guitar, shaped the record's mesmerizing R&B beat by listening to Howlin' Wolf records in Stan Lewis's shop. The drummer used a cowbell to give "Susie-Q" its unusual sound. The song—a true rock 'n' roll ancestor—remains popular on oldies stations. Creedence Clearwater Revival remade the song—a more driving, eerie version—in the summer of 1968. The band's first hit, it reached No. 11 and created a new audience for the song.

Inspiration struck Lewis again one afternoon in 1963, as he drove around Chicago and noticed a chair store named Jewel. "I told Leonard Chess, 'I think that would be a good name for a label. I think I'll start me one.' He said, 'Why don't you?' I was in business. I named my second label Paula, for my wife, and Ronn after my brother. At first I put my country acts on Paula and R&B on Ronn, but then I gave up on that and just put out what I felt like putting out. To me, a record company should make music that matters—music that tells a story. I like gospel, blues, and country because they tell stories. They're about people. Anyway, the reason that labels resorted to creating other, subsidiary labels was simple: If you got real hot, the disc jockeys would play three or four of your records. Then you'd be accused of giving payola. Atlantic started Atco Records and then Cotillion. I started my other labels because Jewel was my gospel-R&B-type label. I recorded every singer on the Bossier City strip. Of course, most of the time I sold only 1,000 copies to jukebox operators. I got Mickey Gilley started, then he left for Playboy Records. Yeah, I still got tons of Mickey in the can. I bought a Willie Nelson album in a tax-shelter deal. I've got a lot of former Chess artists—Willie Dixon, John Lee Hooker, Elmore James. I've got Ike and Tina, Otis Rush. So many R&B acts."

The company's greatest commercial success came on Paula in 1968, when a Baton Rouge rock show group, John Fred and His Playboy Band, cut "Judy in Disguise (with Glasses)" at Robin "Hood" Brians' studio in the mini–music center of Tyler, Texas. Fred liked to record for Jewel because Lewis didn't bother him in the studio. Fred's popular band had already scored a few chart records, but the big one still eluded him. Then came

"Judy." "We were playing in Florida and the girls at that time had these big, old sunglasses," he told writer Steven Rosen years later. "One of the guys was hustling this chick. She took off these glasses, and she could stop a clock. I said, 'That's it.' That's what gave me the idea. I said, 'She's kind of in disguise.'" With its unusual novelty sounds and solid beat, the record exploded across the country. "It just kept going up until it hit No. 1," Lewis said. "But on the next try, with 'Hey Hey Bunny,' we couldn't break John Fred out of the fifties." Lewis didn't stop. He discovered country singers Randy Travis, Joe Stampley (his rock band, the Uniques, recorded "Not Too Long Ago" on Paula), and Nat Stuckey. But once established, they—and other performers—left Jewel for the larger labels in Nashville.

Somehow, Jewel persisted. I like its slogan: "The World's Most Unique Record Company." At the least it is one of the nation's indigenous labels, for Jewel has thrived primarily on roots music. Most people wouldn't recognize its artists. Lewis has no Madonna clones, no alternative bands, no flavor-of-the-month acts. Jewel's artists include bluesmen Jimmy Reed, Toussaint McCall, and Ted Taylor, as well as the older black gospel singers the Soul Stirrers, the Rev. C.L. Franklin, and the Brooklyn All Stars. Even old Lightnin' Hopkins recorded for Jewel. (Lewis complied with Hopkins' unorthodox demands: payment in cash—no royalties necessary, thank you—for one performance. And no retakes!) Many recordings came from labels that Lewis bought in later years, including Chicago's Cobra Records. Other acts led the major labels like refugees from a storm and sought out Jewel, the unpretentious label that appealed to blues singers like a home-cooked meal. Although Lewis did not sell millions of records, he sold enough to transform Jewel from a commercial label heavily dependent on radio airplay into a successful roots-music independent of the late 1990s.

The transformation did not come without turmoil—and it came at a price. As the record business changed in the early 1980s, developing into a more corporate environment, Lewis adapted. He sold 300,000 to 400,000 copies of twelve-inch singles by the Conway Brothers, Magnum Force, and Tony Ballard. But even then, he knew his labels were like small game trying to evade stealthy hunters. As radio increasingly resisted his more commercial records, everything began to unravel for Lewis.

"The majors set out to kill the independents, which in the early days probably comprised 90 percent of the record industry's sales in the roots field," he said. "By the '70s, my distribution business suffered. The majors bought Atlantic, so I lost it. Every six months or so we'd lose another label

for our distributorship. Every time this happened, the independent distributors weakened."

By 1983, his record labels couldn't generate enough income to carry his
entire company. "In this business, we carry on paper," he said. "It's not like a
bank or some store. I had 150 employees, including twelve promotion men
on the road, several salesmen, a sales manager, and many family members in
wholesaling and manufacturing. I got so big that I couldn't watch over it all.
When you get hit with $5 million in receivables, you're hurting. A lot of my
friends in the industry went out of business or hung on by their fingernails.
I had a big team of employees, and all of a sudden I'm in Chapter 11—
bankruptcy. I tried to work it out, but there was a lot of backstabbing. I was
sold down the river. Politics as usual. Thank God I emerged from that mess,
but it almost killed me, mentally and physically. It almost destroyed me. You
see, I went from being a poor boy, hustling all my life, to becoming a multi-
millionaire. And then I lost it, had it taken away. I fell into the bottom of the
pit. That's when you see how many friends you have. There wasn't anybody
there to help me. It wasn't the old days, when I could ask for help. Morris
Levy of Roulette Records helped me at times. He called and said, 'What do
you need?' But I had to struggle."

By the mid-1980s, Lewis emerged with only the record labels and his
music-publishing companies. So he concentrated on his strength, roots
music—the music of Shreveport. He had no choice. "We have some of the
greatest musicians in the country in Shreveport and east Texas and Mississippi," he said. "They play everything from jazz to rock. Imagine what we
could have had here—all the booking agents, managers, studios. But they
never happened. I try to take the music and put it out, but it's a battle. The
majors are just too powerful. Many of the original independents started in
the South, and the others came down here to record our talent. When they
started building more studios on the West Coast, they duplicated our
sounds. Everything changed. Our musicians even went out there. Now not
much is left of the regional-sound cities. Chicago is dead, and it used to be a
huge R&B market. I used to sell tons of records in Detroit. That's changed."

Lewis handed me a box filled with a dozen compact discs released on
Jewel. My favorite title, *Blues Is Killin' Me,* is an anthology from 1951–1953
that features rough-and-tumble singers named Baby Face Leroy ("Pet Rab-
bit"), Floyd Jones ("Skinny Mama"), and Memphis Minnie ("Kissing in the
Dark"). It's the kind of music you won't find too often at the mall's chain
stores. Staring at the black and white cover, I realized that Jewel—with its

indefatigable owner—was one of the last true American record companies, a feisty operation that would not perish with the twenty-first century.

As I prepared to leave, Stan Lewis walked slowly over to a window for a few minutes and watched the people of his hometown. For a moment he saw a simpler time: his record shop, the autograph parties, the *Hayride,* the hamburger and drive-in days.

"I wish I could transfer everything I have in my head into my employees' heads," he said. "All the history and the knowledge. All the ups and downs. But this is a business that everybody learns on the streets and in the back rooms. You can't learn what I've learned from a book."

Houston: Treat Her Right

Under a bright June sky, Roy Head met me in a parking lot in Humble, Texas. The night before, he had told me on the telephone, "Meet me at noon at the IHOP," and I did not know what he meant. But I followed his directions to a strip in suburban Houston lined with malls and fast-food restaurants and discovered the International House of Pancakes. The location seemed incongruent with my expectations of Roy Head country. (Consider the irony: Roy Head, macho soul singer, songwriter, and character, living in a place called *Humble.*) I expected to meet him in a fittingly rustic environment, possibly sitting in a rough-and-tumble roadhouse or at his house, beneath the head of the 250-pound deer that he'd shot and taxidermied, but that was not possible. Two months earlier, a flood had destroyed many of his possessions, including his music awards and records, and made his house temporarily unlivable. So while he cleaned and repaired his house, he and his wife were living in a Humble apartment.

Adversity did not slow him down. He jumped out of his red Blazer (with 150,000 miles on the odometer and a crack running across the windshield), laughed deeply, and announced, "We stayed up until 4:30 A.M. eating crawfish, so excuse my wrinkles." He wore a black T-shirt with "Fortyish" splashed in white across the front. I liked Roy Head the minute I met him. He seemed genuine, friendly, and unpretentious. "Call me Roy," he insisted, a cigarette dangling from his lips. He stood about five feet, ten inches, muscular with a medium build, but smaller than I had expected. "It's not a good day," he said. "I just stopped for a pack of Camels, and the cashier told me, 'That must be an *old* shirt.'"

For this peculiar pleasure, I had driven south from Tyler, Texas, for three hours. This time, all I'd told Cheryl was that I was looking for remnants of the Houston Sound—a rocking blues with a tint of country. The trip was worth it, for I grew up on Head's music—at least what I could find of it in Ohio. When I was in high school in 1965, his single "Treat Her Right" reached No. 2 on *Billboard*'s Hot 100 and R&B charts, and Roy Head helped define the small but growing blue-eyed soul movement. Every time I hear the record, I imagine him wearing his tight gray suit with narrow lapels and black velvet collar and stylish black boots. Bending on one knee, he woos

Roy Head's "Treat Her Right," a No. 2 pop hit in 1965, was recorded in Houston for the independent Back Beat Records.

Peacock Records featured many black gospel and blues singers who often traveled in package tours.

Advertisement for Houston's Peacock Records, a label founded in the
late 1940s by black entrepreneur Don Robey.

"Pledging My Love" turned Johnny Ace, an R&B singer, into a pop
star in 1955, two months after his suicide.

Roy Head's "Drinkin' Them Long Necks" dented the country charts in 1980.
He preferred to sing R&B.

Houston's Roy Head turned to country music in the 1970s, after his R&B stint ended.

women in the crowd with the first verse: "Well, let me tell you a story, every man ought to know. If you want a little lovin', you got to start real slow. . . ." Then I see the Traits' sax men, Danny Gomez and Tom May, blast Roy to the edge of the stage with the force of a Texas twister, as he screams, "Yeah! Yeah! Hey, all right! Every night! All right!"

The frenzied "Treat Her Right" became the impetus for more white soul records of the late 1960s, and in its small way, it helped make it hip for a white guy to sing soul music. Head's record impressed me so much that I followed his career as it sputtered and imploded. I remember ordering Roy's 1970 album *Same People (That You Meet Going Up, You Meet Going Down)*, and thinking that it could be the motto of The Man himself. After all, he had achieved unlikely success when America was suffering from British-band mania. If radio could not have a British band, it would take any band with long hair and a good song (even Doug Sahm and a group of local boys, the Sir Douglas Quintet). Then along came Roy Kent Head, a white guy with slick dark hair and a Ph.D. in roadhouse warfare (he says his broken fingers are his diplomas).

He is still a wild man today, the link between the Texas bluesmen of the 1950s and the modern blues-rockers. Before Stevie Ray Vaughan, there had to be a Roy Head. For forty years he has sung R&B, Texas-style, the way he did when he had the body of a white kid and the voice of a black man. Not that he didn't stray from the faith briefly, cutting country records in the mid-1970s. (My favorite titles are "The Most Wanted Woman in Town" and "Play Another Gettin' Drunk and Take Somebody Home Song.") He placed twenty-four records on the national country charts from 1974 to 1985, many on ABC/Dot, Elektra, Mega, and some short-lived labels named Texas Crude and Shannon, but only three dented the Top 20. Continuing radio airplay brought gigs at country nightclubs and county fairs, but Roy said that he temporarily prostituted himself by singing country music. Since then, he has repented. In his fifties, he sings old R&B as fervently as he did at the start.

I tried to discuss all this with him—anything to make conversation—as we stood in a long line at the IHOP. Local men in their Sunday suits, women in fancy hats. Cheryl incredulous. Hungry tourists from a big Greyhound surged forward, and suddenly Roy bolted to the front of the line and said he had already given his name for the waiting list. People looked at us as if we were wearing ski masks and carrying pistols. Cupping his hands around his mouth, Roy yelled, "The bus departs in five minutes. L-a-s-t call!" A couple of young women in shorts walked past us. Roy slapped me on the chest and said, "Check that out, brother!" Another walked by with small bandages on her legs from a bad shave. "Hail damage!" Roy said. "Oooh. Hail damage!" A woman customer paid her bill, scowled at me, and said, "Why don't you take him away?" He said, "Oh, darlin', it's Father's Day. Indulge me. My family sent me out to get rid of me." He gave his seat to an old woman. A familiar hostess in her forties brought him a cup of black coffee. "Darlin'," he told her, "the only thing I drink from styrofoam cups is *whiskey*."

When the crowd dispersed, we sat down. Breakfast: blueberry pancakes and orange juice for me; steak and eggs for Roy, with a pot of black coffee, biscuits, and gravy. Heavy gravy. So much pepper and Tabasco sauce that the food turned black. He glanced out the window. "Hail damage!" A woman next to me stabbed me with quick glances. Cheryl moaned into her waffles. Unfazed, Roy said that he had returned from New Orleans the night before, after a one-week gig. One night while doing his usual microphone-tossing act and some flip-flops, he landed against a big speaker, fell from the stage, and hurt his knee. He still does his familiar flip-flops, although in the last few years he has had to curtail his number of performances. He said there isn't an overwhelming demand for older white soul singers, but lately he has been singing more often, and a German company—Bear Family Records—has released a compact disc of his better recordings. Sometimes he sings in oldies shows. I think they are a waste of his talent. "Nobody has called me a one-hit wonder yet," he said. "But I know it will happen some-day."

One big pop hit was all Roy Head ever had, at least nationally, but in east and central Texas he became a star. Don Robey's company—including the labels Duke, Peacock, and Back Beat—provided vehicles to reach the people; for Back Beat Head turned out "Apple of My Eye," "Just a Little Bit," and other rocking soul records. When I listen to them now, they sound like music from another world.

Compared with today's record business, Robey's company did operate in another world. When Houston developed into a Gulf Coast center for country and blues artists in the late 1940s, Robey became the entertainment emperor of Texas, opening the city's hippest club, the Bronze Peacock. Already Houston had grown as a recording center, with Bill Quinn, the owner of Gold Star Studios, cutting bluesman Lightnin' Hopkins for Modern Records of Los Angeles. Suddenly Houston rivaled Dallas. At Robey's club, blacks and a few whites dined and gambled in a back room. In 1949 he decided to form a record label, Peacock, to generate more interest in his house performer, the blues singer Gatemouth Brown. Robey learned the business quickly. His first release, Brown's "My Time Is Expensive" and "Mary's Fine," became a double-sided blues hit in 1950. "We looked at our [label's] bank account and I had $35,000 in it," Robey once told *Record World*. "So I said, 'Oh, my stars! This is the business for me! This is better than a nightclub!'" From one artist he developed a roster of the nation's top black gospel groups and blues singers and helped make Houston a national music center. Local performers called him the Godfather because he was a musical power-broker. In the mid-1950s he bought Duke Records, a small Memphis label founded by a white radio executive named David Mattis who worked at WDIA, a radio station with a black announcing staff. Mattis didn't like Robey. He claimed that Robey had pulled a gun during a business meeting. To his credit, Robey turned Bobby "Blue" Bland, Little Junior Parker, and Rosco Gordon into blues stars. Robey found a kid named John M. Alexander Jr. and recorded teenage R&B ballads with him under the name Johnny Ace; he became Broadcast Music Inc.'s most programmed artist of 1954. But the minister's son drank heavily and drove too fast. At a Christmas Eve concert that year, at the height of his career, Ace fatally shot himself in the Houston City Auditorium while playing Russian roulette in front of his girlfriend and Big Mama Thornton. The young star died with $23 in his pocket. Robey, who earned a fortune from Ace's records, quickly issued a memorial album.

Losing Duke's star performer didn't hurt business for long. Robey found new stars. He honed his natural talent for making money. Caucasian record men mistook the light-skinned Robey for white, and when they learned of his race, many rejected him. This hurt Robey, but he continued to record the hits and gamble. He wore expensive sharkskin suits, carried a .45-caliber pistol in a calf holster, spat tobacco juice into a spittoon five feet away and rarely missed, bought race horses, operated the successful Buffalo Booking and Don Music companies, invested in a number of local small businesses, lived in a mansion, and created stars out of the poor blacks who arrived on his company doorstep at 2809 Erastus Street in Houston. "Every artist that we have made, when we got them they weren't known," he once said. "Nobody had ever heard of them. Most of them had patches on their pants. We don't have any artist who was made by another record company and then came to us. It's just intuition. I met them and selected them and recorded them, and they were the right artists."

Record men respected Robey, but they did not understand his ways. "Don was a little uncouth at times," said Stan Lewis, Robey's distributor in Shreveport. "Not so much with me but with his own people, because he felt superior. He had a lovely wife—a sweetheart. But Don was different. He used to book all the shows out here, and he'd always carry a big pistol around with him. If you tried to get into the show without paying, he'd take a guy and hit him up against the side of the head. Oh, he was tough."

In the 1970s, Robey sold his labels and publishing companies to ABC Records, so that he could devote more time to his passion—breeding horses. He died six months later from a heart attack. *Billboard* wrote one paragraph on him.

By then, Roy Head had also joined ABC as a country singer, but through no help from Robey. It seemed a logical progression, for since his birth on September 1, 1941, in Three Rivers, Texas, population 250, Roy had been all country. His father, a farm worker, moved the family around to find work. His mother, an Indian who grew up in Oklahoma, encouraged him to sing. At a young age Roy moved with his family to Crystal City, Texas, near the Mexican border. His mother worked in a spinach factory. "Crystal City is the world's spinach capital," Roy said. "No kidding. They've got a statue of Popeye in the town square. When I lived down there, I had black friends. I listened to Bobby Bland, B.B. King, Elmore James, Junior Parker. But my parents were into country music. In our house, *The Louisiana Hayride* was the really big show."

Later the family moved to San Marcos, between San Antonio and Austin, where Roy entered high school. In 1958 he started singing professionally with some classmates who had formed a band called the Traits. Bill Pennington played bass; Tommy Bolton, guitar; Dan Buie, piano; and Jerry Gibson (later with Sly and the Family Stone), drums. Pennington's father, the owner of the local funeral home, bought them band uniforms—black pants with pink stripes down the sides and spangled shirts with the name TRAITS embroidered across the backs. Mrs. Pennington served as the chauffeur. "We were the hottest band in Central Texas," Roy recalled. "Every place we played we'd draw five hundred to two thousand people, and that's big numbers in a small town. It wasn't unusual for people to drive one hundred miles just to hear us. We played in all these little dance halls in towns that were barely on the map: East Bernard, Needville, Louise, New Boston. You could see the headlights for miles. Some of those dumps were so bad that the owners had to string up chicken wire just to make sure nothing would happen. The audiences were rough, man. They wanted to *rock*. When these old boys got a few beers in them, they mixed it up real good. We didn't dare stop playing; that would make things worse. While the crowds fought, we played. It was like some wild movie. Then we went back to school on

Monday morning. It was tough to study after those hard-drinking weekends."

Ricky Ware, a disc jockey at KTSA in San Antonio, liked what he heard of the Traits, and arranged for them to sign with San Antonio's T-N-T Records (Tanner 'n' Texas), known for an eclectic blend of polka players and the blues of Lightnin' Hopkins. The company released a half-dozen records on Head's group, including the regional hit "One More Time." More records followed on other local labels, and the boys graduated from high school and moved on to their own school of hard knocks. By 1965, some members had left, new ones had arrived, and Roy continued to sing lead. By then he had found a day job in the Westwood Furniture factory in San Marcos. It was a frustrating life, for young Roy lived for the stage. To him it was like being one step ahead of a tornado: He was scared, and he didn't know the significance of what was happening around him, but somehow he loved the thrill. One night a Houston promoter, former television repairman Charlie Booth, saw the group play in a bar in East Bernard. The scene could have been borrowed from a B movie. Booth said, "Roy, I'd like to make you a star." Roy said, "Hell, yes. Do it, man!" Later, Booth asked Huey P. Meaux, a former barber and area disc jockey who produced records, to take the band into Houston's Gold Star Studio to record some blues songs. No logical single emerged. But Booth liked the band's original bar song, "Talking 'bout a Cow," and suggested cleaning up the lyrics. The bawdy song became "Treat Her Right," some manly advice on romance. Roy and the Traits returned to Gold Star to record "Treat Her Right."

"The whole session cost only $500," Roy said. "We gathered around a big old Electro-Voice microphone, and brother, we *cooked*. We sold the master to Don Robey, and he put it out on his Back Beat label. Robey loved us. Man, everything broke loose when I went to a black DJ convention. Because I was white, they didn't want to let me sing. Robey himself had told me not to go on; I guess he wanted everybody to think I was black. Remember, now, this was during a time when race riots were breaking out. There was a lot of racial tension. Nobody knew I was white, because they hadn't seen me on the TV. Anyway, Joe Scott, Bobby Bland's orchestra leader, said, 'Damn it, put him on!' And I said, 'Uh, I don't know, man, it looks awful *dark* out there.' I didn't have much time to think it over; the band started playing the intro to 'Treat Her Right.' Charlie Booth actually had to push me onto the stage. The DJs were surprised to see this honky walk out. The whole place went silent before the music started. I was scared to death, too, but as soon as I started doing my flip-flops and dancing, the crowd went nuts.

"The record became an instant hit with the DJs, who went home and started playing it on their radio stations. The record became a smash. My name's being mentioned all over the country. So I went to L.A. with my promotion manager, an older black guy. We walked into a black radio station, where the record had been No. 1 for weeks. Everybody pointed to him and yelled, 'Roy Head! Roy Head!' I said, 'No, man, *I'm* Roy Head.' They didn't like that one bit. We had one hell of a confrontation. I mean, did you ever see black hair go straight? Well, it happened that day. But the record had already become a stone hit, and nothing could stop it. It had taken on a life of its own by then. Looking back on it, I think it was a success because of the repetition I used at the beginning: 'Hey, hey, hey! All right! Yeah!' I think I was one of the first to yell that, and to sing about screwin' in a *nice* way. Pretty soon, all the blacks, they started hollerin' it, too. 'Hey, hey, hey! All right!'

"Of course, I was going crazy by then. I itched to tour, but the band didn't. Man, they only wanted to play on weekends, so that they could find regular jobs or go to school. I just couldn't believe it. They wanted to become physical education teachers and doctors. All I wanted to do was sing, man. But earlier, I had signed some agreement with them—you see, I loved these guys; we grew up together. So when I told them I wanted to sing, they sued me. Before we could come out with an album for 'Treat Her Right,' Huey Meaux, who also owned the studio, comes up with some tracks we'd cut earlier, and he sells them to Scepter Records in New York. They didn't have our hit song on it, so they called the album *Treat Me Right,* see, and everybody thought my song was on the album. That's all it took, man. I went into hibernation for a year. I had my vocal cords scraped for nodules, and I didn't do any performing. I made a nickel wherever I could. Meanwhile, I don't know what in the hell kind of music came along toward the late '60s. The 13th Floor Elevators and all that psychedelic shit. I didn't know how to do all that stuff. Hell, it's like turning a boy loose in a barn with only a flashlight. I couldn't find that groove; it wasn't my bag anyway. It was all downhill for me."

By this time, Houston had developed into a major regional music center, pulling into its orbit the neighboring cities of Beaumont, Orange, and Port Arthur, and eastern Louisiana. The music was both white and black. Local radio stations broke many new records, and producers cut hits at Houston's ACA and Gold Star studios. Meaux, a former barber, left his radio job and became one of the nation's most prolific independent producers. In 1962 he discovered a young Barbara Lynn and produced her hit

"You'll Lose a Good Thing," which he leased from his local Starfire label to Jamie Records in Philadelphia. In 1963 he produced "Talk to Me" by Sunny and the Sunglows and other chart records on the Tear Drop label. Despite some legal problems with state lines and young women, he managed performers and searched the region for talent. By late 1965 and early 1966, Meaux had cut "She's about a Mover" and "The Rains Came" by the Sir Douglas Quintet and "I'm So Lonesome I Could Cry" by B.J. Thomas and the Triumphs. When he wasn't recording hits for his own nationally distributed Pacemaker, Tribe, and Jet Stream labels, he was leasing masters directly to the majors or recording songs for his local Shane, SOM (Son of Mississippi), and Copyright labels (the latter featured the words "This is the right copy!"). Throughout Texas and Louisiana, Meaux became known as the creator of the Gulf Coast Sound, a soulful blend of black and white music. He recorded all the top talent between Mobile and Houston. Meaux's career climaxed with Freddy Fender's "Before the Next Teardrop Falls" and "Wasted Days and Wasted Nights" in the early 1970s. Later, he was back in prison.

Across town in the 1960s, Don Robey reigned stronger than ever. His best-selling artist, Bobby "Blue" Bland, recorded hits such as "Back in the Same Old Bag Again," "Good Time Charlie," and "Rockin' in the Same Old Boat." Robey signed many black gospel artists and hired impressive local session players, including pianist Teddy Reynolds, guitarists Clarence Hollimon, Johnny Brown, and Wayne Bennett, and trumpeter Joe Scott.

But there was still a little place in the Godfather's organization for Roy. After his legal troubles ended, he joined Robey's black package tours with Ruth Brown, Joe Tex, Al "TNT" Braggs, Joe Hinton, Bobby Bland, Junior Parker, Clyde McPhatter, and others. "There was a bunch of white guys dyin' to do the R&B scene then," Roy said, "but they got found out pretty quick. You have to grow up with black music to sing it right. Joe Tex was my idol. He taught me all my moves, including tossing the microphone and making the cord walk back up my arms. Back then, you'd have five or six big acts per show. You could see them for three bucks a head. People could afford to attend the shows then. Today, one big act comes through for $80,000, and it's $30 to $40 for a ticket. I was lucky enough to be on those tours. We traveled by bus. I also played in a lot of black clubs on my own. During the riots in Detroit, I played in a soul lounge while the streets burned down around us. When I finished playing, I went out to eat some chitlins. That's the way my career has gone. I've always gone off to eat some chitlins. I've tried not to let the craziness of the record business bother me. Sure, I've screwed up my share of times. But it's been a good life. I did what I wanted. I never did have much sense, but I sure had fun. The greatest compliment I ever had came from another performer. He said, 'Roy, you're a stage warrior.' I thought, yeah, that's right. That almost made me cry."

Since he had introduced the delicate subject of having fun, I started asking him questions about his reputation as an original rock wild man. Did Don Robey really slap you on the back and tell you to buy yourself a Cadillac, then charge it to your royalties? On package tours, did you tell the bus driver to stop so that you could cut "road weed" and stuff it into pillowcases? Did you really drink too much late one night and call the president of ABC Records and demand to know why your records weren't available in some mom-and-pop store in rural Texas? Did you really tell your teenage son, Sundance, to slam a foreign music journalist against a wall and frisk him as a joke, and did the incident frighten him so badly that he refused to ride in the car with you? Did they really throw you out of a rodeo in San Antonio because you jokingly grabbed your crotch while singing a country song? Did your wife really smash two eggs on your face the moment some big-city record executives handed you a big contract to sign? And did you really bite the King of Rock 'n' Roll on the leg?

"I was working the Thunderbird Lounge in Memphis," Roy said. "Feeling good. In walked one of Elvis' bodyguards, Richie Davis, and he said, 'Hey, you wanna meet Elvis?' I said, 'Yeah, why not?' So he took me over to the Memphian Theater about three in the mornin'. I still didn't believe him, though. So Richie bet me a steak dinner that he could get me in. On the way he said, 'Do you *really* want to meet The Man?' I said, 'If you can get me in to see Elvis, man, I'll fall down and kiss his ass right on the spot.' Well, we went in there, and I tell you, it wasn't Elvis. It was a bronze Madonna. A guy with so much magnetism, I could feel it. Richie said, 'See, I told you.' Yeah, well, I don't know what overcame me. I guess it was the milkcow blues. For some reason I ran up to Elvis, fell down, and bit him on the ankle. All of a sudden, a bunch of his bodyguards jumped on me. Fists flew. The next thing I knew, I was layin' outside in pain. They like to broke my shoulders. I ached all over. Ended up in the hospital for two days."

Suddenly he turned to me and said, "Say, why don't you folks come back to our apartment tonight and we'll eat a batch of crayfish?" Before I could speak, Cheryl's foot kicked my shin. Roy excused himself for a moment and Cheryl said, "Listen, did you ever eat crayfish? I didn't think you did. You bite off their heads first and suck out their insides! Well, I'm not doing it."

Roy returned, winced, and, as if still aching from the bodyguard thrashing, motioned for us to follow him to his Blazer. We climbed inside. He inserted a cassette into his dashboard tape machine, cranked up the volume, and played several songs that he had sung and produced, including Joe Tex's "I Want to Do (Everything for You)." Horns and guitars and harmonicas blew through the IHOP parking lot like hail. My ears ached, but I didn't want to ask him to turn it down. In the back seat, Cheryl looked stunned. I had to scream questions to Roy. He yelled that he had been recording the tracks for eight years. Stevie Ray Vaughan had played guitar on some of the older ones, he said, and other big-name Texas pickers had helped him. "Brother," Roy said, "I'm just having fun these days."

Often he does it out of town, for Houston's music scene is much different today. There are fewer soul gigs, and national independent labels—the niche-makers—now promote such Texas acts as Santiago Jimenez, Jr. (son of accordion player Don Santiago Jimenez) and roots-rocker Stephen Bruton, formerly a Bonnie Raitt sideman. Houston even has its own national independent, Justice Records, which promotes country singers Willie Nelson and Jesse Dayton. I urged Roy Head to seek a record deal, but he said he doubted if any large record company would take him at his age, and he didn't know if anybody would pay good money to hear a new Roy Head album.

As I drove away, I wondered if there is a place for Roy Head in today's celebrity-driven record market, and if soul music by a white Texan would impress the kids. Before leaving Houston, I stopped on Erastus Street to see Don Robey's old headquarters, now a neatly painted church in an industrial-residential neighborhood. I took a photograph of it and then called Wayne Perry in Nashville to tell him whom I had seen and where I was standing. He didn't believe me at first. Then he said, "Roy Head's still The Man. Hey, all right!"

Memphis: Cry Like a Baby

The lost sounds of Memphis converged in Nashville on a gray autumn afternoon. The heat, which had been unbearable all week, finally retreated for a day. Wayne Perry met me for lunch near Music Row, and afterwards we looked at a car completely covered in outrageous bumper stickers. My favorite was "Elvis is an alien!" Later, we drove around town and heard Carl Perkins' "Blue Suede Shoes" on the radio. The rockabilly anthem's sonic clarity—and the image of a swiveling Elvis emerging from a flying saucer—overcame us as we drove down 17th Avenue South.

While I drove around looking for record shops, Wayne strummed his guitar and tried to write a song. He said, "What do you think of this title? 'Your Old Flame's Goin' Out Tonight.'"

"It's not Memphis," I said. "And it's not rockabilly."

"No, but I think I'll keep it anyway," he said. "Hey, why don't we find the Memphis guys? They know all the old licks."

"I'm too tired to drive to Memphis today," I said.

"Man, you don't have to. They're all over Nashville."

Three decades after Memphis declined as America's fourth-largest recording center, many of its musicians and producers work in Nashville, giving credibility to the old claim that Memphis provides the talent for Music City (a claim that other cities make as well). So later that day we searched for musicians—any kind of Memphis players—on and off Music Row. With no appointments or advance calls, we found songwriter Dickey Lee in his office at a music publisher. His former partner, Allen Reynolds, was working in his own studio, Jack's Tracks. All over town, A-team guitarist Reggie Young and pianist Bobby Wood played on sessions, as they once did in Memphis. Lee, a former Sun vocalist, eventually moved into commercial pop, then country, and along the way wrote the George Jones classic "She Thinks I Still Care." He told us, "Everything shoots out of Memphis: the inspiration to create music that *moves* people."

Its radio hits started with blues records in the early 1950s, rockabilly a few years later, Southern soul in the 1960s, and commercial pop in the 1970s. The city that gave us Johnny Cash and "I Walk the Line" also pro-

Marcus Van Story played his upright bass at home in 1990. Photo by Randy McNutt.

Dan Penn sings his hit song "Cry Like a Baby" at home in 1994. Photo by Randy McNutt.

Producer Allen Reynolds began his career as a Memphis songwriter ("Five O'Clock World") in the mid-1960s. This is how he appeared in 1999, a year before he was elected to the Nashville Songwriters Hall of Fame. Photo by Randy McNutt.

Dickey Lee

The Original Sun Rhythm Section, circa 1989. The band was composed of musicians who were once connected to the Sun label in Memphis.

Ronald "Slim" Wallace, shown here in 1993, founded Fernwood Records in Memphis in the 1950s. *Photo by Randy McNutt.*

Fernwood Records in 1993. The office and makeshift studio operated in a garage on Fernwood Avenue in Memphis. *Photo by Randy McNutt.*

Otis Redding's "The Happy Song" reached No. 25 on *Billboard*'s pop charts in 1968, a year after his death in a plane crash.

Under the direction of Memphis producer Chips Moman, Sandy Posey cut "I Take It Back" and other hits in the late 1960s. She also sang backup on many sessions.

Memphis

B.J. Thomas' "Pass the Apple, Eve" was an underappreciated single cut at American Recording in Memphis in 1969.

"Hooked on a Feeling" was made with the American Recording house band, a group of white players who effectively mingled soul and pop sounds.

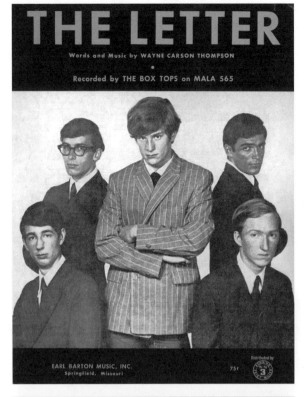

"The Letter," written by Wayne Carson Thompson and recorded by the Box Tops, spent four weeks at No. 1 on the *Billboard* Hot 100.

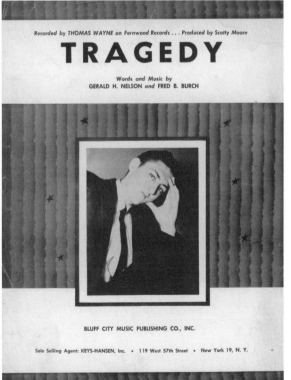

"Tragedy" came out of Memphis on the Fernwood label in early 1959. It was Thomas Wayne's only national hit.

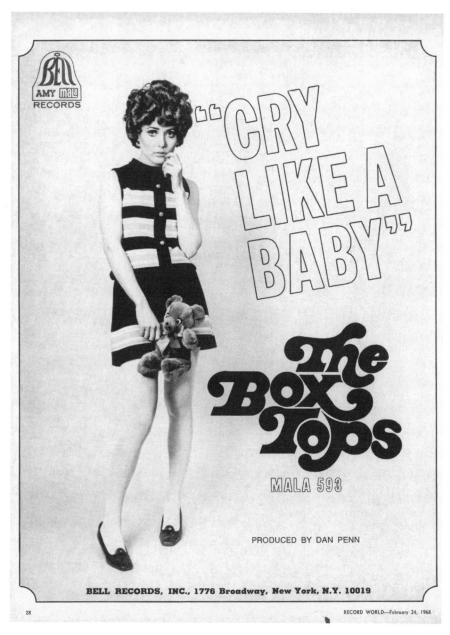

"Cry Like a Baby" returned the Box Tops to the Top 10 in 1968 and
gave producer Dan Penn his second major hit.

duced Isaac Hayes and the "Theme from Shaft." But today, most people remember Memphis for either Elvis or the blues.

The seat of Shelby County, Tennessee, lies on the Mississippi, a wide artery of soul and passion. In the early twentieth century, Beale Street—known as "the Main Street of Negro America"—brimmed with restaurants, vaudeville houses, gambling rooms, and speakeasies, where the blues flourished. W.C. Handy, a black band leader and songwriter, started publishing blues songs in Memphis when no company would do it for him. By 1914 he had established himself as an entrepreneur with "The Memphis Blues," "St. Louis Blues," "Beale Street Blues," and other songs. But Handy didn't invent the blues. He simply adapted the South's rural black music to a more commercial format and, once successful, left for Tin Pan Alley in New York City.

In the late 1940s, Memphis also attracted Sam Phillips, a white man who, like Handy, was born in Florence, Alabama. By 1950, the year Phillips opened his Memphis Recording Service, the city had ripened into a business and commercial center—the world's largest cotton market, and home to 396,000 people. Though Memphis was segregated by law, poor blacks and whites shared a common love of music, which rang inside the little studio at 706 Union Avenue, in a working-class neighborhood near the downtown. "Sam didn't really have all the latest equipment—just an old radio board, a couple of mono tape decks, and a lot of desire," guitarist Scotty Moore told me. "But in those days there wasn't much to it. You just tried to capture a performance on tape."

At first, Phillips recorded anything. But in his spare time, as one of the early independent producers, he made records for black performers—B.B. King, Howlin' Wolf, Rosco Gordon, and Jackie Brenston (Brenston's "Rocket 88" was a hit for Chess Records). A few years later, Phillips started recording white acts on his Sun Records, including teenager Elvis Presley, who in 1955 hit with three Top 10 country singles: "Baby, Let's Play House," "I Forgot to Remember to Forget," and "Mystery Train." Then Phillips sold Presley's contract to RCA Victor Records for $35,000 to help pay for more Sun recordings, including "Blue Suede Shoes." Some people call it the first successful rock 'n' roll record because it hit the country, pop, and R&B charts simultaneously.

Nowadays, Memphis is an international pop-culture icon because of its music. Millions of tourists flock to Graceland, the old Elvis mansion, and other musical attractions. Writers devote books, magazine stories, and albums to the Sun, Stax, and Hi record companies, W.C. Handy and Beale

Street's blues, and even the city's lesser-known performers. But every time I visit there, I still long to know: How did it really *feel* to hang out in Memphis when rock 'n' roll was born and reared? Eventually I sought out four men who experienced the music from the 1950s through the 1970s. Although they don't have a lot in common, they have spread the Memphis Sound around the world. Musically, their lives touch like pages in a book and represent what made Memphis great: independent production, independent record companies, and talented sidemen and songwriters.

⤳

At 1308 16th Avenue South on Music Row, we found a Victorian house with tan brick walls and windows boarded with wide strips of wood. I wondered if it was really Jack's Tracks. Suddenly a small white car pulled into the parking lot, and a bearded man in his early sixties emerged. He wore a rumpled green T-shirt and a broad smile. I said, "Hey, aren't you Allen Reynolds?" He invited us in for a tour, and we ended up staying for two hours. Reynolds is that kind of man—courteous, friendly, and curious. He is also one of the few truly independent producers left.

Like the other independents who worked on every funky corner, Reynolds gambled his own time and money to make records in Memphis. When local music centers withered in the 1970s, independent producers like Reynolds spilled across the country like coffee stains on a map. They had contributed heavily to the success of their cities, and without their investment and guidance, hope evaporated. One of the bigger names, Chips Moman, returned briefly to Memphis from Nashville in the 1980s, only to find that he could not recapture the former hits—or civic support. Other independents, of major and minor proportions, faced the same difficult decision: stay or leave?

I discovered Allen Reynolds when as a high school student I bought scratchy 45s from a neighborhood record shop. I would see his name in parentheses beneath song titles. By the early 1970s, he was also listed as producer. In 1976 I bought his original "Somebody Loves You," a pop-sounding country record by Crystal Gayle. At the bottom of the United Artists disc I saw a curious line: "Recorded at Jack's Tracks, Nashville, Tenn." I never forgot that name—or Reynolds.

Thirty years after going independent in his native Memphis, he now sits atop a country gold mine named Garth Brooks. Except for a live album, Brooks recorded his albums in this small studio, on a twenty-four-track analog recorder. ("I like the warmth of tape," Reynolds said.) Gayle, Don Williams, and Kathy Mattea also recorded albums there. When Brooks initially needed a producer, his label gave him a list of potential candidates. Brooks liked Reynolds because he offered something more than expertise— a personal warmth that's reflected in his songs.

As we sat at the console, lights dimly illuminating instrument stands in the studio, Reynolds recalled when independent record producers could find a sympathetic ear from local and national record company executives, who used the independents as talent scouts.

"Record company presidents came to Memphis to check things out," he said. "They don't go there anymore; they don't see any need to. If they do hear that something's happening, they'll send out a junior A&R man who has no clout. In the 1950s, after I got out of high school, I'd go over to Sun Records and watch them pack and ship records from the studio floor. It was a great time. Dewey Phillips, the disc jockey, was going wild on the air. Sam Phillips was my hero. I met Jack Clement, the Sun producer and engineer, about that time. I learned a lot from those guys. There were many home-made sounds in town then. Studios weren't fancy; some had egg cartons tacked to their walls. But people improvised. They went for the personality of the studio. I come from a time when people were proud to make regional sounds and put a local spin on things. Memphis had a buzz around town then, and record companies responded by beating the bushes in search of local sounds. Producers worked all over town and looked for something different. Over the years, a lot of Memphis hits came out of an old movie house, the Royal; Lyn-Lou, in an old grocery store; the tiny Sun studio; another old theater which became the Stax studio; and other little places that have been long forgotten. Memphis was the crossroads of music then. I'd go over to WDIA, the black station, and visit DJ Rufus Thomas. We felt welcome there. We also had Sleepy-Eyed John, one of the best country disc jockeys. I grew up liking the city's music and wanting to become a committed amateur."

He turned professional when his friend Dickey Lee signed with Sun Records. But the difficulties of life on the road convinced Reynolds to write and produce locally. He and Lee wrote "I Saw Linda Yesterday," a hit for Lee on Mercury's Smash subsidiary in late 1962. In 1966, Reynolds wrote "Five O'Clock World" by the Vogues. The pop song was totally regional, written in Memphis by a Sun fan, sung by a Pennsylvania group, and recorded for Co & Ce Records, owned by two Pittsburgh distributors. (The song later became the theme for *The Drew Carey Show,* a sitcom about a guy living in Cleveland.)

"'Five O'Clock World' came right out of my life," Reynolds said. "I worked in a Memphis bank then and moonlighted as a songwriter and producer. I'd rush out to buy *Billboard* after work. I wanted to be in the business badly. One day I went home and the song just fell out of me. After that I continued to work in the bank and produce records with Dickey. We set up our own company, Rivertown Productions, and we did a lot of writing and recording for Atlantic and other companies. Producing was easier then; you could place things with the labels. We kept at it until 1970, with mixed results, and then I decided to go to Nashville to write. I guess I've always been a writer first. In the back of my mind I knew I wanted to produce, too. I had to make the break. Martin Luther King Jr.'s assassination had polarized the industry in Memphis. Prior to his death, whites and blacks had worked together with mutual appreciation and respect. At least it seemed that way to me. Suddenly, all that changed. One day I said, 'This place is always going to be the boondocks.'"

Reynolds noticed that some crack Nashville studio musicians played as though *they* worked in the bank. They cut hits but couldn't squeeze out much feeling—the soulfulness that Reynolds had come to expect. "In Memphis, our sessions lasted five hours instead of Nashville's three, and it was done with the blessing of the American Federation of Musicians," he said. "Memphis musicians weren't as quick as Nashville's, but they looked for a sound, a uniqueness. It took a little longer for them to get it. Though Nashville had great players, their way of cutting records was less than satisfying to me. I wished they would spend more time on them. So when I moved here, I tried to incorporate more of the Memphis rhythm in our sessions. We wanted more dynamic range. At that time, if you played too loudly, everybody would point to the bouncing console meters and say, 'Wow! Look at that!' I'd say, 'That's no problem. Let it roll.'"

He found a job with Clement, who by now had become a Nashville publisher and studio owner. The Memphis expatriate had come to Nashville years earlier and made a lot of money. By 1976, Reynolds bought the two-year-old Jack's Tracks from Clement, resumed producing records independently, and wrote more songs. Crystal Gayle's "Don't It Make My Brown Eyes Blue," a Top 10 pop hit that Reynolds produced but didn't write, came out of Jack's Tracks and set him up as a major Nashville producer. Reynolds' Forerunner Music has published hits such as Garth Brooks' "That Summer," "Unanswered Prayers," and "The Thunder Rolls." He also wrote Crystal Gayle's "Wrong Road Again," "Somebody Loves You," and "Ready for the Times to Get Better." Waylon Jennings and other acts have recorded Reynolds' "Dreaming My Dreams with You."

Boosted by income from two decades of hits and royalties from Brooks' recordings, Reynolds has been able to close the studio to outside clients and use it as his personal workshop. His biggest success came in the 1990s with Brooks, whose first album sold five million copies. The next two sold ten million each. For Brooks' early albums, Reynolds called upon some experienced studio players, including pianist Wood, who played on dozens of hits at the old American Recording Studios in Memphis. With Brooks' hit albums, Reynolds moved to a new sales level, yet he could not overlook the changes occurring in the industry.

"In the early 1990s, I temporarily stopped trying to develop talent for record companies," he said. "I produced a woman who was extremely talented, but I couldn't do anything with the tape. All of a sudden it hit me that record companies didn't want us, as independent producers, to do this thing anymore. Up until then, independents provided most of the talent for many labels. But things had tightened. Everyone in town passed on Garth before one A&R guy, Lynn Shults, stuck out his neck to sign Garth. The new record industry is run by focus groups and people who never wrote a song, performed, or produced a record. It's the nature of the business to wave you off. It happens, I think, when record company people don't trust their instincts—or know where they're coming from. Now I've got a another new woman singer who's great. I've spent my own money to record her. I took the tape around town, and two-thirds of the labels wouldn't even talk to me. One-third of them did, and said they'd get back to me. That was four months ago, and nobody has called. It's a different world. Record companies and radio would clone today's No. 1 hit forever if they could."

⌒

In suburban Nashville early one night, the sky exploded with lightning. As rain smacked the Eagle's windshield, I remembered the melody to "Raining in Memphis," an album cut recorded by Dan Penn in 1970. Unfortunately, the song is now only a little more obscure than its creative writer and producer, who rode the regional-music train to glory in the 1960s and continues to write good songs without compromising quality.

Actually, I was heading to Penn's house when the storm hit that summer night. My visit achieved a personal goal—to meet the man whose soulful songs and productions influenced me as a kid. Promptly at 7 P.M., Penn—dressed in bib overalls (his favorite attire)—greeted us at the door with his wife, Linda. They are a close couple, who go back to Penn's early days as a songwriter in Alabama.

From 1963 to 1972, he was an integral part of two regional music machines: Rick Hall's FAME Studios in Muscle Shoals, Alabama, and Chips Moman's American Studios in Memphis. In Muscle Shoals Penn wrote songs for Hall's publishing company, engineered a few sessions (including "I'm Your Puppet" by James and Bobby Purify), and even made some records of his own. By the time he left for Memphis, Penn was ready to write and produce for other artists. Without the two music centers, Penn's career might not have happened, and the world would not know "Do Right Woman—Do Right Man," "Dark End of the Street," and other soul hits written by the white boy from Vernon, Alabama.

He was born Daniel Wallace Pennington on November 16, 1941. As a kid in the 1950s, he listened to a little green transistor radio on which he picked up WLAC in Nashville. "I was supposed to be sleeping, but I was listening to that black blues," he said. "I thought, 'Hey, this is pretty good.' Then here comes Jerry Lee and Elvis and all them, and I said, 'Hey, this is great!' But it didn't take rockabilly long to grow real thin."

He started performing as a teenager when the leader of a square-dance band offered him a job. Later he started singing with the group. Even then, Penn could sing with such feeling that it moved people. "I learned to sing in church," he said. "I'd be hollerin', and Dad would say, 'Son, hold it down a little bit.' When I got to read, I was the loudest one in the church. So anything I got, the good Lord gave me. I accept that. But what got me singin' better was just singin'—I did club gigs for a long time. I pushed myself way beyond my limits. I went through the R&B thing and learned from all the black singers."

About 1960, Penn started playing the VFW and campus circuit in Mississippi with a group called the Nomads. Later he joined the Mark V, an eight-piece R&B horn band based in Florence. Eventually the group evolved into Dan Penn and the Pallbearers, featuring vocalist Penn, pianist David Briggs, bassist Norbert Putnam, and drummer Jerry Carrigan—and their trademark 1956 Cadillac hearse. "We played the college circuit," Penn said. "When everybody else played rock 'n' roll, we did R&B. It wiped everything else out. I didn't listen to any rock music, hardly, until way past the Beatles. I liked Jerry Butler, Jimmy Reed, James Brown, and all the King Records people. If they had a hit record and they were black, they were all my bro's.

"I was into R&B music and nothing else. One night Tommy Roe came into FAME Studios in Muscle Shoals from England. He had an acetate. He said, 'Boys, I've got something here that's going to change the world.' We said, 'Put it on! Put it on!' So he put it on a little turntable over in a corner, and we heard this 'I Want to Hold Your Hand.' It sounded so *bad*. He said,

'Well, what do you think?' I said, 'Tommy, if that's going to change the world, I don't know if I want to live in it!' It took me a long time to accept the Beatles as anything but good. I never have accepted that they were wonderful. It ain't as good as black music was, although they did write some wonderful songs."

When Dan Penn and the Pallbearers played on campus, the kids liked R&B, too. "You know how fraternities are," he said. "They laugh at death. So every time we went to Old Miss, those guys would say, 'Where's your casket? You've got a hearse, so Dan, you get into a casket.' Well, we were anybody you wanted us to be. But I told them I *ain't* gettin' into a casket."

In the early 1960s, the band became the session group at Rick Hall's studio, and Penn moved to Muscle Shoals to write songs. He joined pianist Spooner Oldham to write "Let's Do It Over," recorded by Joe South. Dan also wrote the Conway Twitty hit "Is a Bluebird Blue?" But Penn wasn't comfortable with his limited role as a writer. He wanted to produce a hit record; he knew he could do it if he had the opportunity. Moman promised him one at American Studios in Memphis, so Dan and Linda moved there in November 1966.

American, at 827 Danny Thomas Boulevard, was not fancy. Located in a black section of Memphis, the studio was held together by Moman's slim hopes and tenacity. The former member of the Mar-Keys had given up playing in clubs to open his own studio. He worked day and night. By the time Penn settled in there in early 1967, the studio had been "upgraded" to a three-track Ampex tape recorder. (The modern studios had four tracks by then and would soon go to eight.) Moman, a Georgia native, was no stranger to the studio scene. He had played on sessions in Memphis and Muscle Shoals (he was lead guitarist on Wilson Pickett's "Mustang Sally"). In the early '60s he had developed the Stax label with Jim Stewart and his sister, Estelle Axton. Moman helped open the label's studio in the old Capitol Theater and produced some of its early hits, including "Gee Whiz" by Irma Thomas. After a disagreement over compensation, Moman quit to open American, which gave him a base as an independent producer. Soon the hits came, with "Keep On Dancing" by the Gentrys and "Single Girl" and "I Take It Back" by Sandy Posey.

At the time, I bought every record that Chips Moman produced. Like many other people, I was attracted to his sound—something different he brought to vinyl. Maybe it was the studio. Maybe it was the musicians and singers. Or maybe it was his choice of material. Whatever the reason for his success, he continued his streak with "The Eyes of a New York Woman" and "Hooked on a Feeling" by B.J. Thomas. They were records I loved for their simplicity and commercial feel.

Moman recruited his studio band from session players in Memphis: Tommy Cogbill, bass; Mike Leech, bass and arrangements; Gene Chrisman, drums; Reggie Young, lead guitar; Johnny Christopher, rhythm guitar; Bobby Wood, piano; Bobby Emmons, organ; and Ginger Holaday and Donna and Sandy Rhodes, background vocalists. Moman worked them for hours—until he got it right—in the smoky little studio. The Memphis musicians, like their counterparts in Muscle Shoals, were capable of playing anything. But as guitarist Jimmy Johnson explained, the American boys were better at making commercial pop music than their more soulful white brothers in the Shoals.

Finally, as if struck on the head by a brick, New York record chiefs suddenly noticed what was happening in the pop field down in Memphis. Atlantic brought in the Sweet Inspirations and English pop singer Dusty Springfield ("Son of a Preacher Man"). Uni Records sent Neil Diamond ("Holly Holy"). Warner Brothers brought in Petula Clark. Scepter sent Dionne Warwick ("You've Lost That Lovin' Feelin'"). Moman even started a house label, AGP (American Group Productions), distributed nationally by Bell Records in New York. From September 1964 through March 1969, the studio recorded sixty-four hits for many labels. The biggest visiting star, of course, was Elvis Presley, who went from Sun to Hollywood to Nashville and, in January and February of 1969, back to Memphis to find his musical roots at American. He cut "In the Ghetto," "Suspicious Minds," and "Kentucky Rain" with Moman's musicians.

Meanwhile, Dan Penn was feeling frustrated and unwanted. "I was going to cut me a hit," he said. "I was going to move around until I did. I had met Chips, and we were real close at that time. He and I were supposed to be producing together. And we did do a few things. But it ended up in frustration for me because I'd sit behind him in the studio and say, 'A little more bass.' And he'd say, 'No, I don't think so.' It was like clashing. I was trying to get my licks in and couldn't. Finally, I just told him one day. I said, 'Look, we can't produce together. You're a good producer. You don't need me. But I think I can produce records, and I don't need you. But I do need somebody to cut. Give me the worst one you got.' He started thinking. Of course, he didn't have much time for himself. He had big names coming in and out. Then he said, 'I think Roy Banks got this little old group you might be interested in.' Chips was just graspin'. He'd never heard them either. I said, 'They'll do. By the way, who are they?'"

They were five Memphis boys in a band called the Box Tops, discovered by Banks, a disc jockey. Moman handed Penn a tape with some demos written by Wayne Carson Thompson, a talented songwriter based in Missouri. Moman liked several of his songs, including a ballad. But to Penn, only one song stood out: "The Letter," an up-tempo number that started with the singer asking for a ticket for an airplane so that he could get back to his baby. Penn had never heard of a song with "Letter" in the title.

"I told Roy to have the group back at the studio on Saturday to review the tape," he said. "Sure enough, they all came back at 10 A.M. It took me all day, but by 5 o'clock I had cut the track and singer, Alex Chilton, who I'd never laid eyes on before. We're talkin' *faith* recording here. I didn't give him much direction. He was a little timid. I gave him a couple of small lessons in screaming. I said, 'Now, don't say airplane. Say aer-o-plane.' It just came to me. Anyway, from that moment on, he picked it up, exactly as I had in mind, maybe even better. I hadn't even paid any attention to how good he sang because I was busy trying to put the band together. I had a bunch of greenhorns who'd never cut a record, including me. I knew these kids were never going to learn it another way, so I borrowed everything from Wayne Thompson's original demo—drums, bass, guitar. Even that good guitar lick. I added an organ with an 'I'm a Believer' lick. I liked that kind of groove. We cut it all on the studio's three-track Ampex, a great little recording machine. At the end of the tape, the singer's track was empty, so I got some black kid who hung around the studio late at night to help me with a sound-effects record. I put him in a little office next to the control room, and I said, 'All right, now, start it!' I'd try to catch it. It took me a couple of hours to do it, to hit the airplane taking off just right. When I finished, I played the tape for Chips and told him I wanted to put strings on it. To his credit, he agreed. But his words were, 'Dan, I think you got yourself a pretty good little record there if you'll take the airplane sound off at the beginning.' I said, 'Give me that razor blade right there.' He said, 'Why?' I said, 'I'll cut this damn tape up! The airplane stays on it, or we don't have a record.' He said, 'Oh, man, I was just suggesting. It's your record.'"

Moman hired arranger Mike Leech and paid for the strings and horns. Larry Uttal at Mala Records (a Bell subsidiary) released the single, which perched atop *Billboard*'s Hot 100 chart for four consecutive weeks that August. The record clung to the chart for sixteen weeks. It also hit the R&B

chart. Suddenly people at the studio and the record label were pressuring Penn to record another version of "The Letter." He searched for material but found nothing as interesting. What he really liked was another Wayne Carson Thompson song, an intriguing piece called "Neon Rainbow." It was just a happy song, and Penn recorded it on the studio's new four-track Ampex recorder.

"That was my 'sinful' record," he said. "I was in my you-can't-do-it-twice mode. I still believe that. I mean, I liked *Rocky,* but not *Rocky II.* I've always been that way." Because it was a good song, "Neon Rainbow" climbed to No. 24. But the record label gave Penn an obvious comparison: "The Letter," four million copies sold; "Neon Rainbow," 500,000. "So it was a dog," he said. "They made me feel like one too. At the time I was drinking a lot of beer and keeping myself kind of sopped. People around the studio started pointing their fingers. I was not following too many orders. . . ."

"But," Linda interjected, "you didn't follow *any* orders."

"Oh, yeah, well, I didn't *believe* in following orders. I tell you, people will 'committee' you right out of what you think. A record made by committee is not my idea of cutting records."

As pressure mounted for another major hit in early 1968, Penn searched for songs and found nothing worthwhile. If he was to survive as a record producer, he knew he must write his own next hit—and on a deadline. The Box Tops were scheduled for a session the next week. Penn saw the recording date as his personal Waterloo. He had to win.

"I started thinking maybe I am a one-hit man," he said. "But I knew I could come up with another hit record. The session was on a Tuesday morning. By that time I was using the American house band. On the Friday before, Spooner and I started writing. We came up with nothing. We just couldn't write. We stayed up for two or three nights. Pitiful. We finally ended up down at Porky's, a restaurant across the street from the studio. It was 2 or 3 in the morning. We had just about run our roll out. We were in a dejected mood. We had written and written and still came up with nothing, and I had this session coming up later that morning and sure didn't want to cancel it. I knew it was now or never. So we sat there, two bad, sad boys who hadn't slept. Spooner and I looked sick. Suddenly he puts his head on his arm and says, 'I could just cry like a baby.' I said, 'What did you say, Spooner?' He said, 'I could just cry like a baby.' I said, 'That's it!' He said, '*What?*' I said, 'That's the song! Come on!' I didn't even eat my food. I got up, threw some money at the cash register, and headed across the street. By the time we walked through the studio door, we had already written the melody and first line. I fumbled for the lights and told Spooner to turn on the organ, 'cause we're fast-forwardin' now. I turned on the console, grabbed some quarter-inch tape, and fired up the two-track. We wrote the rest of the song very fast—fifteen minutes."

They didn't take time to sleep. They drank coffee and prepared for the second part of the battle—the session. Musicians drifted in, heard the demo, and grabbed their instruments. They liked the song immediately. Groggy but inspired, Penn walked up to lead guitarist Reggie Young and asked him if he had a new guitar in the odd-looking case he'd brought with him. Young said it was an Indian instrument called a sitar. "I said, 'Reggie, you think you can make that thing cry like a baby?' He kind of looked at me funny. He started playing old R&B licks on the sitar, and before long, the record was cut. The sitar added an unusual sound to the record. It sold over a million copies—not as many as 'The Letter,' but a No. 2 record. Suddenly I turned into a real good boy with Bell Records."

Also in 1968, Penn and Oldham wrote an R&B hit, "Sweet Inspiration" by the Sweet Inspirations, featuring Cissy Houston. Penn's next releases for the Box Tops that year, "Choo Choo Train" and "I Met Her in Church," were respectable songs, but they didn't climb above the twenties. After a disagreement with Moman, Penn left American in 1970 to open Beautiful Sounds, the first sixteen-track studio in Memphis. There he recorded *Nobody's Fool,* now considered a cult album. The album included Penn's version of "I Hate You," later a country hit by Ronnie Milsap. Bell Records released "Nobody's Fool" as a single, but it failed to sell. Penn continued to write but stopped recording his own songs.

As the hits declined in Memphis, Stax and American closed, and in time other independents retreated. Penn moved to Nashville in the mid-1970s, where he lived and wrote more songs with Oldham, who toured as a sideman with Neil Young and other nationally known acts. In 1991, Penn and Oldham performed at a writers' night at the Bottom Line in New York. An A&R man from Sire Records heard them and suggested a new album for Penn. They cut it in Muscle Shoals in 1993, and Penn received good reviews.

"I've been writing a lot of songs that have sat on the shelf because nobody is around to do them," Penn said. "You can pitch them, but if the politics just ain't right, they don't get cut. I remember when I walked into some office in Nashville and played 'Tear Joint.' Somebody said, 'That ain't country.' I said, 'That ain't country? Well, do-de-oh!' That's about the time I gave up on country music."

Linda said, "It's the groove, Dan."

"I played some songs for producer Barry Beckett one day," Penn said. "He said, 'Dan, we need more lyrical content, less groove.' I said, 'Barry, you know what you just said? What the hell does that mean?' I know he's trying to help me, because he can't get my funky songs cut. But I ain't going for it. I will *not* be contaminated.

"I hardly ever go down there to Music Row anymore. Why should I when I can be in Memphis in my mind?"

Memphis Redux: Whole Lotta Shakin' Goin' On

Near Spot, Only, and Bucksnort, Tennessee, I wondered how many times Memphis musicians took the back roads to Nashville before the federal interstate highway system was built in the early 1960s. At Jackson, the home of Carl Perkins, we stopped to eat at Suedes, his restaurant. (This was several years before his death on January 19, 1998.) Suedes, a clapboard building with a lighthouse tower that could pass for a New England seaside building, was closed for an afternoon break. As I took a picture, a man came out and asked if I wanted to look around. He handed me a red and white business card with a pair of shoes on it and the name Bart Swift, Perkins' son-in-law. "People come here from all over the world," he said. "Last week we had fourteen from Tokyo and twelve from England. You can spot the people from overseas right away." He bowed, as though the restaurant were a mosque. "This place is important to them. They even ask for *my* autograph. But the locals are interested in only the big three—service, good food, and cleanliness." The restaurant's food was good, but not the down-home Southern cooking I expected. Perkins' guitar memorabilia fascinated us.

Later, as we drove toward Memphis, full and satisfied, the car's air-conditioner broke, and the heat immediately choked us. The skies darkened ahead. Humidity curled my notebook paper and my hair. All along the road, ivy-covered tree limbs looked like ballerina arms stretching toward us. The landscape pitched and rolled in bounteous green until suddenly it came to a nature's no-man's land. Gray trunks of trees—hundreds of them—stood like poles. It was if life refused to enter the area. Then suddenly everything turned green again.

Memphis loomed before us like a big greenhouse. One hundred degrees. We tried to imagine Memphis but could think only of the time in 1970 when we flew into town for one day and night to seek a deal with B.B. Cunningham, who ran Holiday Inn Records. At the time, *Billboard* ranked Memphis the nation's fourth-largest recording center. It turned out a potpourri of hits by Al Green ("Let's Stay Together") and Willie Mitchell ("Soul Serenade") on the locally operated Hi Records; Isaac Hayes ("Walk On By") and Booker T. & the M.G.'s ("Green Onions") on Stax Records; and Neil Diamond ("Holly Holy" and "Brother Love's Traveling Salvation Show") and Merrilee Rush ("Angel of the Morning"), all made over at American Recording.

But this time we had come looking for rockabilly performers who nurtured rock 'n' roll. Still uncomfortable with neglecting the soul men (when I first met Wayne in 1969, he was singing "Knock on Wood"), we drove over to McLemore Street to look for the old Capitol Theater, home of Stax Records. Owners Jim Stewart and Estelle Axton (the first two letters of their last names became Stax) converted the theater into a studio and record shop in the early 1960s, but left the concrete floor intact. Musicians could roll a marble downhill during a session. On arrival we found only a pile of bricks covering an empty lot in a tough urban neighborhood. Under a gray cloud canopy I could almost see the integrated Stax rhythm section (the Booker T. group)—Donald "Duck" Dunn, bass; Al Jackson, drums; Steve Cropper, guitar; and Booker T. Jones, organ—lugging instruments from their cars as they prepared to cut "Time Is Tight" and other spirited instrumentals. I walked over to a silver historical marker. It read:

> STAX RECORDING STUDIOS
> On this site stood Stax Records, Inc.,
> which boasted such stars as Otis Redding,
> Isaac Hayes, the Staple Singers, Albert
> King, the Bar-Kays, and many others.
> It relied upon its deep soul roots to
> carry it through, struggling from a
> back-street garage in 1957 to become
> a multi-million-dollar organization.

The rubble seemed so final. It was no monument to our youth. We didn't say anything as we drove over to 706 Union to visit the Sun Records shrine—a three-room building that features a twenty-by-thirty-foot studio. These days, it doubles as a museum and studio and still provides—as engineer Jack Clement once maintained—a "magical" sound. The place looks much as it did when Sam Phillips rented it, installed acoustic tiles in just the right places, and opened for business as Memphis Recording Service. We could almost sense the ghosts of Elvis, Carl, and Dewey.

If not for the sleek, aerodynamic cars driving past on Union, I could have convinced myself that I was living in the time of shellac and vinyl discs and the man who played them, Dewey Phillips. The rock 'n' roll piper introduced Memphis to "That's All Right," an R&B song recorded by a young

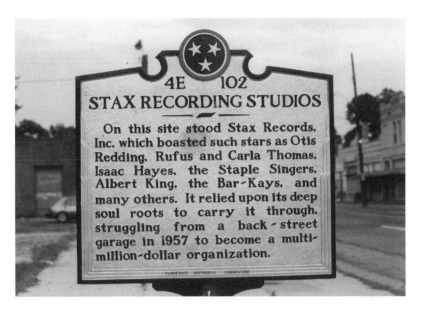

Stax Records historical marker in Memphis, 1993. Photo by Randy McNutt.

truck driver named Presley with guitarist Scotty Moore and bassist Bill Black. Sam Phillips released the disc as Sun 209, which also featured "Blue Moon of Kentucky." As soon as Dewey Phillips (no relation to Sam, but they were good friends) played the record in July 1954, the telephone started ringing. He called Mrs. Presley and told her to send Elvis to the studio for an interview. Phillips became the first DJ to interview the future King of Rock 'n' Roll. Dewey's advice: "Just don't say nothin' dirty, son." Elvis, thinking the microphone was turned off, talked freely. Although it wasn't a national hit, "That's All Right" sold 5,000 copies in two days after Dewey played it.

"Daddy-O-Dewey" set the city's musical tone shortly after joining WHBQ in 1949. Station managers thought he was strange, but they wanted to start an R&B show and didn't know who else to hire. They had noticed the success of WDIA, with the first all-black staff in the nation, and sought to attract the same audience. In those segregated times, WHBQ preferred a disc jockey who sounded black but wasn't. Enter Phillips, who sold records at the W.T. Grant variety store downtown and had gained a following for playing records over a loudspeaker and saying, "Hey, mother!" to everyone he met. WHBQ hired Phillips—they didn't even pay him at first—for a fifteen-minute show. It quickly expanded to three nighttime hours. He played what he liked—the blues, hillbilly, pop, and, later rockabilly. Even a little Sinatra. Phillips became the most influential Memphis DJ when rock was percolating. This unpolished, down-home guy transformed himself into an early personality DJ—one of the first R&B disc jockeys. He just happened to be a white, rural Southerner who drank and smoked too much, took pain pills, and hung around with the stars he helped create.

In 1956, the popular Phillips went on local television—following Lawrence Welk! The show, *Dewey Phillips' Pop Shop*, featured a madcap art student named Harry Fritius, who wore a gorilla mask and a trench coat. Imagine the surprise when middle-aged Welk viewers suddenly went from champagne music to rocking anarchy.

As we drove around late that night, I fumbled for an audio cassette of Phillips' "Red, Hot and Blue" radio show to play in the Eagle's tape player. I told Wayne to imagine that we had time-traveled back to the 1950s. It wasn't difficult to do. The music was the blues, and the announcer was the original Daddy-O-Dewey. "Let's wake up! Whoa! I got a telegram from Truman!" In the high humidity, street lights looked like welding arcs with a dozen concentric circles around them. "Tomorrow night's payday and bath night and that's a good deal. . . . you flat *wake up* out there!" He wolf-whistled and played Rosco Gordon and Piano Red and talked over records—fast, often unintelligibly. "I got a letter from Grandpa today." When he incorrectly attributed a dedication to a certain woman, he said, "I got a morphine shot in me, and I can't see very good." He hawked a Southern beer and always said, "Tell 'em Phillips sentcha!"

By day, he played the DJ role and received the princes of the record industry. At night, he drank and took pills and cough medicine. "Let's dig that boogie!" Surprisingly, Daddy-O-Dewey survived his stream-of-consciousness and achieved cult status in Memphis. As R&B slammed head-on into rockabilly, Phillips picked up on the trend and played white singers' records. "I almost swallowed my gold tooth!" He personally transformed Presley into a local radio star. "Get your girlfriend or somebody else's girlfriend and get over there." He told the kids to honk their horns, despite the police chief's warning, and they did. "Come in here and bring me my bottle! I drink Carnation milk all night long." The show became Phillips' life. He spun out of control, setting up four turntables and playing four copies of the same record at once to create out-of-sync rockabilly. Reportedly he declined an invitation to manage Presley, preferring instead to break new records—Perkins' "Blue Suede Shoes," Jerry Lee Lewis' "Whole Lotta Shakin' Goin' On," and Johnny Cash's "Folsom Prison Blues." The payola flowed to Daddy-O as freely as the whiskey.

By 1957, he had become a kind of crazy caricature. He called people Elvis. He drank more. His television show was canceled after Fritius turned his back to the camera and pretended to get familiar with a cardboard cut-out of buxom Jayne Mansfield. In 1958, as rock 'n' roll evolved into a smoother affair, WHBQ fired Phillips. Although he found work at a couple of other area radio stations, by the 1960s he had become too extreme, too Dewey, to adjust. Radio had changed. One night he went home to his mother's house and went to bed. They found him dead the next morning. He was forty-two. "If you can't sit on it, lay on it!"

⌒

Ronald "Slim" Wallace once cut a record for Dewey Phillips (and many other Memphis music people), so I asked him what it felt like to participate in history. "Why don't you come over to the Southland Mall?" he said. "My wife walks there every day. We can talk." Two hours later, I found him sitting next to a toy store with Dorothy, the walker. He wore heavy plastic glasses and a blue polyester ball cap that said "Retired Teamster" in red letters.

Slim witnessed the early days of Memphis recording glory—firsthand. Not that he ever was a rocker. He was just a country bass player and the founder of Fernwood Records. His label burst across the country in 1959 with "Tragedy" by Thomas Wayne and the DeLons. Though the rockabilly ballad was Fernwood's only big national hit, it placed the label—if only briefly—among the national players. Many Fernwood recordings were cut in his garage.

"I was driving a truck in those days," he said. "I played mostly on Friday and Saturday nights. We'd go to Union City, Tennessee, on Friday night, then to Greenwood, Mississippi, to play for four hours on Saturday. We'd come home and sleep Sunday, and I'd go on the road again on Monday with the truck."

His western swing band, Slim Wallace and the Dixie Ramblers, included Jack Clement and Glenn Honeycutt, a future Sun rockabilly singer. Like his father before him, Slim loved music. He knew from experience that per-forming was easier than working in a coal mine in Kentucky and driving a bus through rural Mississippi. A few years after returning from the navy in 1945, Slim leased the old Fifty-One Club, then just outside the city limits. "Jack Clement had to leave his steel guitar in my house because his dad and mother were true Christian people. He'd say, 'I'm going to the show,' but he'd come to the Fifty-One Club to play with the band and maybe make four or five dollars. After that, I bought the Plantation Club in Paragoud,

Arkansas, and we'd drive over there every Friday and Saturday night. One night—it must have been in '54—we were drivin' home from a gig, and Jack turned to me and said, 'Big Slim, let's go into the record business.' I said, 'Yeah, sure.' I knew he was so serious. I was too. Well, about that time I did a one-night bass gig—I could always get jobs—and met the disc jockey Sleepy-Eyed John. He offered to sell me a mono Magnecord tape recorder. I won't forget that night, because it was the first time I ever saw Elvis. He was a teenager, and he just waltzed into the club wearin' a long, split-tailed coat. Nobody knew him. They let him sing two or three numbers, and the crowd booed him. They let him out through the back door."

Slim installed the recorder in his garage, installed some acoustic tiles, painted the exterior dark brown, and remodeled it into a primitive studio and office for his new label. He called it Fernwood Records because he lived in a brick Cape Cod on Fernwood Avenue. When Clement had learned how to operate the recorder, the new duo produced their first record, for a local singer named Ramon Maupin. The appropriately titled "No Chance" (Fernwood 101) came and went without much notice.

Although Fernwood wasn't a large label, it was important to Memphis—and in retrospect became the perfect independent because it cultivated local talent. In fact, Fernwood was a little incubator for performers such as rockabilly artist Billy Lee Riley, who graduated to Sun and cut the unusual "Flying Saucers Rock 'n' Roll" and other regional hits; Travis Wammack, a thirteen-year-old guitar wonder who would become an expert session player and recording artist ("Scratchy"); and, of course, Scotty Moore himself, who hired Bill Black and D.J. Fontana (Presley's band) to play on the Scotty Moore Trio's "Have Guitar Will Travel."

Slim found singers in unlikely places. One morning, when he was delivering boxes to a frame company in Arkansas, a young employee introduced himself as Bill Rice. He said he sang and wrote songs, and he wanted a chance. Slim took his telephone number and called him the next week. "A man answered, 'County jail!' I thought he was joking, and I laughed real hard. Then the man said, 'This is the jail, fella.' I apologized for dialing the wrong number. The man said, 'Oh, no, you got the right one. I'm Bill's daddy, the sheriff of Corning, Arkansas.'" In the 1960s, Bill Rice started writing dozens of country hits in Nashville. He recorded for Capitol.

Fernwood was outmatched from the start. By 1956, as Memphis music echoed across the country, Clement left Fernwood to become Sun's chief engineer and producer. "Sam Phillips was a good friend, but he hired everybody I had," Slim said. "He hired Jack as soon as he got the know-how as a writer. He also hired away Scotty, Billy Lee—heck, about everybody."

Fernwood released several local records, and Slim continued to haul freight across the country. By 1957 he needed help with the label. Moore, who with Black had recently quit playing for Presley, needed a job. Slim hired him as Fernwood's vice president. "Bill went to work for the Able Appliance store in Memphis," Slim said. "I bought a new washing machine from him just to give him a sale. He was hurting for money. He came over and hooked up the pipes under my house, while Scotty was working in my back yard. You wouldn't think that two musicians who were so famous were so poor."

Moore met disc jockey Gerald Nelson and college student Fred Burch, who had written a haunting love ballad called "Tragedy." Burch took the title from a course on Greek literature. Strumming a ukulele, Nelson auditioned the song for Moore on a Memphis corner. Moore suggested they cut the song with singer Thomas Wayne Perkins, brother of Luther Perkins (Johnny Cash's guitarist) and Moore's former paper boy. Although still in high school, Thomas Wayne could sing convincingly. He brought along his backup singers, the DeLons (three high school girls, including his girlfriend). But Slim's garage studio didn't sound right. "So we took the kids over to the old Royal Theater studio and recorded with two instruments— me on guitar and Bill Black on bass," Moore said. "We cut it in mono. The owners had recently installed a one-track Ampex tape recorder, which the engineer had to kick to start that day. The studio didn't even have an echo chamber, so later we traipsed over to WMPS to add some slapback echo— the delay effect you get when running the tape through two tape machines. That became our echo. The whole record was as basic as you can get."

Disc jockeys promptly ignored the A side, "Saturday Night," also written by the same team. Then a station in Kentucky turned the record over and played "Tragedy." It caused a chain reaction that rippled across the country. One month before Slim's thirty-seventh birthday, on February 26, 1959, "Tragedy" hit No. 5 on *Billboard*'s pop charts. "Suddenly, everybody came looking for Fernwood Records—that little brown building in our back yard," Slim said. "My neighbors never did complain, but it got to be pretty bad, because we'd have people coming from Texas and Chicago and anywhere else to ring our doorbell in the midnight hour. I was trying to sleep so I could drive the truck. That's when we moved to an office downtown. My wife could answer the telephone in a more professional setting. When somebody asked for me, she'd say, 'I'm sorry, but our president is out on the road today.' Yeah, drivin' a *truck*.

"I guess it was a strange situation. Scotty slept on the couch in the studio and borrowed my wife's car to get cigarettes. Scotty is an honest man. He paid us back—every cent. But 'Tragedy' forced us out of the garage. We grew too big. The sad thing is, we could never cut another hit on Thomas Wayne."

Slim opened a folder and lovingly pulled out several yellowed papers. He spread them across a vinyl bench in the mall and pointed to them one by one. "Now, here's where he paid the Jordanaires to come to work in my back yard," he said. "Here's a check for $21 that Scotty wrote to Stan Kesler to play on a session." Then he pulled out a black and white 8 x 10 photograph of Elvis Presley and Dewey Phillips clowning in a Memphis hat shop. "These things all bring back the memories," Slim said. "I was making payments on the house, driving a truck, and launching a million-seller in my back yard. But I never sat down in a truck stop anywhere and told people, 'I'm the owner of Fernwood Records, and I've sold tens of thousands of records.' I'd sit there and listen to 'Tragedy' playing over and over on the jukebox and radio stations from St. Louis to Los Angeles. In Missouri, a waitress said to me, 'Hey, Slim, that record you left for me is a hit! Turn on your radio. They play the record all the time.' Sure enough, I'd turn on one station and then another and hear 'Tragedy.' We never did quit, never gave up on it. When the record got too big, I owed Plastic Products, the pressing plant in Memphis, $40,000, but we hadn't collected any money yet from the record. Sam Phillips told the owner, Buster Williams, 'Let Slim Wallace have up to half the work in the plant. If he can't pay you, I will.' Sam was really a friend. We all knew everybody else in those days, and we all cared about each other's records. They were *Memphis* hits."

Although no other big hits came along, Slim and Dorothy operated Fernwood regularly until 1966, when their twenty-one-year-old daughter, Sandra, died. Suddenly they no longer cared about hits. "We've been on a downhill slide ever since," Slim said.

Before leaving town, I found Marcus Van Story, a bassist who played on sessions at Sun Records and performed in Warren Smith's band. I had met Van Story several years earlier, when I wrote about him in a book on rockabilly. He impressed me as genuine and funny. Some people work at boring jobs all their lives and later regret it. Van Story was different. He did exactly what he loved—play music—until his death on April 24, 1992, not long after I visited him again.

Van Story was a joyful man, ruddy-faced and easily amused. Settling down in a thick chair in his living room, I listened to him talk and laugh while telling the story of Memphis music in the 1950s. He brought out his bass, played it, and invited us to a concert that night at Overton Park Shell, a musical landmark where Elvis Presley and other famous entertainers performed. Van Story was to appear there with the Original Sun Rhythm Section, a group of rockabillies consisting of J.L. "Smoochy" Smith, an original member of the Mar-Keys, on piano; Marcus, nicknamed King of the Slap Bass, on bass, harmonica, and rhythm guitar; Stan Kesler, songwriter and producer, on electric bass; Paul Burlison, member of the Rock 'n' Roll Trio, on lead guitar; Sonny Burgess, former Sun artist, on lead guitar and vocals; and J.M. Van Eaton and D.J. Fontana, alternating on drums. For Van Story, the group was the culmination of a lifetime of performing. In his sixties when I met him, he was finally being recognized for his achievements. The rhythm section even played at the Smithsonian Institution and recorded some albums.

Since childhood, Van Story had played music on the family farm near Grenada, Mississippi, where his mother performed on a radio show. Eight-year-old Marcus joined her. "The station had a bass fiddle, but it was taller than me," he said. "I loved to watch a guy play it. It amazed me. I tried it even then. I never lost my fascination for it. When I went into the service, I played that old bass for USO shows."

After World War II, he went to Memphis to make the bass work for him and his young family. For several years he played in beer joints and worked side jobs. "If it hadn't been for the housing project where the Presleys, Bill Black, and we all lived, we couldn't have made it," he said. "Times were tough for us after the war. There were a lot of taverns to work in, though. I hated them because they had so many drunks. But if you did a song that the customers really liked, they'd let you know it—and tip you. I did a lot of imitations in those days, trying for tips. I really needed the money. I imitated Lefty Frizzell, Hank Williams, Red Foley—even Kitty Wells."

In 1953, Sam Phillips hired Van Story to play on sessions at the Union Avenue studio. "When I started slapping bass for him," Van Story said, "we didn't have any drums, so I did the slap to compensate. The bass, I got to hittin' it real hard, and then I started slappin' the strings against the neck and playin' it at the same time. That's how we came up with the slappin' bass. In those days, musicians put a penny postcard in guitar strings and eggshells on the baby grand piano strings to get different sounds. Anything to be different. Musicians broke the eggs, parched the shells to get a dry, 'rattle-ly' sound. They put towels around the baseboard so the shells wouldn't bounce off. It gave a funky, honky-tonk sound."

Van Story and Black played on many Sun sessions. Taking into account

Black's happy-go-lucky personality and ability, Phillips paired him with a new kid singer, Elvis Presley. Phillips also recruited guitarist Moore to round out the trio of Elvis, Scotty, and Bill. Meanwhile, Van Story played on sessions for Charlie Feathers and the Miller Sisters, performed in local clubs, and worked in a music store as an instrument repairman.

One day an Arkansas man walked into the store clutching a big cotton bag. It contained an old upright bass, broken in two. The man insisted on trading it in on a new instrument. When he left, the store owner handed the bag to Van Story and told him to throw it into the trash can. But Van Story couldn't do it. He took it to the store's basement workshop, glued and clamped the instrument back together, and lovingly restored it until it sounded right. He coated the body with jet-black automobile paint and ivory gloss around the edges.

"I was messin' with it one day, and Elvis came into the workshop with Bill Black," Van Story said. "Bill took one look at the bass and said, 'I like it. Man, I've *got* to have it.' He paid the store owner $175. I got half. When Bill died from a brain hemorrhage in 1965, I tried to buy the bass, but his widow had already sold it. It had sentimental value to me because Bill did the same kind of slap as me. When we recorded over at Sun, you couldn't tell whether it was me or Bill playing. One day I was coming back into Memphis, and I heard a disc jockey say at the end of a record, 'Listen to Bill Black slap that bass!' Of course, I knew better. I did it. Then the disc jockey comes back after a commercial and says, 'Oh, boy, I messed up. A lady just called to say it wasn't Bill Black after all. Mrs. Van Story says it was her husband on that record.'"

Once the rockabilly sound exploded in 1956, musicians traveled across the country to perform. Every few months they'd return to Memphis to play on records. Van Story played for Warren Smith, a Mississippi native who sounded more country than rock. Although his Sun singles were not national hits, two ultimately became rockabilly classics: "Ubangi Stomp" and "Rock 'n' Roll Ruby." The latter, written by Johnny Cash, was the more successful of Smith's early records. He predicted that it would break nationally, so he bought a Cadillac and painted "Warren Smith—the Rock 'n' Roll Ruby Man" on the back. The record didn't live up to his generous expectations, but it did burn across the South.

"We were all very close, like a family," Van Story said. "It was hard work, carrying that big bass around on the road. There were times I wish I had taken up the piccolo or something." He stood up, grabbed his bass, and slapped it rhythmically, to demonstrate the strength he needed to handle it.

"I had to haul this thing on top of the car. I never weighed it, but it must be at least eighty pounds. We used to drive to the *Big D Jamboree* in Dallas and the *Louisiana Hayride* in Shreveport. One day I got the bright idea of going over to a shop that made automobile convertible tops. I thought that material would make me a great cover for my bass. So I fitted the cover over the bass and placed it on top of our car, and we left for Dallas. Man, all of a sudden a horrible rain come up. Warren said, 'Oooh, this is bad.' I said, 'I ain't worried one little bit. That cover's waterproof!' Boy, we got to Dallas, and I reached up to get the bass and I couldn't move it. It took the three of us to get it down. It was full of water. I said, 'Man, this can't be. It'll fall apart.' So we laid it down to drain, and it never came apart. You know, I never did figure out how all that water got into that covered bass."

Actually, Van Story kept two instruments—one for the road and one for the Sun studio. He traveled with Smith, who played acoustic guitar and sang; Al Hobson, who played electric guitar; and Johnny Bernero or Jimmie Lott, who played drums. During Smith's four years with Sun, and later with Liberty Records, the band went across the country. Smith recorded some attractive songs, but they were little more than local hits. "Sam Phillips had so many artists, he didn't have time to push them all," Van Story said. "A lot of them were great artists. Warren was a little bitter about it. He felt let down. I loved Warren like a brother. We had some great times. We used to travel on the road as a package tour—Warren, Johnny Cash, Carl Perkins, and others. It was a convoy. The trips were monotonous. You lived in them cars twenty-four hours a day. There were few chances to stay in a hotel two, three days. It was mostly one-nighters. To offset the boredom, we'd light firecrackers and throw them out the window so they'd blow up under the cars behind us—our cars, that is. But firecrackers blew too quickly, so we graduated to cherry bombs.

"Jerry Lee had just brought a brand-new Chrysler, which swelled out on the sides where the windows rolled in. The windows were so clear. Up in Missouri somewhere, a guy lit a cherry bomb and tried to toss it out on Jerry Lee's side from the back seat. But the window wasn't down, and he didn't notice. We were riding in the car right behind. All of a sudden— boom! Man, it looked like that Chrysler rose up and come back down and swerved like a bird in flight. Smoke all inside. Those boys couldn't do a damned thing that night at the show."

Another time, Van Story and the band traveled to a show with Clayton Perkins, who was to join his famous brother, Carl, at a gig in Missouri. Van Story describes Clayton as "a first-class nut." They all rode in Smith's

Cadillac. It had been a particularly boring drive, so the musicians set off their share of cherry bombs along the way. A police officer noticed and followed them without their knowledge. Not far from Memphis, somewhere in northern Mississippi, the band stopped to eat breakfast in a large restaurant. Ham, eggs, pancakes—the works. The place was filled with people. Suddenly, police cars surrounded the building. Women, dressed in pearls and high heels, gasped in horror.

"Oh, Lord!" Marcus said. "Cops was everywhere. At every door—even the kitchen. One of the cops comes up and announces, 'Who owns that black Cadillac out there with a teardrop trailer behind it?' Well, I was driving, but I wasn't going to say nothing. Then the cop said it again. Nobody said a word. Then the cop said, 'I WANT TO KNOW WHO OWNS THAT CADDY!' Finally, Warren looked up from his eggs and said sheepishly, 'I guess I do.' The cop said, 'You're goin' downtown.' I knew we were in trouble. Then a cop shoved Clayton, and he kicked the guy in the shins. Well, Clayton was no stranger to the law. Officers had to lock up poor Clayton so many times for racing that they didn't even bother to chase him down anymore. They'd just go straight to his house and wait for him to return. So, of course, once they got old Clayton downtown, the cops looked up his traffic record. Oh, Lord, I knew we were all headed to jail. Fortunately, we knew one of the cops. He used to come hear us play. So the captain said, 'You guys got any more of them cherry bombs out in that car?' We said 'No, sir!' Our friend the cop pipes up and says, 'I'll go out to search the car just in case.' He came back and said, 'No, there ain't no more out there.' But there was—a five-pound bag of 'em right on the back seat! So they let us out of jail. We finally got to the gig really late, just as Carl was finishing up a set. He said to Clayton, 'Where in the heck have you been? I had to get somebody else to play bass.' They got into one heck of an argument. Never a dull moment around that Clayton Perkins."

In time, the days of cherry bombs and rockabilly faded. Smith joined Liberty Records in 1960 and became a temporary star with "I Don't Believe I'll Fall in Love Today" and "Odds and Ends." By 1965, it was about over. He suffered injuries in a car accident and left music for a decade. Van Story found gigs wherever he could. Later, after Smith relocated to Texas, the two resumed playing at times. Then one bitterly cold night in 1988, Van Story received a telephone call from Smith's wife. "She said, 'Marcus, Warren's dead.' Man, I couldn't believe it. He was not quite forty-seven years old. The last thing he told her was to comb his hair. He was keen about his hair. I drove all night to get there. I miss him, I really do. A lot of times I think I can see him."

Early that night, we met Van Story before the concert at Overton Park. It's like a small version of Central Park in urban Memphis. As we walked around, I finally noticed the Shell—an amphitheater that looks like a big white seashell beached on an island of green. It appeared much the same as it did on July 30, 1954, when Elvis, Scotty, and Bill played their first advertised gig there, with Slim Whitman. When Presley walked on stage, he nervously gyrated, and the crowed loved it. He was on to something.

Backstage, we met members of the Original Sun Rhythm Section, who invited us to watch them perform from a small alcove. They wore black chinos and black long-sleeved shirts with red ties on that humid evening, but I saw no trace of perspiration on their clothing or faces. The band members had all played on Sun sessions or for Sun artists, and they loved their rediscovery.

"I sure hope you guys didn't come here expecting to hear some old guys reminisce about the good old days," said drummer D.J. Fontana. "'Cause man, we gonna rock this place tonight."

"We do feel like kids again," said guitarist Paul Burlison, who played for the Rock 'n' Roll Trio in the 1950s. "But I don't regret leaving the music business back in the early days. I started my own electrical contracting business, and I've done all right for myself. I got to see my five kids grow up. I got to take time to live."

Although he left the music business early, he made history by introducing the familiar rock 'n' roll "fuzz-tone" guitar sound—a rumbling and growling that attracted Jeff Beck and other guitarists who followed Burlison in the next decade. Burlison did it by simply loosening a tube on his amplifier.

Promptly at 7 P.M., the band played "Whole Lotta Shakin' Goin' On" and other songs from the dawn of the big beat. Van Story, King of the Slap Bass, kept perfect time with Fontana. They moved a little slower, but they worked as two men with one mind.

When the show ended and we walked to my car, I felt privileged to know Marcus Van Story and to have shared his music and stories. He made me laugh and cry and, somehow, feel closer to those sweltering Memphis nights at the dawn of rock 'n' roll.

Muscle Shoals: Funky Fever

I rolled into Florence on the Fourth of July. By 6 P.M., families had lined up on a big iron bridge to watch fireworks explode above the Tennessee River later that night. I didn't bother to join them, for I had come to northern Alabama looking for hits—or what's left of them—in the hometown of W.C. Handy, father of the blues, and Sam Phillips, father of rock 'n' roll.

Florence, population about 40,000, is the larger of the developing Quad Cities: Sheffield, 13,000; Tuscumbia, 10,000; and Muscle Shoals, 10,000, are the other three. Their borders seem to blend; I couldn't tell when I left one city and entered another. I stopped in Florence first, because it is the mother of the Muscle Shoals Sound. In the late 1950s, James Joiner founded Tune Records, downtown on Court Street, and Tom Stafford, Rick Hall, and Billy Sherrill started Spar Music on Tennessee Street. They slept on cots in their little one-track studio, piled egg cartons up against the walls (the poor man's soundproofing), and searched the countryside for songs. "Florence was where it was happening," pianist David Briggs said.

But not anymore. I ended up driving around in circles until I stopped in quiet Tuscumbia. The city is the home of three attractions: the Alabama Music Hall of Fame, the birthplace of Helen Keller, and the Coon Dog Cemetery on State Route 247. When I saw the latter, I *knew* I had reached the Deep South. It began in 1837 when a man named Keg Underwood buried his beloved Troop at this special site. Touched by his gesture, other people buried their coon dogs there, too. About one hundred dogs now rest at the cemetery, surrounded by a park with picnic tables and a shelter. On Labor Day, the Coon Hunters Association hosts a liars' contest and a remembrance celebration. To me, the coon dog cemetery reflects something intangible that also flows through the music—a rural feeling, and devotion.

I'm not a coon dog man, so I moved on to the Hall of Fame and looked around for an hour or so at the photographs, artifacts, and displays of the Delmore Brothers, Tammy Wynette, Nat "King" Cole, Hank Williams, and various other nationally known natives. The hall is a music lover's dream— a first-rate museum. As I stood in line at the cash register to buy the hall's special compilation album of area rock bands, a friendly stranger in his late

Renowned session guitarist Jimmy Johnson at his office in Sheffield, Alabama, in 2000. Photo by Randy McNutt.

The original Muscle Shoals Sound Studio, at 3614 Jackson Highway in Sheffield, Ala., as it looked in 1993. Although only 25 feet wide, the studio turned out dozens of hits from 1969 to 1978. Photo by Randy McNutt.

(*Top*) Bassist David Hood at the second Muscle Shoals Sound Studio in Sheffield, Ala., in 2000. Photo by Randy McNutt.

The second Muscle Shoals Sound Studio, 1000 Alabama Avenue in Sheffield, Ala., was built as a naval reserve center. It became a recording studio in 1978. Photo by Randy McNutt.

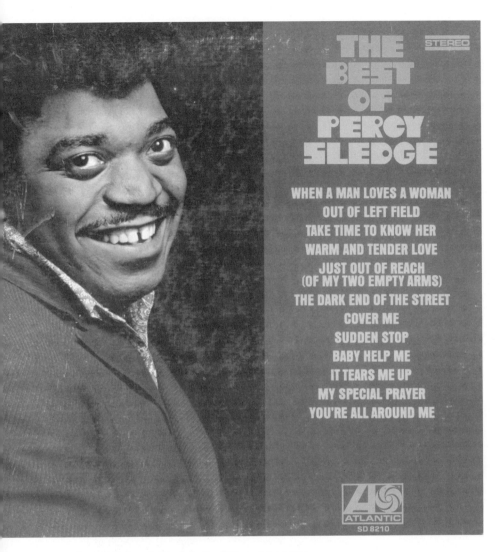

Percy Sledge's early hits, including "When a Man Loves a Woman" in 1966, came out of northern Alabama, where he lived.

twenties walked up to me and said, "Man, Dan Penn's performance on that CD is worth the price alone!"

Around here, people obviously take their music as seriously as their coon dogs. Legend has it that the music is in the soil somehow, and that the early inhabitants—Shawnee, Cherokee, Chickasaw—were more musical than other tribes. The first wave of white settlers arrived about 1818, when developers started Lauderdale County, named for Tennessee colonel James Lauderdale, who was killed at the Battle of New Orleans. Through the 1850s, the region produced cotton, but the Civil War destroyed the plantation economy. After the war, Sheffield took up iron production. By 1888 it had five blast furnaces. In 1916, Congress approved construction of the world's largest munitions plant and Wilson Dam, which during the Depression was absorbed by the Tennessee Valley Authority. World War I encouraged more people to work in the factories. Nevertheless, the area remained rural through the 1970s, and the name Muscle Shoals sounded more like a fishing lake than a city. (The name comes from the mussels that grew on the shoals of the Tennessee.)

Thanks to its catchy name, Muscle Shoals receives most of the notoriety for what's generally called the Muscle Shoals Sound, a brand of commercial R&B that's adaptable to about any style of song and artist. It's a homegrown sound made by Alabama boys who grew up on the blues, rock 'n' roll, and a little country music. It's also profitable. By the early 1970s, local musicians had played on and produced hit records by the hundreds. It's difficult to explain the appeal of their music. I can describe it as soulful, encompassing singers such as Arthur Conley and James and Bobby Purify, but then it becomes a musical chameleon for pop acts such as Mary MacGregor and Tony Orlando. The changeability comes from within the players themselves, whose styles and abilities seem greater as a whole than as individuals.

In Muscle Shoals, proud officials decided to erect a white metal sign with black letters on the edge of town: "Welcome to Muscle Shoals, Hit Recording Capital of the World." This was no hillbilly hyperbole, either, for Muscle Shoals and the Quad Cities once welcomed everyone from Cher to Wilson Pickett. They stayed at the Florence Holiday Inn—or in a trailer.

Musicians from area towns are an extended family who've created a distinctive sound from their environment. The story of the "Muscle Shoals Sound" is, in fact, the story of a few musicians, producers, and arrangers who have fought like alley cats and made up and worked together and made music that the world has come to love.

Unfortunately, when I arrived for the first time in 1993, the Muscle Shoals Sound had grown quiet. Several studios had closed, and musicians no longer worked every day. On a brilliant afternoon I went to the original Muscle Shoals Sound Studio, a former venetian blind factory at 3614 Jackson Highway in neighboring Sheffield. I found a long concrete-block building covered in front by a stone facade with a rusting address sign mounted on the side (just as it looked on a Cher album in 1969). Gravel crunched under my tires as I pulled into the little parking lot and looked around. I wondered why the front door was propped open on such an unbearable day—101 degrees and as still as death. As I entered the building, humidity pressed against my face like the breath of an overeager hound. "Howdy!" somebody shouted from the back. Suddenly a man in his fifties with no legs approached me in a wheelchair. Spots of perspiration bled through his dusty denim overalls, and he wiped his face with a paper napkin. He told me that the studio housed his used appliance shop, and that his family lived in the basement. The news stunned me momentarily. My eyes quickly scanned the room that gave the world many hit records—Paul Simon's "Kodachrome" and "Loves Me Like a Rock," R.B. Greaves' "Take a Letter, Maria," and Bob Seger's "Night Moves," to name just a few. "Yeah, I guess this place used to be famous," the man drawled.

The control room and its big glass window were still intact, without the old recording equipment. In fact, the interior still looked something like a studio, except that every inch of space in the small building—only twenty-five feet wide—was crammed with white washing machines. I asked the man if he ever receives visitors, and he said, "Oh, sure. A few years ago some guy stopped in here and said he's Mac Davis. He got out of a Cadillac and looked around. I said, 'So who's Mac Davis?' He seemed a little peeved at that remark and said, 'Well, I used to be on the TV.'" Laughing uproariously, the man rolled over to a dark wooden door and grabbed the tarnished brass-plated doorknob. He looked into my eyes as if he were ready to make some serious announcement and said, "I suppose you'll want to see my john." I shrugged. He pushed open the door slowly to reveal a room no larger than a small home closet. Cheap brown paneled walls revealed hundreds of musicians' signatures and naughty commentary. I didn't know whether to laugh. I turned around, surveyed the room filled with washers, and wondered aloud how such a musical landmark could be left to obscurity. "Easy," the man said. "Nobody cares."

Of course, he didn't understand that some people still revere the Muscle Shoals Sound Studio and consider its musician-entrepreneurs the real stars of those old records: David Hood, bass; Jimmy Johnson, guitar; Barry Beckett, piano; Roger Hawkins, drums. Thirty years later, I can better appreciate that their financial and artistic success came solely from making good music—songs crafted in the traditional sense, with pleasing hook lines and haunting melodies that have been overshadowed in recent years by rapping and raving and electronic instruments. The Muscle Shoals Sound was always about the music. Not marketing. Not advertising. This was pure picking by musicians who never did care about being stars or moving to the big city. They wanted to earn a living back home, to better enjoy their beloved Alabama.

But many others did leave, and some became internationally known. Briggs and bassist Norbert Putnam, two early players at Muscle Shoals' FAME Studios, went to Nashville and started their own studios after playing on many hits. Briggs, of Killen, Alabama, started doing sessions for Tune Records at age fourteen. The boy couldn't even drive himself to the studio, but he earned $5 an hour, more than tradesmen in the early 1960s.

I wanted to find the remaining musicians, to prove that their sound isn't dead, so I drove into downtown Sheffield in mid-morning. The streets were quiet on a Wednesday. Mothers took their kids into the two-room library that was once some kind of a store. Old men strolled by on their way to a coffee shop. Actually, Sheffield looks like Anywhere, U.S.A.—a place worn and tired as it lumbers into the twenty-first century. Like the buildings in thousands of other American downtowns, Sheffield's are mostly brick, from the late 1800s and early 1900s. Faded white letters spelling out long-forgotten brand names in fancy script appear high up on the sides of the buildings, like ghosts revealing past lives. On side streets, Victorian houses of all sizes dominate the neighborhood, and kids ride bicycles past the tree-lined Vietnam Veterans Park and a sign that reads: "This community is a bird sanctuary."

A few blocks away I find Riverside Park on the Tennessee, a river as tranquil as any lake. Near the water, at 1000 Alabama Avenue, I stop at a sprawling concrete building, painted tan and white with double glass doors bearing the logo MSSS—Muscle Shoals Sound Studios. It's the second incarnation of the famous studio, set in Sheffield's former Naval Reserve Center, which was built in sections from the early 1900s through the 1940s. When it closed in the mid-1970s, members of the Muscle Shoals Rhythm Section decided to buy it from the city at an auction and renovate it as a studio. Their long-term lease at the old Jackson Highway studio was nearly up, and they didn't think the owner would sell. So they hired a Nashville studio consultant to design two twenty-four-track studios in the reserve building. At 31,000 square feet, it provided more than enough space for meeting rooms, loading docks, and offices. In fact, the musicians felt at home because they had performed at dances there when they were young. When the new studio opened in 1978, it continued the hit streak with "We've Got Tonight" and "Old Time Rock 'n' Roll" by Bob Seger and "Giving It Up for Your Love" by Delbert McClinton.

Hood, the world-famous bass player, greeted me at the front door. He is a friendly man with curly brown hair going gray and, to my relief, a big talent with a small ego. At his desk I kept staring at his nameplate, which read "Rednu Gnilbbub." "It's not my name in Polish," he said. "It used to sit on Jerry Wexler's desk at Atlantic Records in New York. It spells 'bubbling under' backwards. I thought it must be his name from the old country or something. But I guess he wanted to remember all those records that just bubbled under the Hot 100."

As I sat in front of Hood, one of my favorite musicians, I wondered how four guys who couldn't read music ever turned so many songs into hits. "We never really tried to make a certain sound," he said. "We were just trying to cut hit records with whatever artist walked in the door. If it was a black artist, we tried to sound like his band. If it was a white artist, we tried to sound like his band. Over the years, it evolved to the point that there was a sound. But at first we were just trying to do the job."

Hood grew up in Sheffield and went to high school with Jimmy Johnson. His father, a local tire dealer, wanted David to take over the family business. He preferred to attend what is now the University of North Alabama, "but accounting just about finished me." He also played trombone and a little guitar in a rock band called the Mystics. "We copied parts of records," he said. "I remember hearing 'Walk Don't Run' by the Ventures. I loved it. It was my goal to play it perfectly." Hood, who had played trombone in high school, felt a special kinship with the band members. One day the lead singer convinced his father to pay for a session at Rick Hall's new FAME Recording in Muscle Shoals, one of a few studios in the area. When they arrived, Hall wasn't there. The boys pushed back a plywood sheet and squeezed into the studio and called Hall. He came over to record them. "Recording was fun, and it got into my blood," Hood said. "That session attracted Rick Hall's attention to me as a player. There weren't too many people interested in recording at the time, so he would use me when he wanted something done and he didn't want to pay."

As the Mystics gained a larger following, Hood left college to concentrate on music. "Playing with the Mystics was just like *Animal House*—a four-man band playing at fraternity parties and proms and school dances," he said. "We were wild and crazy and thought we'd be the next Beatles. The other guys in the band were a little bit more serious students than me, and about 1966 they all started graduating. That ended the band. They went out to get regular jobs. Here I was working at my father's tire store and playing in the band on weekends. I wasn't ready to quit. I was loving it."

The day after the Mystics' final performance, May 15, 1966, Hood played trombone on his first union-scale session, Percy Sledge's "A Warm and Tender Love." "That did it for me," Hood said. "I said, 'Man, I've *got* to do this.' From then on, any chance I had to get back into the studio, I took it. When I was supposed to be managing the store, I'd get a call from Rick Hall to come over to play on a session. I'd grab my instrument and head over there. My father used to get so mad at me. Eventually I told him, 'Forget the tire store, Dad. I'm going to be a musician.' He thought I was throwing my life away. I haven't looked back, really. At times it's been slow and rough, and I've thought that maybe I should have stayed at the tire store. Then I go down to a tire store and I say, 'Nah, not for me.'"

In northern Alabama, people call Rick Hall the Godfather because he makes deals and hits. He is known for his handlebar mustache, twirled on the ends, and for his tenacity. In photographs from the 1970s, he looks like a member of a barbershop quartet in a business suit. Hall is local talent. He took raw black music from his home state and made it his signature sound. He showed that it was first and foremost *American* music, made for all races, and then he proved his point by adapting it to white pop singers.

Hall grew up poor on a sharecropper's farm near Phil Campbell, Alabama, in the 1930s and '40s. His father taught him to work hard. At age three, Hall picked up a harmonica; at age six, a mandolin. In high school he won first prize in a contest of the Future Farmers of America. But he preferred to plant musical seeds, and after graduation he headed to Illinois to play bass in a country band and work in a factory. Disillusioned with life in the North, he came home to a factory job in Sheffield.

At the time, the early 1950s, there was no record industry in the Quad Cities. In fact, most of the area counties were dry, and would remain so for years, forcing musicians to work away from home. But Hall was destined to work close to home, in a local record industry that started early one night in the spring of 1955. After country musician James Joiner finished playing a baseball game, he drove home on Route 64 and saw a falling star between

Greenhill and Lexington. Fifteen minutes after arriving home, he finished writing a country song called "A Fallen Star."

He decided to match it with an amateur band featuring singer Bobby Denton, who cut the song between broadcasts in the WLAY radio studio. The session cost less than $5. Joiner pressed the tape on his own Tune Records, and turned it into a regional hit. Later, country singers Ferlin Husky and Jimmy "C" Newman also recorded the song. Excited by the experience, Joiner opened a studio and searched for talent. He didn't cut any big hits, but he gave local people an opportunity to record. He also invested in another studio, opened above the Florence City Drug Store in 1959 by Stafford, Sherrill, and Hall. They called the place Florence, Alabama Music Enterprises, now better known by its acronym, FAME. By 1960 they had split up, as the result of a dispute, and Hall retained the name. (Sherrill would become the head of Columbia Records' Nashville office in the 1960s.) It would be the most important factor in Alabama music for the next decade.

Hall started his own music-publishing company. As he once put it, "With getting married and having mouths to feed, I had to find me a new cotton patch." He published "You Better Move On," written by black singer Arthur Alexander, a bellhop at an area motel. "I really dug that song," Hall said. "I thought it was sure to go someplace." When no Nashville record company would cut it, Hall decided to record it himself. He bought a used console from WLAY and a one-track recorder and opened FAME Recording in an abandoned tobacco warehouse on Wilson Dam Road. He organized some local musicians (from a band called Dan Penn and the Pallbearers) and recorded the song. Suddenly Hall was a record producer, a term that wasn't in widespread use yet. He played the master for nearly every label in Nashville, and again they rejected him. Then Randy Wood, owner of Dot Records in Los Angeles, accepted the recording, which landed in the twenties on the national pop charts and earned Hall enough royalties to build a new studio at 603 East Avalon Avenue in Muscle Shoals. He carefully built it to achieve the sound he wanted—a deep, funky sound, to enhance the R&B music that he planned to record. He built a special echo chamber using a plaster coating, then installed a three-track Ampex recorder. He opened the doors in 1962.

The FAME sound came as much from Hall's ingenuity as from his creativity. Of course, his musicians lent a distinctive ingredient. Since 1960, Hall has employed four house bands. The first two are the most famous. The first band included Briggs on piano, Putnam on bass, Jerry Carrigan on drums, and Terry Thompson on guitar. Band members credit Thompson, who died in 1965, with being the best musician of the group. As they played on more sessions, they became as tight as a fist. They sensed where each man was going, as though they walked as one. I'm aware of their talent, but its full depth didn't strike me until I listened to them play with area musicians on the Hall of Fame compact disc. The live performance sounded better than most studio cuts.

When matched with Alexander's emotional vocals, the band created a muddy yet memorable track in "You Better Move On." Alexander's song would be remade by the Rolling Stones and other groups. The Beatles cut his "Anna (Go to Him)," and Bob Dylan his "Sally Sue Brown." Alexander told reporters that the only thing he knew to write about was his own experiences. "This guy had been going with this girl since grade school," he said of his hit, "and I met her after graduation. I thought I had the best hand, and he thought he had the best hand with her. And I just put my feelings into that song." Unfortunately, years later Alexander ended up disillusioned with the music business. He moved to Cleveland and took a job as a school bus driver. Shortly before his death in 1993, he recorded a fine album in Muscle Shoals with many of his old Alabama friends.

Alexander's hit single attracted his friend Jimmy Hughes, a local tire worker and R&B singer, who had written a song called "Steal Away." Hall liked it, but knew that he'd face a difficult time placing the master. So he recorded the song and released it on his own FAME Records. Hall obtained distribution through Vee-Jay Records of Chicago and headed out on a national promotional tour. He gave each disc jockey a record and a bottle of whiskey. "Steal Away" sold 500,000 copies and set FAME Records into motion. Soon word spread about the studio's sound. In 1963, Tommy Roe cut "Everybody" and the Tams "What Kind of Fool Do You Think I Am?"

In 1965, record store owner Quin Ivy opened a studio in Sheffield to record the acts that Hall didn't have time to accommodate. Ivy, who for years had worked as a disc jockey across the South, knew commercial songs. So when Percy Sledge, a twenty-five-year-old orderly at Colbert County Hospital, arrived with "When a Man Loves a Woman," Ivy agreed to record it. The identifiable soul song, written by two members of Sledge's band, came from the heart. Ivy and guitarist Marlin Greene produced it at Ivy's Norala Recording Studios on two one-track tape recorders. (The second one was used for primitive overdubbing by freelance engineer Jimmy Johnson, FAME's session guitarist and Hall's apprentice.) Ivy took the tape to Hall, who pitched it to Jerry Wexler at Atlantic. Wexler liked it, but he insisted that the producers record the song again, because the horns—and Sledge—were slightly out of tune. So they re-recorded it. When the song reached No. 1 on the pop and R&B charts in April 1966, Ivy was surprised to hear the *original* version, apparently released in confusion. Nobody cared if the horns were slightly out of tune. "When a Man Loves a Woman" went on to become one of the era's most enduring songs, even inspiring a Meg Ryan film of the same name in the 1990s. It earned the Shoals its first gold record and popped up on charts across the world. Sledge followed it with more chart records: "Take Time to Know Her," "Cover Me," and "Out of Left Field." But it is on the strength of his initial soul ballad that Percy Sledge still performs.

Also in 1966, Arthur Conley came to Hall's studio to cut "Sweet Soul Music" with producer Otis Redding. Florida DJ "Papa" Don Schroeder came in to record R&B singers James and Bobby Purify. Hall offered them "I'm Your Puppet," written by FAME staff writers Dan Penn and Spooner Oldham. The Purifys used Hall's rhythm band, including Oldham on piano, Albert "Junior" Lowe on guitar, Roger Hawkins on drums, and Barry Beckett on organ. David Hood played trombone, with Charlie Chalmers and Ed Logan on saxophone. The record reached the Top 10 on the pop and R&B charts in September 1966, and forced the world to notice this little place called Muscle Shoals.

Jerry Wexler, *Billboard* reporter-turned-producer, did as much as anyone to ignite the regional recording fires. He brought Atlantic acts to Muscle Shoals, Memphis, New Orleans, and other Southern cities. The company's money enabled studio owners to buy better equipment. But Wexler came not to see the tourist spots but to hear new sounds. By the mid-1960s, he had grown tired of predictable New York arrangements. He found the un-predictable—Rick Hall—in the fields of northern Alabama. He describes Muscle Shoals as "that karmic place saturated with soul and sprit."

Atlantic sent Wilson Pickett to FAME to cut what are considered soul classics: "In the Midnight Hour," "Mustang Sally," and "Funky Broadway." Hall picked him up at the Florence airport, and as they drove through the rural area, Pickett cringed at the sight of blacks working in the cotton fields. After all, this *was* Alabama in 1966. But the session, like others during the early days of the Muscle Shoals Sound, would bring anything but racial trouble. In fact, it represented racial togetherness, for again black singers worked well with Hall's white house band. The "Mustang Sally" session, pro-duced by Hall, turned out to be a combination of the best of Muscle Shoals and Memphis players: Oldham played organ; Chips Moman, lead guitar;

Jimmy Johnson, rhythm guitar; and Tommy Cogbill, bass. The Sweet Inspirations, a black female group, sang background vocals. The sessions also
inspired Pickett's nickname, "the Wicked Pickett," which the label chose as
an album title. One day he entered his record company's New York office
and saw a girl in a miniskirt bending over a desk. He strolled up and, with
soul-man bravado, pinched her buttock. A secretary scolded him for his
wicked behavior. Executive Jerry Wexler overheard the comment and ex-
claimed, "That's the name of the album—*The Wicked Pickett!*"

Back in Muscle Shoals, Hall continued to search for white soul musicians. He knew how to find the best studio players. He hired guitarists Eddie
Hinton and Duane Allman, "the redneck hippie" who suggested that Pickett
record the Beatles' "Hey Jude." Improbable as it sounded, the record worked.
Allman looked out of place standing next to FAME's mostly short-haired
musicians, who in turn looked unusual in the era's long-haired music business. Hall pushed his musicians hard, and they responded—or left. As his
latest studio band became artistically successful, it started breaking up in
the late 1960s. Then Hall turned to Hood, Beckett, Johnson, and Hawkins—
the new A team—without sacrificing quality. In fact, their hiring brought
about the halcyon days of FAME and sessions by Aretha Franklin. Wexler
brought Franklin to FAME to record "I Never Loved a Man (the Way I Love
You)" in early 1967. But after this song and part of another were recorded, a
white horn player got into an argument with Franklin's husband, Ted White.
White took her back to their motel in Florence and prepared to leave town.
Hall went over to straighten out the problem, but ended up in a fistfight
with White. Racial problems were not as common in northern Alabama,
and especially not in its studios, despite the stormy political climate across
the country. As David Hood pointed out, "Black entertainers were our he-
roes. We looked up to them. Around town, it was a little unusual to go to a
restaurant with a mixed crowd, but it was never a problem." But Franklin's
work in Muscle Shoals was over. Weeks later, Wexler brought Hall's musicians to Atlantic's studios in New York to finish the Franklin sessions, which
included the hits "Respect" and "Think."

Hall didn't lose business as a result of the argument. All the national
attention brought him more offers to produce records. Hits followed: "Up
Tight Good Man" by Laura Lee; "Tell Mama" by Etta James; "Slip Away" and
"Funky Fever" by Clarence Carter; and dozens of lesser but money-making
hits. Hall was so concerned that Carter would be offended by the idea of the
song "Patches"—a poor boy helps his family on the farm after his father
dies—that the producer told an associate to whisper the words to Carter as

he recorded the song. He didn't even know what he had cut that day in 1970.

By then, Hall sensed that Southern rural soul was slipping in favor of more polished music. He installed an eight-track recorder and brought in the Osmond Brothers, a white act from Las Vegas that had been gaining in popularity. The group wanted to record something other than their predictable pop material, and Hall allowed them the freedom, using Merrill Osmond on lead vocals on "One Bad Apple," a song suited to Motown's Jackson Five. The hit version nearly failed to make it to the pressing plant. After recording it, the Osmonds sat around eating fast food with sauce while Hall edited the quarter-inch master tape. Somehow an important piece fell into a trash can while Hall was busily working. The singers tossed their leftover food into the can on top of the tape. When Hall realized that the piece was missing, everyone searched the studio. Finally, somebody reached into the can and pulled out the piece of tape, which Hall wiped off and spliced onto the rest of the song. That greasy little piece of quarter-inch tape became a part of the final master.

While recording at FAME, the Osmonds lived in a trailer in a field. Donny Osmond, then twelve, thought the studio—with "recreation-room wood paneling and location somewhere close to the middle of nowhere"— looked surprisingly modest compared to its reputation as a palace of hits. Hall worked closely with the group to develop a solid vocal delivery and find commercial material. Osmond and his brothers delivered more hits for him: "Double Lovin'," "Sweet and Innocent" (written years earlier by Hall and Billy Sherrill), and Joe South's "Yo-Yo." As session engineer and producer, Hall demanded that each voice stand out in the final mix. The records showed versatility and turned the Osmonds into one of America's more popular acts.

Hall's ironic success with white pop brought offers for more pop records. In 1972 he recorded "Baby Don't Get Hooked on Me" for Mac Davis, followed by "One Hell of a Woman" and "Stop and Smell the Roses." In 1974, Hall returned 1950s teen star Paul Anka to No. 1—for the first time since 1959—with "(You're) Having My Baby," then with "One Man Woman/One Woman Man." Hall even brought crooner Andy Williams back to the charts with a remake of Aaron Neville's "Tell It Like It Is," and Bobby Gentry with "Fancy," which Hall believed was his best work.

By this time, Muscle Shoals was defying the gravity of musical trends. Disco was booming, yet the Quad Cities' studios operated as though they hadn't heard the news. Hall, producer of the year in 1971 and a Grammy nominee in 1974 and 1975, had just entered semi-retirement. When he returned to producing full-time a few years later, disco was gone, but tastes and radio programming had changed. He ignored an industry recession and started building his publishing empire. In later years he published the hit "I Swear" and produced Billy Joe Royal and Shenandoah while his sons, Mark and Rodney, entered the business. Mark, who co-wrote Tim McGraw's "I Like It, I Love It," manages FAME's publishing office on Music Row in Nashville. Rodney manages the studio, the one his father built with royalties from his first hit.

I visited FAME on my last trip to Muscle Shoals. It was just as I had imagined it. When I walked through the front door, I noticed a sign above the entrance to the studio: "Through these doors walk the finest musicians, songwriters, artists, and producers in the world." Forty years and hundreds of hits after the old tobacco warehouse first echoed with song, the words still ring true.

After lunch at Pizza Hut, I wanted some Muscle Shoals music. I drove around lost until I finally ended up on a street of older homes, then found Jimmy Johnson's little white house in Sheffield. While the sun burned like a laser and humidity drenched the city, I rested in the car for ten minutes with the air-conditioner running and a damp towel wrapped across my perspiring face. Finally I went to the back door of the one-story house, which had no sign but was called Swamper Sound Studio. Two women in their late twenties sat on the back step. One was playing an acoustic guitar. They both tried to act hip. One kept saying, "Well, hey!" Soon Johnson came to the door and welcomed me inside. He said he had planned to record some demos with the women, but they could wait. He showed me his little studio, a bedroom transformed by digital equipment and compressors and microphones that were being operated that day by veteran engineer Steve Melton. He insisted on playing a track for me, which was flat-out rock 'n' roll. "I started working at Muscle Shoals Sound Studio when I was only seventeen," Melton said. "I was a musician in a band. Of course, I had heard all those great records by Wilson Pickett and Aretha Franklin. I loved them. Then I found out that Jimmy and the rhythm section had helped create those sounds. I said, 'This is where I want to be.'"

As he took me into his office, I couldn't take my eyes off more than a dozen gold and platinum singles and albums that hung on his walls. He said he lacks sufficient wall space to hang his whole collection. He spoke slowly, with the assurance of a local historian: "Everything started with 'A Fallen Star.' Through that notoriety, musicians from a 50-to-100-mile radius were willing to move here when they weren't willing to move to Nashville. They thought that if they were to associate with James Joiner, that somehow success would rub off on them, too. About a dozen writers and artists came in, including Billy Sherrill and Rick Hall. They slept in their car, under a bridge. They liked to starve to death. Slowly, they started a publishing company. It was all built around that one song, the catalyst, which now has been recorded more than three hundred times. Everybody was so impressed that a song could be done here. They thought something like that had to come from New York or Nashville or Los Angeles. There's something mystical about it. Some people suggest that it's because of the water from the Tennessee River, but nobody really knows. People say they come here and *feel* something."

Johnson's inspiration came from his musician father, known as Cowboy Ray. When Johnson's aunt bought him his first guitar at age eleven, he was hooked. His father encouraged him to play it. Cowboy Ray had played on the radio for years, but stopped performing when Jimmy was born in 1943. (Forty years later, eighty-year-old Cowboy Ray was encouraged to perform by Johnson and his son, Jay, who in 2000 produced an album for the family's elder musician.) By the time Johnson reached his early teens, he was ready for a dose of more youthful inspiration. It came directly from guitarist Donnie Srygley of Spring Valley, near Sheffield. While a student in junior high school, Johnson heard Srygley's band perform. "I was so impressed," Johnson said. "It was the first sock hop I'd ever been to. They were playing 'Johnny B. Goode.' I was really into Chuck Berry, Jimmy Reed, Bo Diddley. I was mesmerized. I realize now that everybody who plays an instrument has one moment of inspiration. I said, 'I've got to learn how to do this.' I stood there with my mouth open the whole night. I'd never seen a Fender guitar before. Right then, I made plans to get associated with Donnie. We're great friends to this day."

In the early 1960s, Johnson met Roger Hawkins in a rock and soul band called the Delrays, which toured the South. They ended up working as session players at FAME and were later joined by Hood. As his confidence in Johnson grew, Hall offered the guitarist the job of apprentice. He cleaned the studio, played on sessions, did some engineering. Johnson, always a keen observer, learned well from the man who was determined not to fail. When Johnson finally started earning his living exclusively from session work, he knew he would never do anything else.

As FAME's hits continued, Johnson and the band worked with major acts. They called themselves the Swampers, a name they received from admiring musicians. The world looked bright. Then, abruptly, life hit a sour note in 1969. "Rick was in the midst of going closed-shop, which meant he would hire us as full-time players exclusively for his studio and label," Johnson said. "We couldn't imagine doing that. At the time, you see, we were playing for labels from New York, L.A., Nashville—even Shreveport. And Rick didn't offer us as much money as he did the year before, when we each made $17,000. So Rick offered $10,000. Nobody was happy about that. It was take it or leave it. We decided to leave it. That was Rick's fatal error. If he had just offered us what we made the year before, we would have probably stayed. We didn't dislike him; we thought of him as an older brother. But Roger and I saw that opening our own studio was an opportunity.

"Nobody on the outside knew what was going on behind the scenes. Jerry Wexler, one of the most powerful men in the record business, didn't even know that Rick was fixin' to shut the door on us. We had trouble finding a place to call Wexler where two of us guys could talk to him, 'cause none of our houses were wired for multiple phones. Heck, we couldn't call him from FAME. This was before people had more than one phone in their house, at least down here. But we ended up learning what the meaning of conference call was."

After talking to Wexler, Johnson and Hawkins met in a pizza parlor to discuss their plans for insurrection. They agreed that they *should* lease the little Fred Bevis Studio on Jackson Highway, but they worried about the future. Could they make their mortgage payments and the studio rent, too? The rent, $150 a month, was a lot of money to them. By agreeing to buy the studio, they fashioned an unusual arrangement, for generally musicians can't agree on anything but what songs to play. But then, this was not a band of average musicians.

"It was probably our last chance," Johnson said. "I had $3,500 in the bank and a new home. Roger had the same amount of money. I was too afraid to ask my wife about the deal. Fred wanted $7,000 down, so it was $3,500 for Roger and me. I had $200 left in my savings account. I had never been a gambler. I was afraid it wouldn't work, but I knew I had to try. Something made me do it. Then we had the big problem of talking our other two partners into it. We had to guarantee them something we didn't have— money. We felt the only way we could get them to join us was to make them an offer they couldn't refuse, and we hadn't heard of the Godfather yet. So we offered them five percent of the studio in stock—free. Just gave it to them. And we guaranteed them $30,000 a year each, after one year. Roger and I were standing good for the money on paper. But we had reached the point where we just said, 'Hey, let's go for it.'"

As new business owners, they faced problems. What to call the place? Hood suggested, half-jokingly, that they call it Muscle Shoals Sound Studio. Who'd ever heard of Muscle Shoals? The name was wacky enough to work. Each member took a job in the studio. One man cleaned the toilets; another kept the books. Until then, few people across the country—let alone the music business—had even heard of Muscle Shoals, but that was about to change. The Jackson Highway studio would nourish the Muscle Shoals Rhythm Section, and musicians all across northern Alabama would ultimately benefit.

Nothing happened for six months. They sat around and worried some more. The ceiling leaked near the recording console; the musicians patched it temporarily with tampons. Bills rolled in on time. Then, just as everything was looking increasingly bleak, Atlantic came in and cut two hits by an unknown singer named R.B. Greaves—"Take a Letter, Maria" and "There's Always Something There to Remind Me." Lulu followed with "Oh Me Oh My (I'm a Fool for You Baby)." More hits exploded across the country.

As the studio's financial state improved, the band started a publishing company, a production company, and a label. They worked with Art Garfunkel, Cat Stevens, and Kim Carnes. Performers waited in line for a chance to record with the band. "We all had the same goal," Johnson said. "That's why it worked. We never had a stalemate on any vote, and we had pressure votes each week. Isn't that bloody amazing? It's almost beyond my imagination."

At first, Hall reacted as Johnson expected—with tough competition. Then he did the unexpected. He added these words to the front of his recording studio: "Home of the Muscle Shoals Sound." Despite the confusion, more than enough work existed for FAME and Muscle Shoals Sound. By 1973, the band and the funky studio, despite its limitations, were established. Paul Simon called one day, and Hawkins thought somebody was joking. But Simon came to Alabama to record "Kodachrome."

When the new Muscle Shoals studio opened in the old Naval Reserve Building in 1978, the band hired a full-time employee just to work in the parts department. They recorded an inaugural hit, Dr. Hook's "When You're in Love with a Beautiful Woman."

Meanwhile, other studios opened in the area. Terry Woodford, another former member of the Mystics, opened Wishbone Studios with pianist Clayton Ivey, and they cut "Angel in Your Arms" by Hot and "Falling" by LeBlanc and Carr. They wore out the recording machine doing sessions for Glenn Frey, Roy Orbison, and other stars.

But gradually the musical times changed, and the "Hit Recording Capital" sign came down. Jimmy Johnson and partners sold their studio to Malaco Records of Jackson, Mississippi. The musicians wanted to play, not prepare more accounting spreadsheets. "Even when we sold the catalog and the studio, we were all in agreement," he said. "Our accountant said, 'There is $350,000 in the band's account. What will you do with it?' I said, 'How much is owed to the writers?' He said, 'Most of it.' We could have kept the money. But everybody said in unison, 'Pay the writers!' We couldn't even think of walking off with that money. We sleep real good at night."

Today, Muscle Shoals as a recording center is still active but not busy. The Alabama Music Hall of Fame is a success, having inducted members of the Muscle Shoals Rhythm Section *and* Rick Hall. Johnson works on his latest dream—a company that intends to sell recordings through the Internet as well as retail stores. "We're tired of having no middle class in our industry," he said. "It's so bad that an artist must sell a million records just to be broke, while the record company makes $7 million." Meanwhile, over in Muscle Shoals, sixty-nine-year-old Hall has earned the right to work when he wants. His legacy is independence; he knew good songs and musicians— and when to change.

But these days, fewer sessions around Muscle Shoals mean that musicians must go to Nashville if they want to work regularly. Through all the changes, the Swampers have stayed together, even after Beckett's departure for Nashville. Johnson and Hood, local boys to the end, plan to stay in Sheffield with Hawkins, whose physical problems limit him to fewer sessions these days.

"We've done more than anybody ever expected," Johnson said. "We made hit records in our hometown. We made a good living and we're happy. We're still just a bunch of rednecks who want to play."

Norfolk, Virginia: If You Wanna Be Happy

In early June, Norfolk bloomed with tulip magnolias and camellias. Downtown, pile drivers boomed as construction crews built the twenty-one-acre MacArthur Center shopping mall. I drove through downtown and out to Granby Street, looking for Frank Guida's Rockmasters Music office, then in an industrial and commercial area filled with worn buildings. I cruised back and forth until I came to a white square building made of concrete blocks and surrounded by a high security fence with an automatic gate. The office reminded me of a large guard shack. It sat next to a motel and nightclub that promoted its "Wednesday night cigar social and lingerie party" on a big marquee. As I stood perplexed in front of the building that morning, the gate opened slowly, and a trim man in his early seventies motioned for me to enter the lot. He led me down a narrow hall and into a small white office with gold trim and beige carpet. On the wall hung a poster for *Rigoletto* and framed *Cashbox* and *Billboard* stories. I glanced at a calypso drum, a red and gold shield with "Familia Guida" on the front, vinyl discs, songwriting awards, and varied Italian memorabilia. The man finally turned, shook my hand, and introduced himself as Frank Joseph Guida, record producer. He told his assistant, a black woman in her forties named Rosetta, to listen to our conversation. Guida sat behind a tidy wooden desk, leaned back in his chair, and said, "So what's the story?"

"You," I said.

"Well, I don't know why," he said. "I'm not one of the more popular guys in the record business. I used to sue everybody."

The story is also the Norfolk Sound—part rock, part R&B, part pop, with a calypso beat, low-down saxophone riffs, and good-time lyrics. Norfolk's hits—"New Orleans" and "Quarter to Three" come to mind—helped fill the musical void between the demise of rockabilly in the late 1950s and the arrival of the Beatles in 1964. Guida's music can still be heard today in films ("If You Wanna Be Happy" was in *My Best Friend's Wedding*) and on oldies radio.

Mysteriously, maybe miraculously, things all came together over at 408 West Princess Anne Road in Norfolk, where Guida's Norfolk Recording Studio rocked with tempestuous players in August 1960. Imagine the scene:

Norfolk record producer Frank Guida stands with his
early-1960s recording equipment in 1997. Photo by
Randy McNutt.

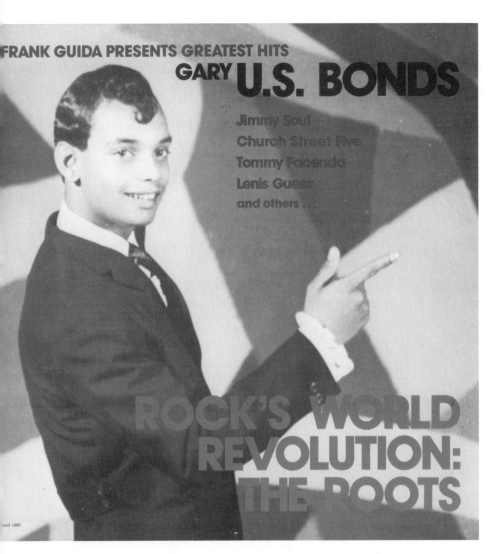

Norfolk's 1960s hits were repackaged by producer Frank Guida
on this vinyl album.

Guida, a self-assured Italian who once billed himself the Calypso Kid, had turned to producing records and collided head-on with streetwise black musicians who preferred jazz and R&B. The studio's untested engineer, a clothing salesman who preferred country music, worked with a one-track tape recorder that was not designed for professional use. Singers disliked Guida's original songs. "I can't tell you the words they used to describe my music," he said. "But then, they never liked anything I ever did, 'New Orleans' included. And that bothers me. Do you realize the heartbreaks and insults that one endures when he's producing? Sometimes you see things your way, and that's the way it's got to be."

That could be Guida's motto. His career reads like either the plot for a situation comedy or the greatest miracle in the record business—maybe both. Nevertheless, Guida became about the hottest producer and songwriter in any regional music center, turning out a driving sound perfectly suited to mono car radios and good-time night rides. Even his lyrics were different. As Jimmy Soul warned us, "If you wanna be happy for the rest of your life, never make a pretty woman your wife; so from my personal point of view, get an ugly girl to marry you." Guida also made money in every other corner of the record business—retail sales, publishing, and management. His recordings impressed the Beatles, Bruce Springsteen, and producer Kenny Gamble of Philadelphia, and introduced some unusual names into the American radio vocabulary—Jimmy Soul, Gary U.S. Bonds, Daddy G.

Guida's hits exploded quickly, like a cannon salute: "High School U.S.A." by Tommy Facenda, 1959; "New Orleans" by Gary U.S. Bonds, 1960; "Quarter to Three," "School Is Out," "School Is In," and "Dear Lady Twist," also by Bonds in 1961. The next year came Jimmy Soul's "Twistin' Matilda" and "If You Wanna Be Happy." Bonds returned with "Twist, Twist Senora" and "Seven Day Weekend." Between 1960 and 1963, Guida produced and co-wrote fourteen national chart records, all but one released on his own labels.

He understood the music business—and the young customers at his record shop. "I predicted Elvis Presley's rise, even though I'd never met him," Guida said. "At the time, I was contemplating finding a white kid to sing black music. By the time I got into the business, though, Elvis' career was at a standstill and rock and R&B were receding. Pop was coming back; 'Volare' was a monster, three or four million copies sold worldwide. Then two of my songs had a real impact: 'New Orleans' and 'Quarter to Three.' It was like a whole rebirth of music. Any of my artists could appear on Dick Clark's show. We owned Philadelphia. (But not Norfolk. Its stations wouldn't break our records.) Anything we did, radio immediately played all over the country. This was a shot in the arm for the record business. What records sounded like ours? None. We had some quality musicians, even though I had to bang some heads to make my points. For you see, what we did was not R&B. As a matter of fact, Berry Gordy Jr. used to keep our records in his sound booth in Detroit. 'Where Did Our Love Go?' was not really R&B. It was Frank Guida! I got seven awards from BMI in one year back in those days, and at an awards ceremony some Motown writers told me I was the only one in the room who was doing anything different. But one inspiration brings on another. And when they realized that this Frank Guida's got a black artist selling to white kids, they thought: How come we can't do that? In those early days, Gordy couldn't give away records to white kids. We, on the other hand, sold seventy-five percent of our records to white kids, because the records really weren't R&B. How would I describe the music? A Norfolk concoction, a combination of everything."

His first release on Legrand Records, "High School U.S.A.," attracted the attention of Atlantic, which re-recorded the song in New York. It was unlike Guida's later hits in that it was simple teenage fare consisting of twenty-eight simultaneous releases targeted to different parts of the country.

"I was straining to figure out something that would make an impact on the market," Guida said. "I had a record shop, so I knew what was selling. I came up with this idea: a record for each city—Cleveland, Cincinnati, Memphis, and others. We mentioned a lot of local high schools in each one. I knew the guys at Atlantic because I helped break some of their big hits with my record shop. When they heard about my record, they came to me to do the thing over in New York. The head man, Ahmet Ertegun, finished the session and said, 'What do you think, Frank?' I said, 'The tempo is too fast.' He said, 'Oh, no, no, no.' But, sure enough, the record went to only No. 28. We were ready to put out thirty-eight different versions if things had gone better. Years later, I took the master tape back and slowed it down. We get calls for it all the time because it was a revolutionary idea."

At age seventy-seven, Frank Guida still loves a little revolution, loves to rankle music-business elitists while creating different sounds. He has been doing things his way since he performed calypso at the Port of Spain USO during World War II. When he returned home to New York, he knocked on record company doors—all in vain. "While in the service in Trinidad, I became an expert on West Indian music," he said. "I decided to make this music popular in the U.S. I knew I was on to something. Harry Belafonte saw me perform and, impressed by my audience participation number, decided to try calypso for RCA. It worked. I pounded the pavement as a canned goods salesman and sang calypso on weekends in Harlem. I appeared on NBC in New York. Red Skelton's manager, Uncle Jim Harkins, went crazy about me because he couldn't believe that I, a white man, could sing in such a Trinidadian accent. I was probably the only white calypso singer in the country, but, unfortunately, few people paid much attention. I thought they were all crazy."

To change direction, Guida moved to Norfolk in 1953 with a suitcase and a dream—to enter the record business through a calypso portal. It was not an idle impulse. He planned every step: buy a record shop, find musicians and singers, start his own record company. Guida chose Norfolk for convenience more than music. His sister and uncle already lived in Virginia's second-largest city, which seemed a good place to start over. Soon after arriving, he took a job as a part-time disc jockey and bought a struggling business, the Groove Record Shop, which he renamed Frankie's Birdland (after Morris Levy's famous New York nightclub), and sold jazz and R&B records.

From behind the counter, Guida studied the record business. As sales increased, his name became synonymous with music in Norfolk, then a city of 215,000 people on the Elizabeth River, ninety miles southeast of Richmond. Like the rest of the South, Norfolk was ripe for a music harvest by 1955. WCMS radio booked Elvis Presley at Norfolk's City Auditorium, at Ninth and Granby streets. For $1.50 ($1 for children), the audience also heard country performers Hank Snow, the Rainbow Ranch Boys, Cowboy Copas, and the Louvin Brothers. That year, "Sheriff" Tex Davis, a local disc jockey and promoter, discovered Norfolk native Gene Vincent, who had sat in with the WCMS house band. Davis thought that tough-boy Vincent could become another Elvis. So did Capitol Records, which invited Vincent and his band, the Blue Caps, to Nashville to record a master on "Be-Bop-A-Lula." The rockabilly classic hit in 1956.

Until then, Norfolk was known mainly as a seafaring city, where the first ironclads—the U.S.S. *Monitor* and the C.S.S. *Virginia*—battled to a draw during the Civil War. About a century later, a new battle raged—for the airwaves. Disc jockey Guida stood on the front lines. Across Norfolk and neighboring Hampton Roads and Portsmouth, R&B and rockabilly bands flourished in small clubs and VFW halls. Their sounds echoed from the clubs all the way to Frankie's Birdland, 817 Church Street, in a black neighborhood near downtown Norfolk. Guida learned every facet of the business and met many of the new independent label owners. He conducted amateur night contests and greeted black singers who stopped to buy records. One artist he discovered, a Florida native named Gary Anderson, stood out. An old-fashioned spitcurl hung over the top of his forehead. The young man seemed a good fit for Guida's new song, "New Orleans."

"I decided the time was right to get into the production side, which was why I came into the business in the first place," he said. "Then a little studio, Norfolk Recording, was going bankrupt. In 1960, I decided to buy it. It was a decision that would affect me for the rest of my life. The owner said, 'So what will you do with it?' I said, 'Three months from now, I'm going to cut a hit.'"

"New Orleans," a powerful single pushed by saxophones, came out of the studio right on schedule. Everything about the record seemed different. Contrasting with the powerful musical tracks, Anderson's voice sounded thin but effective. The master tape was not impressive by New York standards. In fact, when executives at Guida's distributing label first received the tape, dubbed at $7\frac{1}{2}$ inches per second instead of the customary 15, they refused to release it until the RCA mastering lab could improve it. Fortunately, RCA technicians could do nothing, and after some pleading and shoving between Guida and the distributor, "New Orleans" finally came out on Legrand Records, audio warts and all. Guida claims that it was the first rock record to feature a double bass drum beat, an overmodulated sound (now called a "hot" recording), and chord progressions with twenty notes with rhythmic suspension.

"Joe Royster and I had already written the song when I bought the studio," Guida said. "Nobody had ever heard of my Legrand Records, so I knew I had to do something different if I wanted some attention. I broke my own first record. One day I thought, Now how am I ever going to get this record played? So I walked out onto the street near my office and happened to see a sign promoting U.S. Savings Bonds. I thought, Holy Moses, that's it! I went back into the office and told Joe, 'Buy U.S. Bonds!' He said, 'What did you say?' I said, 'Bonds, man!' I fooled around and decided to promote Gary as U.S. Bonds. I pressed some records and sent one to Nick Cenci of Standard Distributing in Pittsburgh. Pretty soon he called and said, 'I'd like to order some of that Legrand 1003.' I said, 'Well, how many do you want?' He said, 'Oh, how about 5,000?' Anyhow, by then the radio stations had jumped on the record, at first thinking it was a public-service disc. They were fooled because on the outside of the mailing envelope I had stamped 'Buy U.S. Bonds.' I used the name U.S. Bonds on the record, but Joe Glaser, who used to be Louis Armstrong's manager, told me I couldn't call an artist simply U.S. Bonds. He said, 'Frank, a singer *has* to have a name.' So I tacked Gary's first name to U.S. Bonds and that was that. You know, I should have left it just U.S. Bonds. But I had to listen to Joe Glaser."

Guida's hits probably could not have originated anywhere else in the South, for Norfolk was one of the region's more cosmopolitan cities. Legrand's fancy red-label discs (with a gold crown) arrived in stores across the world. This company's name projected exactly the image that Guida was seeking. "I like names with real meaning and nobility," he said. "And at the time, all of them were taken—King, Regal, Imperial. Legrand means 'the great.' Then I came up with S.P.Q.R. Records, which in Latin means 'Senatus Populus Que Romanus,' the Senate and the People of Rome. Later, I even had a label called Romulus. In my names I wanted something different, something with importance, so I chose what reflected my heritage. I still own all my own publishing and masters, so everybody has to come to me. I was the first one to fuse West Indian rhythms with operatic chord progressions, yet all I hear about is Phil Spector and his bullshit Wall of Sound and the Beatles and how they supposedly started it all. I don't want to sound immodest. I just want to know: How come nobody hears about me?"

Because he worked in Norfolk, for one thing. Other local music centers, including Memphis, were more powerful and influential, supporting a number of independent producers, studios, and labels. Guida succeeded because he developed a narrowly focused vision and sound. He also arrived at a time when the competition was less intense. When he entered the business in 1959, Memphis had hit a brief slump, Cincinnati had started to burn out, and New Orleans was about to enter its period of decline. Muscle Shoals was in its infancy. Because Guida was a powerful record salesman, Rust Records of New York asked to distribute his new Legrand label nationally— before it had proved itself. This coup freed Guida to concentrate on songwriting. Unable to forget calypso, he wrote as though it had officially merged with rock and R&B. He collaborated with Royster, a trusted friend and confidant, to compose most of the material for Legrand.

Considering Guida's ethnic background and age (thirty-six in 1960), it's a wonder he ever wanted to try rock music. The native of Palermo, Italy, arrived in New York when he was two and a half years old and grew up on Italian music and big bands. He remembers his father whistling the hits of the day. By the time Guida arrived in Norfolk, he already had a family. He was not a hip swinger. But his long-time obsession with entertaining would not go away. He tried to explain his undying passion for West Indian music to the musicians he assembled in Norfolk, but they didn't understand. He called them the Church Street Five because they came together around his record shop. At times the band included Earl Swanson and Gene "Daddy G" Barge, tenor saxophone; Leonard Barks, trombone; Emmett "Nab" Shields, drums; Willie Burnell, piano; Melvin Glover, drums; Junior Farley, upright bass and tuba; Wayne Bickner, electric guitar; and Sonny Tongue, acoustic guitar. Guida credits Shields with providing the beat for the Norfolk Sound, and Barks with the "churchiest-sounding licks" needed to attract young record buyers.

A distinctive sound came from saxophonist Barge, a former Atlantic Records sideman who played on Chuck Willis' classic "C.C. Rider." After returning home to Virginia in 1957, Barge taught social studies and directed a school band hear Norfolk. On weekends he played R&B in nightclubs and on recording sessions. Guida nicknamed him Daddy G, after a flamboyant preacher on Church Street named Daddy Grace. Guida enjoyed the music that poured from Grace's House of Prayer near the record shop. "I wanted to record with that kind of excitement," Guida said. At first he tried it with "A Nite With Daddy G," a minor hit on Legrand. "We were trying to get what you'd call a happy sound," Barge recalled. "It was strictly what you would call spontaneous music, although we had a format. If you did something wrong, you had to start all over again. Sometimes we had twenty-five or thirty false starts. By the time you got through thirty takes, you knew pretty well what you're going to do."

Barge's record influenced Guida when he produced Bonds' "Quarter to Three," which took a rocky path to No. 1 in May 1963. The session relied heavily on Bare and his honking sax. When Bonds sang about going out to hear Daddy G play, people around Norfolk and even Philadelphia understood the reference. The rest of us had no clue. Despite Bonds' and Daddy G's talents, the record initially sold only 50,000 copies, most around Philadelphia. Guida knew he'd done something wrong. So he went back into the studio, slowed down the tempo, invited a group of neighborhood kids in for a new session, and recorded 'Quarter to Three' as a party song. "Without Gene's saxophone," Guida said, "I don't think the record would have been a hit."

When I asked him if he recorded his hits on a three-track recorder (an industry standard in those days), he laughed at me.

"We had a monaural Concertone! It was trickery that pulled it off. Pure recording trickery! My recording process is still a secret. Another part of the sound came from the musicians. I used a combination of players from the area, white and black. I had to find people who would do what I wanted them to do. Just think about what we did here in the South. How would I get Southern musicians to do Latin classical things? It wasn't easy. In fact, my artists never agreed with anything I ever did. We still don't see eye to eye. For example, when I first offered Gary Anderson 'If You Wanna Be Happy' he said, 'No, it has no soul.' So I found Jimmy McCleese and deliberately changed his name to Jimmy Soul, just to be sarcastic, facetious, to get my point across. The record went to No. 1, my biggest recording of all. To this day, it sounds as fresh as it did then."

McCleese came from a family of fifteen children in North Carolina, where he was a boy preacher. He moved to Portsmouth to sing in doo-wop groups and came to Guida's offices looking for an opportunity. After making several unsuccessful records, he hit with "Twistin' Matilda," which sold 700,000 copies and earned him an appearance on *American Bandstand*. The record also opened up a whole world of carnal temptations. As his career declined in 1967, he was drafted into the army and sent to Vietnam, where he was shot in the chest, knee, and calf. He drank heavily and took opium and heroin. When he returned home, he was arrested for buying drugs and writing bad checks. On June 25, 1988, he died of a heart attack at Otisville Correctional Facility, Otisville, New York. "He was a wonderful singer but a wild fellow," Guida said. "Nobody could have sung 'Twistin' Matilda' the way he did."

Jimmy Soul was one of only a few artists who recorded for Guida's labels. He preferred to maintain a slim roster so that he could better concentrate on each act individually. At the peak of his chart successes, Guida refused to accept independent masters for release on Legrand and S.P.Q.R. He told me that the ban extended to everyone, including a then unknown band named the Beatles, whose representatives were seeking a record deal in the U.S. In 1964, after Philadelphia's Swan Records turned "She Loves You" into a No. 1 record and Chicago's Vee-Jay followed with "Twist and Shout" at No. 2, Guida had second thoughts. "It was stupid of me," he said. "But I said, 'Who needs a version of what I did with "New Orleans"'? But I felt at the time that I should keep our sound in Norfolk. So I never took a record off the streets. We made our own hits."

Guida continued to release more records through the 1960s, but nothing big happened. He remained in the retail business, opening a new record shop and a one-stop called Frankie's Got It! He gave away black jacket patches featuring a golden woman holding a large platter over her head.

Unfortunately, Jimmy Soul's decline signaled the end of Guida's—and

Norfolk's—national hits. The Norfolk Sound, so influential in 1961, sounded antiquated by the time the hippies arrived five years later. In retrospect, perhaps Legrand's downfall started as early as 1961, when Guida squabbled with his distributing label, owned by New York's Laurie Records. Guida maintained that Laurie's No. 1 hit "Runaround Sue" by Dion sounded too much like "New Orleans." To give Laurie the message, he pressed some 45s by Daddy G and listed the artist as I'm Gonna Sue. Though the matter was ultimately resolved without a lawsuit, their relationship soured, and Guida concentrated on promoting S.P.Q.R. Records through the London family of labels.

By the late 1960s, many of Legrand's studio musicians started drifting away, with Daddy G going to Chicago to work for Chess Records. By the 1980s, Guida seemed a musical dinosaur. But he continues to operate Rockmasters Music, leasing old masters for reissue albums. He even wrote a musical that played in Norfolk. He still reports to the office every day to take calls from people across the world. Like me, they remember the Norfolk Sound and what they were doing the moment they first heard his songs. As I prepared to leave, Guida took me into a back room, his personal contemplation chamber, painted white with Roman columns and detailed gold and red trim. The room is his own little piece of Italy. He waved his hand, like an emperor looking over his empire, and said: "I've been appointed a cavalier, you know, the equivalent of a knight."

These days, Norfolk's record industry has gone silent. Jimmy Soul's name is rarely mentioned, and interest in Gary U.S. Bonds has ranged from the oldies circuit to hit status (he recorded "This Little Girl" in 1981 with producer Bruce Springsteen) to obscurity. The most interest in the town comes from English music fans who publish a fanzine, *The Norfolk Echo,* dedicated to Legrand's glory days—and to Guida himself. "I made R&B change to what we were doing," he said. "I introduced the 'live' sound. But being in Norfolk, Virginia, is somewhat detrimental to me and my so-called contributions. It's so easy to bury me. My pupils are going into the Rock 'n' Roll Hall of Fame, and all of a sudden people discover that there is a guy named Frank Guida and that he had a lot to do with this music."

While standing in the Roman room, basking in a fluorescent glow near the plaster columns, Frank Guida, the Calypso Kid and self-proclaimed master of rock 'n' roll, seemed perfectly content in the Old Dominion. Perfectly happy to sell the memories. "I'm a groundbreaker," he said, all modesty aside. "I never followed anybody else. The only way to succeed is to set the world on its heels. Shock it!"

Bakersfield: Act Naturally

From the moment I entered Bakersfield, California, I felt heat and music surround me. I remembered Joan Didion's caveat that the region can become "so hot that the air shimmers and the grass bleaches white and the blinds stay down all day, so hot that August comes on not like a month but an affliction." On a morning in early June, the affliction had already started displaying symptoms: sidewalks reflected the sun's rays like lines of horizontal mirrors, and the steering wheel seared my hands. (On my first day in town, the temperature reached 97 degrees, but without the debilitating humidity of Memphis and Muscle Shoals.)

Heat notwithstanding, vast green fields of lettuce grew on the periphery of the Mojave Desert. Along two-lane Route 58, the arms of small black derricks pumped oil next door to driving ranges and car washes and convenience stores. I expected to find a smaller, drier city, an unsophisticated place where rednecks wear pistols like old-time cowboys and spit tobacco juice on unsuspecting visitors, but instead I found a modern community of 170,000 people with clean streets, new public and private buildings, and major highway-construction projects extending west to Interstate 5. My false assumptions came mostly from Bakersfield's roughhouse reputation and from Buck Owens' "The Streets of Bakersfield," a song about walking lonely streets.

Owens defines everything that is Bakersfield, musically and culturally. I always thought he was having too much fun to be country. Listen to "Act Naturally" (remade by the Beatles in 1965), "I've Got a Tiger by the Tail," and "Under Your Spell Again." His early sound, sort of a honky-tonk rockabilly, offset Merle Haggard's more serious songs, which captured the essence of Bakersfield so well that the *Bakersfield Californian* called them musical postcards from home.

When both singers were hot in the late 1960s, I was more interested in rock bands, but I couldn't have ignored Owens if I'd tried. A couple of his records popped up on Cincinnati's Top 40 station, and their feeling intrigued me. For country records they carried a powerful energy, with a driving "freight train" rhythm from the Fender Telecasters played by Owens and his band, the Buckaroos. By then, Bakersfield music had already matured

Bakersfield singer Red Simpson recorded several
country chart records, including the No. 4 *Billboard* hit
"I'm a Truck" in 1971.

Red Simpson in Bakersfield. Photo by Randy McNutt.

Trout's, a Bakersfield area nightclub, as it was in 1999. Photo by
Randy McNutt.

Buck Owens sang at the Blackboard, a raucous Bakersfield nightclub in the early 1950s.

Buck Owens made Bakersfield a recognizable name in country music, even when he sang about Kansas City.

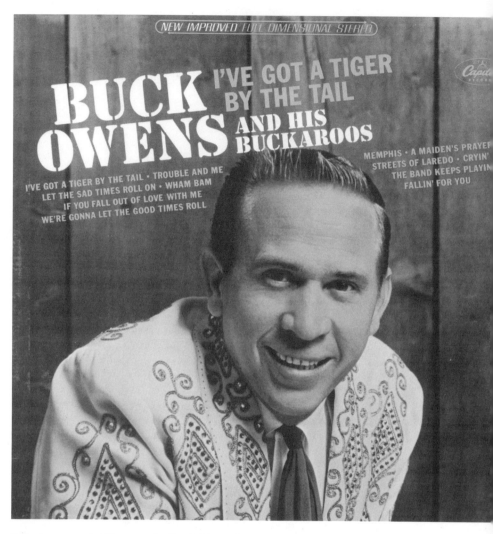

Buck Owens recorded 25 consecutive Top 10 hits on the
Billboard country charts from 1963 to 1972, including "I've Got
a Tiger by the Tail" in 1965.

and expanded far beyond its native honky-tonks, traveling three thousand miles across the country to become the working man's music. During a complicated time of war protests, free love, and psychedelic music, people identified with Bakersfield's real-life songs, which in turn provided musicians with plenty of work at home. Unfortunately, the jobs didn't last. By the mid-1980s, the city once called Nashville West was doing little in the record business. By the time I arrived in 1999, musicians couldn't even generate enough community interest to build a local country music museum.

I first flew to Los Angeles and rented a red Monte Carlo and headed north, toward the ghosts of country music and neighboring towns called Pumpkin Center, Greenacres, Old River, and Weed Patch. My journey didn't start on a whim. Bakersfield's music meant something special to me, and I wanted to occupy the same space, if only briefly, with its respected musicians and writers and see the nightclubs that once helped influence the direction of country music. For years I had admired the city's performers, because they bypassed Nashville's star-making machine to create their own pocket of country music. By 1968, as country was evolving from its rural roots, Bakersfield performers glided across the country like rhinestone hummingbirds, pollinating local music with their sounds. Sufficiently impressed, industry observers predicted that Bakersfield would become an increasingly important regional music center.

The reason was the Bakersfield Sound. I can't define it precisely, but it's a much closer approximation of country music than what's coming out of Nashville today. The Bakersfield Sound is both fast and slow, thoughtful and playful, electric and acoustic, but mostly it's music with a true hillbilly heart. From the 1950s to the 1970s, when it occupied a prominent place in Los Angeles recording studios and on the national charts, Bakersfield supplied an army of session musicians for Capitol Records. Owens, Red Simpson, Bill Woods, Jelly Sanders, and their friends piled into cars and drove one hundred miles south to Los Angeles to play on singles and albums for producer Ken Nelson. Woods estimates that he has played on five hundred records. Because they were accomplished but not full-time session players, Bakersfield's musicians brought a fresh approach that sounded uncluttered. After a session, they'd head north to the potato fields and factories and honky-tonks—to home.

In smoky little joints, Bakersfield musicians forged their own peculiar brand of country, borrowing liberally from the western swing of Bob Wills and the hillbilly songs of Jimmie Rodgers of the 1930s. Owens contributed a driving electric guitar, which he had bought for $30. By 1958, a Spartan brand of country had taken root to satisfy the musical cravings of Kern County's field and factory workers. While the pop-influenced Nashville Sound often featured strings and woodwinds, the Bakersfield Sound remained hard-edged and true to its roots—music about losing the land and true love.

If the latest fad in country music involves rocking out—using heavy drums, dancing on stage, wearing tiny microphones, exposing a smooth midriff—then the Bakersfield Sound ignores everything that's happening. Bakersfield lyrics are poignant and funny and built on melodies that evoke emotion. Although the Bakersfield Sound has faded from the radio, it still echoes in the brand of neo-country played in Austin, San Antonio, and Dallas; in such performers as the Derailers and the Hollisters; and, of course, in the many reissued compact discs by Owens, Haggard, Simpson, Ferlin Husky, and other older stars who made southern California a country music center in the 1960s.

The music is underappreciated these days. Sometimes you'll see Owens driving around town, but no longer in his customized convertible with a Winchester rifle mounted on the trunk, pearl-handled pistols on the hood, and steer horns on the front bumper (the car is in his Crystal Palace now). Gone are Bakersfield's three recording studios (including Owens'), several small record companies, music-publishing offices, and about twenty honky-tonks that introduced new country stars to the world. Gone is the excitement.

Not that Bakersfield is boring. Far from it. Just a two-hour drive from the Pacific, I found hospitality almost Southern in its warmth and generosity. In fact, the whole town and its musical heritage felt Southern to me. Culturally and geographically, the city lies in what writer Gerald Haslam, an Oildale native, calls the "Other California," the Great Central Valley between the Sierra Madre and Sierra Nevada. Here the powerful Kern River, a golden ribbon flowing across the arid land, gives life and purpose to oil worker and musician alike. The unyielding environment and the music are difficult to separate, for the land is filled with families who came out of the Southwest and Midwest during the Dust Bowl days. Their assimilation into California didn't come without trouble. Haslam recalls a sign on a Bakersfield movie theater in 1939: "Niggers and Okies upstairs." Contiguous Oildale was "an enclave of oil-company camps, attracting a disproportionate number of males who did hard, physical labor, and pursued rough, masculine diversions," he wrote. Since the 1870s, Bakersfield has attracted hard-working immigrants—all kinds of whites, Chinese, Japanese, East Indians, Mexicans, Filipinos, and blacks.

Looking for my lunch, I noticed signs of diversity: restaurants offering Basque cuisine (a reflection of the city's French-Spanish heritage), urban storefront diners advertising biscuits and gravy (pure hillbilly fare), and other restaurants reflecting the city's strong Hispanic, Native American, and Chinese cultures. In 1899, a new wave of immigrants came to town looking for water. They found a growing community named for Colonel Thomas Baker, who in 1869 helped found the city when he planted ten acres of alfalfa to feed the horses of travelers going from Visalia to Los Angeles. During the Depression, thousands of families arrived from Oklahoma and north Texas with no more than a mattress, an automobile, and a slim hope for the future. They also brought country music, their diversion. It fit perfectly with the oil-rig workers, who needed more than a stiff drink on Friday night.

In 1953, disc jockey "Cousin" Herb Henson reasoned that country music and the new television were compatible. He asked KERO-TV for his own show, the *Tradin' Post,* and invited local entertainers such as Owens, Woods, Bonnie Owens, and Billy Mize, as well as West Coast favorites the Maddox Brothers and Rose, Tommy Collins, Joe and Rose Lee Maphis, and others. Viewers who didn't even like country music tuned in to see the local faces—and the entertainers who acted like family. Herb dressed like a cowboy and talked like a hick, but his show turned into a genuine hit, and formerly "uncouth" hillbilly singers became regional stars. Seemingly overnight, their popularity leaped from honky-tonks to living rooms and influenced Merle Haggard, then a local singer, and anybody else who wanted to be a country player.

By the time we arrived in town, Haggard had moved to northern California and Owens had stopped performing full-time. On our first day in town, we checked into the Best Western Inn, next to Owens' Crystal Palace, a $7 million complex that includes a restaurant, memorabilia shop, and dance hall on Buck Owens Boulevard. It looks like a big ranch house inserted awkwardly into the suburban strip. Buck himself performs there at times, but I had come to town to find other local talent—the performers who stayed behind after many of the clubs folded in the 1970s. I drove around town to see how many remained. At the former Bakersfield Inn on Union Avenue, a dealer in recreational vehicles had just removed two hundred palm trees, planted fifty years ago when Bakersfield was ready to kick loose. The dealer intended to replant some at his new location and sell the rest as souvenirs of Bakersfield's night life. And what a life it was: in the early 1960s, Bakersfield's better nightclubs (or, if you prefer, honky-tonks) included the Clover Club, the Barrel House, High Pockets, the Lucky Spot, the Pumpkin Center Barn Dance (in Quonset huts), the Beardsley Ballroom, the Rhythm Ranch, the Rainbow Garden, and, of course, Kern County's most famous, the old Blackboard Cafe, 3601 Chester Avenue, in Oildale, a community on Bakersfield's north side, where Haggard grew up.

Aside from Tootsie's Orchid Lounge in Nashville, the Blackboard might be the most iconic tavern in country music. It started as a restaurant for oil workers, then reopened in 1949 as a nightclub under new owners Joe Limi and Frank Zabelata. Within months, the Blackboard was the roughest, and hippest, club in town. The only food left on the menu was pickled eggs. The regulars didn't mind. They represented every shade in the social spectrum, from lawyers to bricklayers, and they came to drink and dance, in that order. It's difficult to imagine a performer of Owens' stature playing in this dumpy little tavern for seven years, even if they were his formative times. But from the experience, he learned how to entertain. "Television wasn't a big deal then," he told a writer years later. "And there wasn't a radio station that was all-country music. You had guys like Bill Woods at KERN and Jimmy Thomason at KAFY doing country music things in the morning. The door was wide open for live country music. I remember going to the Rainbow Gardens in '51 and seeing Hank Williams and Bob Wills. . . . Wills played at the Beardsley dance hall in Oildale every Tuesday night. They'd get one thousand people on a week night."

The Blackboard's bandstand became a launching pad for country music's sparse, electrified alternative. Despite the club's small size, visiting performers recognized its influence. They also noticed the sheer craziness of the place. Where else but the Blackboard would singer Bonnie Owens, future wife of Owens and Merle Haggard, work as a cocktail waitress and write songs at her table when business was slow? Where else could you find women clawing at each other from under the tables, and husbands saying, "Let them fight it out"? Where else could you hear tomorrow's stars for the price of a beer? Where else could you find established stars, such as Patsy Cline, Little Jimmy Dickens, and Tex Ritter, on Thursday nights?

Although many stars performed on the Blackboard's tiny stage, dozens of other acts remained only local celebrities, including Bill Woods and His

Orange Blossom Playboys, Lewis Tally and the Whackers, Jolly Jody and His Go-Daddies, and "Little" Lois Souders and the Western Starlighters. Each night they peered into a gray cloud of smoke and wondered when national fame would come. The place was so dark and smoky that after playing at the Blackboard one night, guitarist Joe Maphis wrote "Dim Lights, Thick Smoke (and Loud, Loud Music)" while driving home. He had never seen a club that loud and dark. But customers liked it that way. "They'd just walk up to a table, and if a guy didn't look right they'd knock him down, right there," bartender Adolph Limi once said. "Of course, they were permanently 86'd. But people would let them back in through the escape doors."

My visit to the Blackboard was less eventful. I pulled up in front and discovered that it had become a Domino's. Missing were its big block-glass windows and the old sign out front. Nobody inside even knew about the history of the building. "You lookin' for a beer joint, mister?" a man asked me. "Why don't you try Trout's, up the street?" Trout's Cocktail Lounge was exactly what I was looking for—a country music anachronism. Outside, a big red neon trout leaped above the weathered front door on Chester Avenue in Oildale, which seamlessly adheres to Bakersfield in border and history. When it opened in 1944, Trout's was considered among the B team of clubs, but since Bakersfield's night life has declined, Trout's is one of the few places to hear real country music.

We arrived at six P.M. The sun shone brightly, and seventy-five cars packed the rear lot. "They must start swinging early around here," Cheryl said. Inside, I asked the bartender why the average age of the customers was sixty-five. "Monday is senior night," he said in a monotone, and Cheryl and I felt like teenagers. I glanced up to see a small homemade white poster announcing "Red Simpson—Every Monday Night!" We wandered around, finally found an empty table, and ordered two Coca-Colas. Five minutes later, a woman who works behind the bar asked us to move. "A couple have been coming in here for four years on Monday night," she said, "and you're sitting at their favorite table."

Regulars come to hear a singer who began his career during the heyday of the Blackboard, still lives near Bakersfield, and has not abandoned the local country music sound. For their loyalty, the regulars receive a meal and discounts on drinks, and Red Simpson a steady gig. Women dress smartly; many dangle cigarettes from manicured fingers. Some wear sandals, some Western boots. Men dress casually, but not in jeans: open-neck shirts and chinos for them. Though they move slower than they did forty years ago, they carry the same zeal for the music and the city. We decided to watch them and imagine that we were in the Bakersfield of 1959, when a poor singer could dream of national acclaim and possibly achieve it.

"Where you folks from?" asked a man who sat on the barstool behind us. "I know *you're* not regulars." He introduced himself as Henry McCullen, a widower and Bakersfield native who'd had a window seat to country music's history. He told us that he'd seen every star in every club in town, and appreciated the opportunity. "Back then, you didn't come out to Trout's unless you were a big drinker," he said. "Depending on your tastes in music, you could hear all kinds of bands. There were open-air dances at the Rainbow Gardens and Coconut Grove. Then there was the Saddle and Sirloin, the Hacienda, the Sands Inn. Hey, I should remember all those places. As a bank appraiser, I closed up eight clubs in five years in the 1970s, when Union Avenue—at the time it was our strip—was rerouted. Route 99 bypassed them and country music. At one time, though, we had a lot of choices. Let's see, above the Saddle and Sirloin was the Penthouse Club, which had a Negro big band. The place was a local hideaway where you took somebody else's wife. Of course, everybody went to Tex's Barrel House, Rancho Bakersfield, and the Blackboard. We had a lot of potato and oil workers, you see, and they all pulled into town on Friday and Saturday night to blow off steam. At the Blackboard, guys danced with their hands on the girls' butts. Now you might not get away with that behavior everywhere, but you could at the Blackboard. It was a boisterous place that had its scuffles, but the bouncers were tough and did their jobs. Despite the free-hands policy over at the Blackboard, I actually preferred the Rancho Bakersfield. I could order waffles there."

Old Bakersfield was a music fan's delight. Rose Maddox, a Capitol artist since 1959, worked there frequently. Others lived in and near Bakersfield. By the early 1970s, Capitol had signed so many local acts that their records were popping up across the national charts. In a single issue of *Billboard* in 1970, three full-page advertisements touted Bakersfield artists. Buddy Alan, Buck's son, had some hits. So did Susan Raye, Tony Booth, the Hagers, Don Rich, and Red Simpson. Owens, who joined Capitol in 1957, exercised plenty of influence on the label. His first hit came in 1959 with "Under Your Spell Again." He went on to place twenty-five consecutive Top 10 hits on the country charts for Capitol between 1963 and 1972. As he gained prominence, he built a studio in Bakersfield's old Riverside Theater and recorded local acts. During one week in 1972, twelve of *Billboard*'s Top 100 country singles had come out of Owens' studio. In retrospect, the singers were lucky to find such a relaxed musical oasis away from autocratic Nashville, where performers had to use session musicians on their records and songwriters had to compose with an ear cocked toward the radio—or else. Bakersfield had no directives from label bureaucrats, no judgmental record-business establishment, no preconceived ideas about what sounded commercial. The music came straight from the hearts and streets of a city that nurtured its entertainers.

As the music played at Trout's that night, a youthful-looking woman in her fifties said hello and identified herself as Inez Savage. She and her husband, Donald Savage, have worked in their own country band, the Savage Sound, for thirty years. When Kern County's unofficial music promoter isn't working in the office of the Clarion Hotel, she's trying to set up a Bakersfield music exhibit at the Kern County Historical Society and assisting the tourism board. The idea of a country music museum started in the late 1970s, but never developed. Many performers gave up on the idea and later became reluctant to contribute memorabilia that might get lost. Then somebody suggested a scaled-down version: a music exhibit at the Kern County Museum. It's not much, Inez Savage admitted, but it's better than nothing. She understands the irony. "Bakersfield has this huge country music reputation," she explained, "but when people come to town and ask me to send them to hear some bands, I have to tell them that there's no place to go. In the '60s, there were up to twenty nightclubs with music, seven nights a week. I could give people a whole list of clubs. Today that's no longer true. I never in my life thought I'd see Bakersfield in this shape. Of course, we're not alone. A part of the trouble is karaoke bars, club DJs, and other distractions. Radio doesn't help us, either. They're marketing to the thirteen-to-twenty-one-year-olds, who are easily brainwashed. Lately we're trying to encourage tourism, but our town didn't even recognize country music until Buck built the Crystal Palace a couple of years ago. Suddenly the city fathers said, 'Country music! Wow!' Bakersfield should have recognized its music thirty years ago. It makes you sick. Without Buck, bless him, there would be no country music in Bakersfield today."

She sees the music as another natural resource that, like oil, must be preserved. But she fears it will be lost in a nation that's losing its local heritage to shopping malls and chain stores. "I come from a family of musicians," she said. "My father was a musician—and an oil-field man. My youngest son, Willie, is a guitar player in Las Vegas. He plays three nights a week and works a sit-down job the rest of the time. This music runs in our veins. It has been with me all my life, though I've never had the nerve to quit my sit-down job and perform full-time. Hey, I have four kids. But Kern County is something special musically. We want to tell its story from A to Z, so some years back we formed the Bakersfield Country Music Museum. Sad to say, it's a museum without walls. But at least we'll have a display case over at the county museum. They've got so many other local exhibits—a wooden oil derrick, a general store, a ranch blacksmith shop, a log cabin, and even a railroad jail. Why not put in some music memorabilia? We all know the stories of Merle and Buck and Ferlin Husky, but they're not the whole story. The regular musicians are the ones who keep the music going in any community; they keep it alive while the other folks are out on the road. Each person has a story to tell. It gives me shivers when I think about all the musicians who've worked around here. Guys like Red are real assets to our city today. Why, I've been in Bakersfield so long that it has become a part of my heart. I want this display case installed so that someday, when I'm dead and gone, the story of our music will go on for future generations."

Simpson has been a part of the Bakersfield story, so he too wants to preserve local music history. In the early days, he said during a break, Bakersfield was a great place for a musician. "There was plenty of work in the clubs and in the potato and oil fields. The fields are what made Bakersfield such a big music town. They gave us an audience. It was a wide-open town with many clubs then, and I was hired and fired in all of them. The Blackboard stayed open from two in the afternoon until two in the morning. Now, that was a *long* shift. If you wanted to record, Capitol Records was just down the road in L.A. We did a lot of sessions there. I started playing on some of Buck's, and writing a lot of songs, and that led to me getting my own contract with Capitol. I was signed to Cliffie Stone's Central Songs. Him and Ken Nelson, the Capitol producer, were pretty close. I used to go down to Buck's sessions, and then I'd take some songs over to Cliffie. I got into a truck-drivin' bag. When Merle turned down some of my songs, preferring to stay in his country and prison thing, Cliffie called me on a Friday morning and said, 'Do you want to sign with Capitol?' I said, reluctantly, 'Well, I guess so. . . .' See, I thought he was kidding. Then he said, 'Well, can you be down here on Monday?' I said, 'Cliffie, I can be down there this afternoon.'"

Red Simpson, a genuinely warm person who picked cotton before turning to music, played special requests for Trout's capacity crowd of about two hundred people. On this night he was joined by Mize, but he couldn't sing because he was recovering from a stroke. So he strummed an electric guitar while Red played a small electronic Concertmate 990 keyboard, which he'd bought for $215. They made an interesting duo. Mize looked sophisticated in a long-sleeved khaki dress shirt, brown slacks, and white straw cowboy hat. More relaxed, Red wore a red and white golf shirt and a crisply pressed pair of jeans, accented by snakeskin cowboy boots and his red hair. As he played a slow song, an old woman yelled, "Go, Red, honey!" He yelled back, "Liberace, eat your heart out." Behind him, brown-paneled walls were covered with pictures, a poster for a man-and-wife band named the Tex Pistols, and a big green and red neon Budweiser sign. With a lighted cigarette hanging from his lips, Simpson grinned and hummed to the music. His voice sounded small and muddy on the tiny speakers. "Play 'Tulsa Time'!" shouted a blonde woman with a beehive hairdo, who was moving in a dance line that looked as if it were stuck in slow motion. Then Simpson played the opening chords of "Tulsa Time" and grinned as the little keyboard created a symphony of horns, strings, piano, and drums. "If you hear only the music," he said, "that means I put it on automatic while I go to the bathroom."

He knows the crowds in Bakersfield as well as family. They have helped support him since his youth, when, after a stint in the navy, he gave up plans to become a sheet-metal worker and became a musician. His first gig, at the Wagon Wheel in neighboring Lamont in 1955, paid him $5 a night. But he was hooked. In those days, he played guitar. When he realized that Bakersfield had a crowded field of guitarists, and he wasn't among the city's best on the instrument, he switched to keyboards. "I couldn't afford to buy a piano then," he recalled, "but I knew they had one over at the church, so I went there and started banging on it. People thought I sure was being good. I stayed around that church a lot—and got more than religion."

As a young man, writing songs came to him as naturally as sports do for some people. Songs came to him at the oddest times. Engrossed in writing while on furlough in Bakersfield, he would sometimes forget to catch the train and end up in the brig upon his untimely return to his base. After his navy days ended, he took up music full-time. As his playing improved, he joined Owens' Buckaroos and wrote songs with the boss. In 1966, after a concert at Carnegie Hall, Simpson quarreled with Owens' manager and left the band. He decided to go out on his own, as a writer and performer. As usual, writing occupied most of his time. He and Haggard wrote "You Don't Have Very Far to Go," and Simpson and Owens wrote Owens' hit "The Kansas City Song."

Woods recalled that Red's performing sometimes interfered with his writing: "In order to stay out of the clubs to write, he'd put some of his prize possessions in an old suitcase and make all the hock shops in Bakersfield and borrow money on them. This inspired one of the television newsmen to tag the name Suitcase Simpson on him." His persistence helped, and songs flowed. Owens cut thirty-five, Haggard six. Rosanne Cash recorded "You Don't Have Very Far to Go," Shelly West cut Simpson's "Love Me Again," and Annette Funicello recorded his "Lucky Ole Colorado." Out of an estimated 1,000 compositions, he says 150 were recorded, by Ferlin Husky, Connie Smith, Jeannie Seely, Homer and Jethro, Dave Dudley, and Roy Clark.

But if Red Simpson is remembered nationally, it will be for his own records on Capitol in the early 1970s. He became known as the Bard of Bakersfield for recording the hit "I'm a Truck," "Highway Patrol," and other road-related material. In the late 1990s he recorded with Junior Brown, a Texan who revived "Highway Patrol." Simpson felt rejuvenated. "I think there's something about this place that inspires us," he said of Bakersfield. "We've had our share of songwriters; most of them weren't born here, but they have chosen to live here. Buck came from Texas, and still lives here. I came from Higby, Arizona. Bill Woods came from Texas. We had a lot going on out here for years. Then around 1985, things started slowing down, and country music went off in a pop direction. But you never know what will happen. One night somebody came up to me at Trout's and told me Junior had recorded 'Highway Patrol.' I got on the telephone to Gene Moles, who played guitar on my original version, and he couldn't get over how Junior had matched the old record, note for note."

One of many Bakersfield session men, Moles played often for Capitol. Bakersfield became a musical oil well, shooting pickers down to L.A. as fast as any gusher. (Owens, in his other life as a session guitarist from about 1956 to 1960, played on Wanda Jackson's rockabilly classics "Hot Dog! That Made Him Mad," "Fujiyama Mama," and "Honey Bop.") Moles wrote songs and played lead guitar on the *Tradin' Post* and *The Billy Mize Show.* He even wrote a couple of songs for the Ventures before turning full-time to his guitar-repair business. Another session legend, Oildale guitarist Roy Nichols, also played for Haggard's band, the Strangers. He started playing music at age fourteen, earning $25 a night, and by sixteen he was playing for the popular Maddox Brothers and Rose. His fluid style helped propel the group into one of the West's top acts, but Nichols was able to transfer his creativity to the studio as well. In a career that has spanned six decades, he has played for Lefty Frizzell, Johnny Cash, Wynn Stewart, and others, and his playing has influenced everyone from Lee Roy Parnell to Vince Gill. Nichols was inducted into the Western Swing Society Hall of Fame in 1988. "If you are bitten by this thing we have come to call the Bakersfield Sound, it becomes a part of you," he told a reporter. "It reaches out to every part of your heart and your soul and becomes the thing that you need to survive. . . . It goes beyond logic. It is something that feeds your spirit."

Woods is universally respected in Bakersfield for his work. He never had a hit, but he played on many and helped dozens of musicians, including Haggard, Owens, and Simpson. Simpson wrote a tribute song called "Bill Woods Of Bakersfield." Haggard recorded it. Woods' popularity could have occurred only in a regional music capital. He became so well known that his reputation spread to other areas. While performing with Tommy Duncan, the band arrived in a small Texas town in a converted army bus. Two young men walked by and said, "Hey, you got Bill Woods in there?" In mock frustration, Duncan threw his hat on the floor and stomped on it.

Sadly, fame is missing in Bakersfield today. What happened—or, more precisely, what didn't happen—is history. Woods is still around, though. "I get calls from Sweden, England, France, all over the world," he said. "They want to know about the Bakersfield Sound, but the attention is tiring me out." What they seek is the past—a past unfulfilled. In 1973, Buck Owens' manager, Jack McFadden, who helped Owens convert the old theater in Oildale into a twenty-four-track recording studio, predicted that Chester Avenue would become "Music Row West" in ten years. But neither the major labels nor the music publishers arrived. Even Owens slowed his frantic pace, devastated by the death of band member and friend Don Rich in 1974 and country music's drift toward blandness. But neither McFadden nor anybody else in town could envision that by 1983, interest in the Nashville of the West would end. Country music had room for only one Nashville, and it was in Tennessee.

⌒

I called Red Simpson before leaving town, and he invited me to his home just outside of Bakersfield, in an attractive mobile home park. He and his wife, Joyce, greeted us at the door. Their yard abounded with colorful flowers, ranging from common petunias to exotic ginger and shrimp plants. Red does the planting; Joyce prunes them to keep new flowers blooming. They enjoy the garden, and they exchange plants with friends. Joyce said, "I used to wonder why anybody would choose to live out here in the desert. The bugs, the heat. Then I started seeing the four seasons, in a subtle and beautiful way, and loved it. It's the beauty in life that counts, you see. It's all about the beauty."

She gave Cheryl some seeds from pink and red hollyhocks and bulbs from a rich peach gladiolus while Red talked with me. Old Blue, one of Red's favorite bluebirds, flew in for peanuts. Red feeds him by hand, and Blue brings other birds to visit.

He took me inside to see paintings in the living room. One of Red and Roy Rogers hangs prominently, near photographs of Simpson with Johnny Paycheck, Crystal Gayle, and other country stars with whom he has performed. By then, at age sixty-five, he was limiting most of his appearances to Trout's, where he had been performing for five years, and the Rasmussen Senior Center, where the visitors pulled back the carpet on Tuesday morning and danced to Red's songs. Sometimes Red performs at Moose lodges in California and Las Vegas.

While Joyce discussed plants with Cheryl, Red took me to his dining room table to play some new songs on his little keyboard. He sang gospel, country, and pop. He doesn't restrict himself to any one kind; he writes "novelty songs, ballads, peppy songs—a little of everything." As he played some witty, original songs, I wondered if anybody would ever hear them. I wondered how big Simpson could have become if he had moved to Nashville in the early 1970s, at the height of his popularity as a writer and performer. A country songwriter living in Bakersfield can do only so much, yet Simpson doesn't stop to contemplate the past. "I've got enough to keep me busy," he said. "And I'm living where I want to be. People assume I'm rich because I've worked with Buck and Merle and I've written some hit songs, but that's not the case. We didn't earn as much in royalties back then. I don't complain, though. When I was young, I saw a bunch of guys performing and making what I thought was easy money. Well, I found it's more difficult than that. But hey, I'm happy."

As we drove away, I watched Red Simpson in my rearview mirror. He sat on the patio swing to feed Old Blue. Probably Red would take some time to savor the brown earth around him, hug his wife, and turn an everyday occurrence into a new song. As I watched him fade away, I knew he had made the right decision to stay in Bakersfield, for it's a city of real people and a place where country music might one day bloom again.

McGonigle, Ohio: Lonnie on the Move

Before the interstate highways were built, McGonigle, Ohio, was a dancing town. Its main street, U.S. Route 27, brimmed with wild kids, vacationing families, and harried sidemen who could relieve the monotony of long rides by listening to the melodies in their heads. Singers might appear in town one week and at the Hollywood Bowl the next—or at least in Cincinnati, thirty-five miles to the southeast. In McGonigle in the early 1960s, the bands always played fast and bluesy, and the small town overflowed with road boats, muscle cars, and 1940s hot rods. At midnight, lines of perspiring young women danced outside in twenty-degree weather, while the beat pounded into the stubble of neighboring cornfields.

The clubs operated only four miles south of what had been set up as a training camp for civil-rights workers. Their mission: travel to the Deep South to register blacks to vote. In June 1964, eight hundred student activists gathered on the pastoral campus of Western College for Women in Oxford, Ohio. They included Michael Schwerner, James Chaney, and Andrew Goodman, who would disappear within days after arriving in Mississippi. Weeks later, acting on a tip from an informant, authorities removed their bodies from an earthen dam near Philadelphia, Mississippi. The murders helped strengthen the civil-rights movement. During their Ohio training, "Freedom Summer" activists sang folk songs and played acoustic guitars and tried to work up the courage to stay in the program, while people the same age rocked in McGonigle with an equally passionate agenda—beer and good times. Probably the two camps never knew the other existed.

When I visited McGonigle decades later, the funky groove capital of rural Ohio had gone stone country. Visitors wore alligator boots and suede cowboy hats, and only one club, then called the Rusty Nail, remained open. Across the road, the old Twilite Inn, an ugly rectangle of concrete blocks, sat empty. It featured a dark brown wooden facade that gave the place the look of a cheap Italian restaurant. Most people drove past without offering a glance, unaware that a small part of America's blues-rock and country music heritage had long ago emerged from the two buildings.

Other than music, McGonigle never had much—a grain elevator, a mobile home park, and a body shop. But the unincorporated town of about

Pianist Denzil "Dumpy" Rice played guitar on a session at Tip Toe
Recording in Cincinnati in 1989. Photo by Randy McNutt.

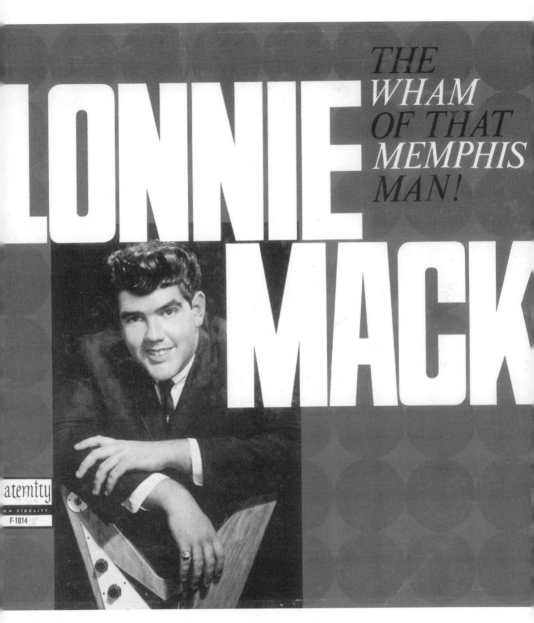

Lonnie Mack's album *The Wham of That Memphis Man!* is an example of the bluesy Cincinnati Sound.

five hundred people didn't need anything fancy; its reputation came from dangerous curves and skin-tight sweaters. In those days, kids called Route 27 the Rock 'n' Roll Highway, but adults knew it as the Highway to Heaven. The narrow road left no margin for drunken mistakes; every night on the way to work, musicians passed a series of white crosses to commemorate the dead. Car crashes added to the illicit lure for kids in my high school in Hamilton, about six miles to the southeast. I never went near the place; my father, despite his love for music, would have blown a transistor. So I settled for McGonigle tales that circulated like Arthurian legends. I ignored the more lurid ones and cut to the point: Did the bands wear matching suits? How many horn players did they bring? Who played the organ? Usually, visitors remembered nothing but the girls' tight sweaters.

Intrigued on a winter's night, I parked my car in the empty lot and imagined the Twilite on a Friday night in 1963. I could almost see the action: hordes of hungry guys in tight jeans and young women with beehive hairdos crammed onto a scuffed oaken dance floor that quaked like a stiff trampoline. In my mind I saw Lonnie Mack and Troy Seals dueling with sleek guitars, some roughneck breaking a chair over a rival's head, and a half-dozen little tube amplifiers blaring so loudly that eardrums and beer bottles cracked. I counted every song that McGonigle's players eventually wrote on their way to Nashville's Music Row, and wondered if the town inspired Seals to write Ronnie Milsap's "Lost in the Fifties Tonight (In the Still of the Night)." I tried to look inside the Twilite, but its windows were boarded, so I drove around town and watched people. The only action was at the convenience store: Million-Dollar Lotto tickets had just gone on sale.

On the other side of the highway, at the Rusty Nail, I noticed a flashing yellow sign: "This week . . . Lonnie Mack!" The roadhouse looked rustic—wooden, faded red, with a gravel parking lot and a cracked telephone booth. Originally named the Blacksmith Shop, it attracted every dance band within 250 miles and served as a regional bastion of instrumental music. Local guitarists received as much attention there as big-name singers. Although instrumentals soon lost favor with Top 40 radio programmers and all but vanished from the airwaves, in McGonigle Lonnie continued to play them—and anything else he pleased.

This time, he transformed the Rusty Nail into a time machine and temporarily revived the old Cincinnati Sound, blues-rock and soul music prevalent in southern Ohio from the 1950s to about 1975. Lonnie helped shape the sound; local bands considered him a spiritual leader. He is a good example of a regional artist who went on to achieve a national following. Inspired by Chicago blues musicians, Lonnie's early bands participated in a musical cross-pollination that impressed teenagers like me, who had never heard of Muddy Waters—or of any other blues players. A few years later, kids my age formed bands and produced their own records, carrying with them the germ of Lonnie's sound and maintaining the original blues influence. A guitar genealogy evolved: Texan Stevie Ray Vaughan absorbed Lonnie's music and eventually produced an album for his hero; and the 1990s blues kids Jonny Lang and Kenny Wayne Shepherd learned from Vaughan's records. But Lonnie does not consider himself a great guitarist or a teacher. "I got style," he once told a reporter, "but it's oversimplified and pretty obvious."

When I opened the front door of the Rusty Nail, a ball of gray smoke rolled into the parking lot. Lonnie stood on the red-carpeted bandstand, his eyes closed, and tuned his red Gibson Flying V guitar. Since I had last seen him, in the 1970s, his beard had turned gray, and he protruded from a red flannel shirt, sleeves rolled up to the elbows. For him this night was like the others: darkness covering darkness, faceless people laughing to themselves and moving in slow motion on a dimly lit dance floor. Lonnie hallooed deeply into a silver microphone, surveyed the young crowd, and twirled the furry animal tail hanging from the neck of his guitar. Drenched in feedback, he boomed, "I was sittin' home in Aurora, Indiana, a few years ago, so broke I was tradin' knives for food. Then one day I went to the mailbox, and there was a royalty check for $18,000. Baby, I've loved them mailboxes ever since." On cue, Denzil "Dumpy" Rice hit the keyboard, and the band played an old Bobby "Blue" Bland number. Dumpy sat hunched over his small electric piano, like he'd been sucker-punched, then Lonnie signaled for a tempo change and the band rollicked with "We Still Play Rock 'n' Roll Like We Used To." Hot licks ricocheted across black vinyl-topped tables, and Lonnie clutched his guitar as tightly as a live fire hose. Every time his popularity has waned, Lonnie has strummed his V a little harder, until it brought him more notoriety and another gig. He refused to join fads in folk rock, surf, psychedelia, bubblegum, progressive rock, disco, and punk, until his music—American roots music—outlasted them all and achieved its own following.

On that night in McGonigle, he seemed vulnerable to only one enemy—time. He stood there wondering whether twenty-one-year-old nightclub customers could relate to 1963. It seemed so long ago that he could hardly remember it himself. The year President Kennedy died. The year the Beatles arrived. The year an unknown Lonnie Mack, already a veteran of the bar wars at twenty-two years old, accidentally bumped into fame with a hit instrumental called "Memphis." It is one of rock's great instrumental singles, and Lonnie Mack is the missing link between late-1950s rockabilly and mid-1960s blues-rock. Other musicians would record instrumental singles, but few would equal the originality and widespread influence of "Memphis."

Today, the Lonnie Mack sound is original roadhouse rock. Dumpy describes it this way: "Loud, full of emotion, and authoritative, because Lonnie is authoritative in his private life and a forceful figure. The man and the music go together." That hasn't changed since music critic Dale Stevens wrote on Lonnie's first album: "His guitar style is low-down, dirty, twangy . . . his approach is basic and sincere, untainted by professional advice and polish." Never mind that Lonnie could not read music, nor that he had no training. As he broadened his playing style, incorporating country elements with blues and rock, he created a forum for 1970s Southern rock and influenced Eric Clapton and the Allman Brothers. Lonnie's first album, *The Wham of That Memphis Man!,* is a touchstone for any rock guitarist worth his picks. The record is a vinyl conduit, sending pure energy from his callused fingertips into listeners' ears. Lonnie glares from the red cover, his black wavy hair slicked back and his dark eyes penetrating like twin lasers.

When "Memphis" broke, I was incarcerated in Garfield High School in Hamilton. I knew nothing about Lonnie Mack. I was too busy trying to pass sophomore Spanish. But when I heard "Memphis" blaring over the cafeteria loudspeaker, I knew I had to buy the record. It sounded unlike anything I had heard. Obviously, this Lonnie Mack was no musical kin to Jan and Dean. We ran around the cafeteria, pretending to strum electric guitars and watching the girls snicker. After "Memphis" and his second hit, "Wham!," came a flurry of Fraternity Records singles, all obscure now. I remember Lonnie's vocals on "Where There's a Will There's a Way" and "Baby What's Wrong." For me, his vocal records became a metaphor for soul music; when I heard them, I finally understood what the term meant. Over time he released more instrumentals, including "Bounce," "Honky Tonk '65," "Lonnie on the Move," "Tension," and "Chicken Pickin'." On one of my Southern trips, I found his most unusual "I Left My Heart in San Francisco," featuring a funky Hammond B-3 organ interplaying with Lonnie's bluesy guitar leads and unlikely big-band horn riffs. At any time I expected Tony Bennett to shout, "Right on, Lonnie!"

He was born Lonnie McIntosh on July 18, 1941, in Harrison, Ohio, and grew up about twenty miles to the south in Aurora, Indiana, an Ohio River town known for severe floods and tough citizens. He was named after Lonnie Glosson, a harmonica man. The McIntosh family enjoyed music.

His father played the banjo, and his mother the guitar. In a home full of gospel and country music, Lonnie's mother taught him to play a $9.95 Lone Ranger model guitar, which became another appendage. (A few years later, younger brother Bill also picked up a guitar, sensing that he would join Lonnie on stage.) At age six, an already confident Lonnie told his mother that one day she would hear him play on the radio. He disliked school, except when he joined his music teacher in playing "Silver Bells" and Gene Autry songs. At thirteen, he dropped out of the sixth grade—after fighting with another teacher—and joined a band led by drummer Hoot Smith. A year later, Lonnie was earning $300 a week—more than most workers in the area's casket and whiskey factories. He played rockabilly, but soon that evolved into a mixture of country and blues riffs that he heard on WCIN, a black radio station in Cincinnati. The more he played, the better he sounded. Bar owners assumed that Lonnie was eighteen, for he already stood five feet, eleven inches and shaved a dark stubble. Armed with a fake I.D. and a strong right hook, he traveled thirty miles east to work in Walt's Barn, a nightclub in Alexandria, Kentucky. There he honed a vocal style influenced by his favorite singers, Bobby Bland and George Jones.

When Lonnie turned fifteen, he drove up Route 27 to McGonigle and asked for a job at the Twilite. The bar owner, Frog Childs, happened to need a new house band.

"What's the name of your band?"

"We don't have a name."

"What's *your* name?"

"Lonnie McIntosh."

"That'll never work. We'll call you Lonnie Mack. How's that?"

"Fine."

"And it's the Twilite, so we'll call you Lonnie Mack and the Twiliters."

By day he played on sessions at the King Records studio for James Brown, Freddy King, and R&B star Hank Ballard. On a session in 1963 his band backed the Charmaines, three girls who recorded for Fraternity Records, Cincinnati's other independent. They finished twenty minutes early. Producer Carl Edmondson told Lonnie to record something for himself, and he cut "Memphis" in one take. "It didn't mean a thing to me," Lonnie said. "I left to go on the road. We hit every roadhouse between Cincinnati and Miami. We had such a tight band. But we didn't have much time to listen to the radio, so I didn't know what was going on. Months later we were in Dayton, Ohio, backin' Chubby Checker one night, and the disc jockeys came runnin' up to me saying, 'You got the No. 1 record at our station!'

They wanted to interview me. I didn't know what they were talkin' about. I thought I'd better get on the phone to Fraternity."

After a slow start, "Memphis" reached the Top 5 on *Billboard*'s pop and R&B charts, sold 500,000 copies, and temporarily pushed the creditors away from Fraternity's door. Suddenly, unexpectedly, the burly kid from Aurora had thrust Fraternity into the national arena again, and owner Harry Carlson never forgot it. Until his death in 1986, he loved Lonnie like a son.

The hit enabled Lonnie to perform anywhere. From Cincinnati's Flamingo Club to the Inner Circle, he worked with top musicians. One night he played for 300 people in Cincinnati, the next night in a Minnesota arena for 17,000. "I did seven nights of one-nighters for seven years," he said. "Had a Cadillac pullin' a trailer. Bought two Cadillacs a year and wore 'em all out. Put several million miles on that trailer. At home in Aurora, I kept seven Harley-Davidsons, one for each day of the week. On Sunday I'd drive the fanciest one, and I'd even wear a suit and tie with it. To me, the '60s were one continuous road run. I performed with just about everybody: Jimi Hendrix, the Everly Brothers, Chuck Berry, Dick and Dee Dee—hey, man, we're talkin' a long time. Eternity."

While Lonnie experimented with the blues and rock and country, the Beatles and other commercial rock bands were changing the music and the record business. The industry became complicated, expensive, self-indulgent. Musician friends scattered. When it seemed that every kid in Cincinnati had formed a rock band and grown his hair long, dancing became secondary to the new, hipper music. Once-popular white soul groups sounded too funky and square. They had difficulty adjusting; to them, the British Invasion meant the Revolutionary War. "Lonnie hated the Beatles," Dumpy recalled. "A lot of musicians didn't care for them because their music was too thin. It didn't have the bottom that we liked."

Lonnie left for Los Angeles after Carlson, recognizing Fraternity's limitations, sold his contract to Elektra Records. He played on the Doors' *Morrison Hotel*. After a stint as an Elektra A&R man, he recorded the first of three albums for the company, *Glad I'm in the Band*. It is pure Lonnie: a blend of soul, gospel, and country—an emotional expression pressed in vinyl. Then he returned to Cincinnati, rounded up Troy Seals and some other old friends, and cut *Whatever's Right*, a collection of blues and country songs that became Lonnie's tribute to the fading Cincinnati Sound. A dozen musicians packed into Jewel Recording in nearby Mount Healthy. "We put seven horn players out in the hall, in the office, in the restroom," said guitarist Rusty York. "When they blew, the whole building shook." The album generated little interest, but by then radio had moved on to other diversions. AM stations, losing ground to hipper FM, had embraced ultra-commercial sounds. New faces arrived, appeared briefly on television screens, then disappeared. Lonnie cut a third album for Elektra, *The Hills of Indiana,* on which he played soft songs and acoustic guitar. A song collaborator, Dan Penn, said the album shows that Lonnie can play the acoustic guitar even better than the electric.

In 1971, Lonnie quit the A&R gig and retreated to Indiana; he went into semi-retirement during the disco years. He turned a Friendship, Indiana, campground into a monthly music stage and barbecued chickens and hogs on an old 275-gallon oil drum. He lost good friends to death, passed on a $100,000 offer to join Neil Young and similar offers for his Flying V, stopped on the road to go fishing, received a bullet in the leg courtesy of a Cincinnati police officer, and waited for another chance. It came in 1985 with *Strike Like Lightning,* an album produced by a fan—Stevie Ray Vaughan. Again, Lonnie left for the road with his precious Flying V, serial No. 7, which he bought for $300 in 1958. It has traveled with him all over the world. No sooner had the album hit than he accidentally broke the V's neck on stage. Gibson rebuilt it using original 1950s wood. "The guitar," Lonnie said, "is more famous than I am. It went through the side of a van one time, in a wreck. It ended up in a field fifty feet away. And it was still in tune."

The V has become a symbol of rock 'n' roll. It and Dumpy Rice, another McGonigle instrumentalist-in-exile, seem Lonnie's only constants. On a break at the Rusty Nail, the old friends sat at a small round table and grinned at each other through a nicotine fog. They are holdouts against commercial excess and veterans of the time when good licks alone could carry a record. No print hype, no music video, no talk-show appearances—not even a vocal. Just expert picking shoved into microgrooves and a musical heritage rooted in country and the blues. The old friends still slide comfortably between genres, forging their own sound with each new gig.

Once there had been five of them on stage at the Twilite and Blacksmith Shop, boys with shotglass wisdom and an ear for melody, but as the more sober notes of factory jobs and mortgages took over, other band members drifted. Averse to the routine of the workaday world, Lonnie and Dumpy continued to play in smoke-filled roadhouses and lonesome honky-tonks. They worked separately at times, but never for long. Just before "Memphis" came out in 1963, Dumpy left for Conway Twitty's band, which traveled 125,000 miles a year. Life away from home upset Dumpy, so he returned to play in Hamilton's Bean Pot and in other clubs he would rather forget. "We worked in some places where, after you hit a note, you glanced up to see if anything was comin' at you," he said. Eventually he reunited with Lonnie, who had received his fifteen minutes of fame. Dumpy missed out on his, but he didn't care. "I have no ambition for personal stardom," he said. "I stay behind the scenes. I don't like pressure or obligations."

In contrast, Lonnie remains a determined, hulking figure, still full of Aurora; Dumpy, a small, disheveled man who is rarely perturbed. Lonnie is a lumberjack swinging a big ax, and Dumpy is a cross between Floyd Cramer and Little Richard. Their musical and personal relationships remind me of some marriages—on and off, but forever.

"Remember the night we met in McGonigle, Dump?" Lonnie asked.

"I don't remember," Dumpy replied, "but I know you fired me after the first month, then rehired me. And one night I went to the drive-in with some chick I never was with before, and I ———"

"There was a lot of them," Lonnie said, laughing.

"No, Lonnie, we went and saw this movie with Bill Haley and the Comets and Chuck Berry. I heard the song 'Memphis,' see, and I loved it, so I ordered Chuck Berry's 45 from Imfeld's Record Shop in Hamilton. Lonnie, you liked that boom, boom, boom so much that you started jammin.' You started doin' 'Memphis' as an instrumental."

Lonnie stared at him incredulously. "No, no, that ain't it, Dumpy. You started playin' it. And one night you didn't come to work, and I had to play guitar on it myself. You were my guitar player then. I usually played bass on it."

Dumpy shook his head knowingly and insisted, "No, you started playin' it."

"You learned it first!" growled Lonnie, with a look that showed the discussion was finished.

Conveniently moving on, they remembered a night in 1958 when, on a break at the Twilite, Lonnie walked across Route 27 to see some rag-tag players on stage at the Blacksmith Shop. He asked Troy Seals to join his band—for more money. Troy accepted, but only if the offer extended to his friend Dumpy, then a mediocre guitarist. Lonnie agreed, but suggested that Dumpy switch to the piano.

"You didn't sound so good," Lonnie said. "But I hired you and I never regretted it. Though I am glad you switched to piano. Besides, I already had a guitar player—me."

"Piano suits me," Dumpy said.

"Yeah, but you won't leave Hamilton long enough to show other people what you can do."

Dumpy sat there and grinned as though he knew a secret.

"We played knock-you-over-in-your-chair music," he said. "But for me, it was rough the first few years. Trial and error—mostly error. Back then, McGonigle was one big happy carryings-on. We actually played to be playin'. The money was secondary. Fifteen dollars a night. If you got twelve dollars, well, fine. You played for the fun of it."

"Yeah, and you used to be the clown, Dumpy, and do backflips and land on your feet," Lonnie said. "We'd march five or six hundred people out of here and down the road and back. You'd bust your tail every time you flipped through the window and hit the dance floor."

"Lonnie, remember the time I came to work in shorts?"

"Remember? One of your trademarks was bein' late, and when the band dressed in matching suits, you'd show up in a T-shirt and jeans."

"Aw, Lonnie, I just came to play."

"And you always tried to steal my women."

"Aw, Lonnie, I never did take any of your women."

Lonnie grunted and tapped a pack of Marlboros on the table. He said Dumpy had a keen eye for the women, sometimes to his detriment. Lonnie recalled a night in the 1960s when his band was backing Jackie DeShannon, and she wore one of those new miniskirts. Dumpy was fascinated.

"Your hair was longer then, and you always kept a cigarette in your mouth and two lighted ones behind your ears," Lonnie told him. "You kept leanin' back farther and farther at the piano, tryin' to get a good look, and pretty soon—BANG! Off your seat, and you set your hair on fire. I guess you really had the hots."

"Aw, Lonnie," Dumpy said, staring at the tabletop in embarrassment.

But Dumpy isn't so easily distracted anymore. He has managed to carve a small career out of instrumental music and songwriting. He estimates that he has played on three hundred albums and countless singles for all kinds of performers. He has stayed alive on long-forgotten country and gospel sessions and the occasional royalty check from his song "There's a Honky-Tonk Angel (Who Will Take Me Back In)," which he co-wrote with Troy Seals. Although Conway Twitty and Elvis Presley both took the song to the Top 10 on the country charts in the 1970s, it did not generate the large royalties that country songs do today. A man can't support himself on one hit anyway, and that's one reason why Dumpy played at the Rusty Nail. The other reason, of course, was Lonnie Mack, the overqualified guitarist who that week returned briefly to his roots, musically and geographically, in yet another respite between fame and obscurity.

Cincinnati: Honky Tonk

Each time I drive into a music town at night, I imagine I'm there to cut a soul record. For this purpose, one city excites me most—Cincinnati. Other towns might have bigger musical reputations, but to me Cincinnati will always mean horn bands and a downtown that lights up the night with the special glow of musicians' souls. By early July, millions of white lights reflect against a blanket of exhaust fumes and humidity, and glass offices hug a darkened sky and the Ohio River's edge. Although the hilly skyline has changed over the years, it still feels much as it did when James Brown and the Famous Flames arrived to record "Please, Please, Please" for King Records in 1956.

Wedged between the North and the South, Cincinnati has held a peculiar geographic and social perspective for two centuries. Steamboats once stopped regularly, picking up bugles and drums made by German immigrant Rudolph Wurlitzer, whose instruments were used, appropriately, by both Union and Confederate soldiers. Runaway slaves avoided the city (and roaming bounty hunters), preferring to cross the Ohio upstream at small towns involved in the Underground Railroad. Soon after the Civil War, black men came to Cincinnati's riverfront to work. Their songs echoed across the landing. In the early 1900s, Appalachians flowed into Cincinnati to work in area paper mills and steel factories. During World War II, Southern blacks joined the migration. Both groups brought their own music and traditions.

By the early 1940s, Cincinnati was a force in radio and the jukebox trade. Powerful WLW (once an incredible 500,000 watts) and WKRC broadcast a variety of live music programs, and influential jukebox operators hustled their own hits. "On Saturdays we'd pick up our 78-rpm records in Cincinnati and load them into a big station wagon, where we'd keep a title-making machine," recalled Lewis Cisle, a veteran juke man. "We'd stay out on the road overnight and crank out title strips at each stop. Towns around here were wide open then. There were jukeboxes in *those houses,* and my job was to go into them with new records. But I felt funny going in. I mean, I had a wife and two children. What if somebody should see me?"

Because Wurlitzer built the popular 1015 model, nicknamed the Bubbler, Cincinnati became a jukebox center at the end of World War II. Jukeboxes respected neither color line nor social register. They turned struggling performers into neighborhood stars. As popular music began to change, splintering off into hillbilly and the blues, small nightclubs popped up across the city, and varied musicians borrowed from one another, pollinating new licks.

In the late 1940s, rough-edged country and R&B discs emerged in record shops across the country. Conservative Cincinnati became an unlikely source for the musical insurrection. Suddenly, tranquil airwaves that had carried the melodies of Como and Sinatra rang with risqué songs called "Sixty Minute Man" and "Annie Had a Baby" and instrumentals called "Honky Tonk (Parts 1 & 2)," "Blues for the Red Boy," and "Pot Likker." They came from Cincinnati's feisty independent, King Records, one of the nation's most important R&B and country labels of the mid-twentieth century. The firm became an odd corner of cultures and races in a town that practiced de facto segregation. As country singers Lloyd "Cowboy" Copas and Hawkshaw Hawkins arrived at King to record more national hits, Bull

Randy McNutt (*left*) and Wayne Perry at a session at Counterpart Creative Studios in Cincinnati, 1971.

James Brown, Soul Brother No. 1, recorded "Cold Sweat" and other hits for King Records of Cincinnati.

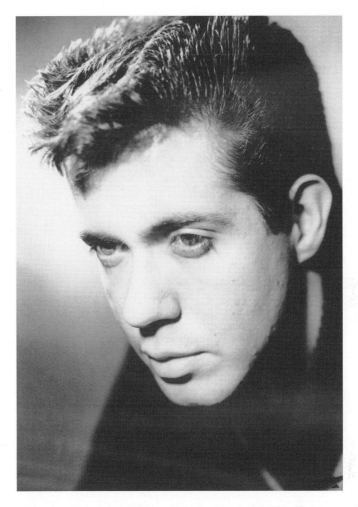

Regional teenage star Dale Wright and the Rock-Its cut "She's Neat" for Fraternity Records of Cincinnati. The record reached No. 38 on *Billboard*'s pop chart in 1958.

The former King Records factory in 1991. Photo by Randy McNutt.

Sydney Nathan, founder of King Records in Cincinnati, started a musical empire on country and the blues in the 1940s.

Harry Carlson, founder of Cincinnati's Fraternity Records, released his first pop hits in the mid-1950s.

Cincinnati guitarist Rusty York stands in the lobby of his Jewel Recording in Mt. Healthy, Ohio, near Cincinnati, in 2001. In 1959 he recorded the rockabilly cult classic "Sugaree" for Chess Records of Chicago. Photo by Randy McNutt.

Rusty York opened Jewel Recording in Mt. Healthy, Ohio, in the early 1960s. It continues to operate. Photo by Randy McNutt.

The Midwestern Hayride was Cincinnati's first country-music television show.
It gained regional popularity by the mid-1950s.

Organist Bill Doggett recorded the hit "Honky Tonk (Pts. 1 & 2)" for King
Records of Cincinnati in 1956.

Moose Jackson, Ivory Joe Hunter, and other blues artists finished their sessions. Black and white studio musicians worked together as King tapped its hometown's steaming vat of blues, R&B, hillbilly, and pop. Local radio stations employed such diverse acts as Andy Williams and his brothers, Fats Waller, Grandpa Jones, and Homer and Jethro. Stations also hired crack hillbilly bands for daily shows and, later, the television show *The Midwestern Hayride*. It turned its twenty-one cast members into regional stars and attracted musicians to area nightclubs.

But gradually the live radio shows faded, and as a result, the city lost its pool of studio musicians. Then radio stopped playing local records, and the independents fell upon tough times. Lacking outlets for their work, talented songwriters, musicians, and producers fled to Nashville. Sadly, by 1970 the local record business had declined. By then, Memphis, Philadelphia, and Detroit overshadowed Cincinnati as soul towns, but James Brown continued to keep an office at King, record in its studio, shop for mod suits at Dino's clothing store, and sit in with bands at the Inner Circle and other nightclubs.

Soul music was only one part of the Cincinnati story. The city once boomed with everything from boogie-woogie piano to yodeling, which I grew up hearing on the radio. In 1950, when I was two years old and Cincinnati still reigned as an important music center, my father dreamed of singing his song. But reality intervened. In the years when hillbilly musicians ran the small roads by car, he laid down his guitar and took up a milk route. The job required a strong back to load wood and metal milk crates and the patience to use an old manual adding machine. While musicians tuned up for gigs on Friday nights, my father sat dutifully at our chrome and gray kitchen table, tapped red and white keys, and pulled the big black crank. His hot licks became the machine's constant clanking; his rhythm, the smooth strokes of his fat yellow pencil. For years our front-porch entertainer worked steadily on the milk route. (There were no convenience stores then; customers entrusted their back-door keys to milkmen.) Yet in the permanence of our family life he yearned for a little impermanence—singing in public. Once, he and his friends had played for tips on Cincinnati street corners, but the war and children and thirty-year mortgages had changed their tunes. To earn additional income, one friend joined the *Hayride*, Cincinnati's first country music television show. Others played on sessions for King, which recorded hillbilly stars Wayne Raney, Hank Penny, and the Delmore Brothers. On Saturday my father would take me down to the *Hayride* set to meet the musicians. If on the street we'd drive past a pedestrian wearing a cowboy hat, my father would say, "Cowboy Copas!" I'd look out the car window and ask, "Where, Dad, where?" After all, I had seen Cowboy's easy smile on television and album covers at my Uncle Bob's house. The discs carried King's silver crown logo and the words "The King of Them All."

King mined Cincinnati nightclubs from 1943, when Sydney Nathan founded the label, until 1971, when its Cincinnati office closed. A visionary, Nathan bypassed independent distributors—and potential trouble—by setting up his own national offices and assembled one of the early studio bands, then consisting of some of the best country players in the business. Many worked in town regularly on radio and television shows. They included Louis Innes, bassist and rhythm guitarist, who also performed on the *Hayride*; Zeke Turner, lead guitarist and a *Hayride* comedic star (with partner Red Turner); Kenneth "Jethro" Burns, the accomplished mandolinist; Tommy Jackson, fiddler; and Jerry Byrd, steel guitarist. Nathan rounded out the band with guitarists Henry "Homer" Haynes, Hank Garland, and Jackie Phelps. These musicians were white and considered country, but Nathan didn't mind mixing his white and black players for various sessions. In fact, blacks were equal at King, even if they could not yet enter Coney Island, the city's old amusement park on the Ohio. Nathan hired talented saxophonist Rufus Gore and promising members of black vocal groups. Henry Glover, a trumpeter in Lucky Millinder's big band, quickly rose to chief producer and writer—and became one of the early black A&R men.

King's session players contributed to the development of the Cincinnati Sound: rock with roots in the blues and country. The Cincinnati Sound's heyday was brief, 1960 to 1975, but it grew swiftly under the influence of blues guitarist Freddy King, James Brown, and Hank Ballard and the Midnighters. Their music blended with the sounds of white rock musicians, who brought along horn sections. Blues-rock spread through area nightclubs and into the King studio, at 1540 Brewster Avenue in the older Evanston neighborhood. The studio turned out hundreds of national chart records, including "Memphis" by Lonnie Mack (Fraternity), "Honky Tonk (Parts 1 & 2)" by Bill Doggett (King), and "Cold Sweat" by James Brown (King).

"Cincinnati had its own sound," said Dale Wright, who sang for Fraternity Records in the 1950s. "A lot of people don't realize that. The Cincinnati Sound is creative—one you still hear all over the world. It's a little jazz, country, soul—a melting pot of music. I think this is because a lot of different kinds of people lived there. Used to be, the city rocked with music in all kinds of clubs. I remember when Cal Collins, the jazz guitarist, played country. Unfortunately, right now the Cincinnati Sound is in a down period."

King Records made many of Cincinnati's hundreds of hits in a nineteenth-century icehouse and molasses factory. Nathan convinced several friends and relatives to invest in his label. It was a crazy notion; few new independents started during the war. Nathan, a gruff man who had once operated a shooting gallery, was short, heavy, bald, and Jewish. He seemed driven by his own demons. When he spoke, he growled; and he ran around the concrete offices in suit and tie and stocking feet. He founded the label while operating a used record store on Central Avenue, in a mixed neighborhood near downtown. At first he knew little about hillbilly and race music, as country and blues were called then, but he learned quickly from his customers. He built a company on what he called "the music of the little people," songs for blacks and Appalachians. He had a new idea: country songs could be blues hits, and vice versa. Nathan also recorded doo-wop, rockabilly, big band, gospel, polka, pop, bluegrass, jazz—any music from which he could make money.

His perseverance—and success against heavy odds—has always intrigued me. I sought out dozens of his artists and employees just to ask them one question: "What was Sydney Nathan really like?" Each person gave a different answer. "His reputation was that of a mean man," the late Jim Wilson, a King promotion man, once told me, "but beneath that exterior was another man who I saw stop in the middle of the road to save a turtle from being smashed by a car. He was a good man. Odd, maybe, but good."

Nathan strung intercom speakers—they gave new meaning to the term "squawk box"—throughout the massive building to talk to employees from his office telephone. "He suffered from emphysema, and used to walk around the plant carrying an oxygen tank and smoking a cigar," said recording engineer Mike Stone, King's quality-control chief in the late 1960s. "Actually, he was a neat guy. There was something bizarre about him. He was one of the few men who could bring all the odd parts of King together. His office was on the second floor, above the pressing plant. He had a barber's chair in his office bathroom. That was his 'think tank.' Well, one day Mr. Nathan was looking out the window when some material became unstable in the pressing plant immediately beneath his office. The force of the explosion shot a big metal object—it was shaped like a missile—up through the floor. We thought it might have killed poor Mr. Nathan. Employees ran for their lives. Total silence in the plant. Suddenly we heard the familiar sound of the intercom clicking on and a gravelly voice booming through the plant and out onto Brewster Avenue: "What in the hell was *that*?"

It would take more than a missile to kill Syd Nathan. He was as hard as a railroad spike and often as blunt. Since the mid-1940s he had worked long hours to build an empire on music that for decades had been ignored—country and the blues. He didn't care what the Queen City bluebloods thought of him, or even his neighbors. With his fancy suits and ties, he must have appeared the perfect businessman to the white world. If only people had known what he did behind closed doors! One night in 1947, he and King executive Howard Kessel signed singer Wynonie "Mr. Blues" Harris to a contract in a New York City hotel room while Harris, clad in pink silk boxer shorts, relaxed in bed with two hot women and a bottle of cold champagne. The record men invited Harris to Ohio. Kessel recalled that when Harris finally arrived at a club in Dayton, the first thing he did was shout, "Everybody, the drinks are on King Records!" Nathan grimaced.

Recording raucous black singers didn't win Nathan many friends among Cincinnati's genteel elite, but then he didn't need their help. He financed his empire's expansion by publishing hit songs such as "Kansas City" and "Finger Poppin' Time," manufacturing millions of discs for custom labels all over the country, and producing dozens of national hits for King and its allied labels.

Among the biggest hits was organist Bill Doggett's "Honky Tonk." It originated at a performance in northern Ohio, when Doggett's combo played some intriguing riffs. Doggett, a Philadelphia native, had once worked for Lucky Millinder's band. He later formed his own blues combo and signed with King. When Doggett's band left their Ohio gig for a New York recording session, the musicians developed the riffs and cut the tracks. King released the song as a two-sided record, parts one and two. Oddly enough, the cherubic-looking Doggett had no organ or piano solo. The bluesy record featured a tenor sax solo by Clifford Scott. Bassist Shep Sheppard and guitarist Billy Butler also helped write the song. Several months later, "Honky Tonk" stormed the pop and R&B charts to become one of the decade's biggest hits, reportedly selling four million copies and influencing musicians in and out of Cincinnati, including young Lonnie Mack.

Although by 1967 King had scored with an occasional hit by an R&B or country act, James Brown was the label's most prolific and consistent star—and the self-proclaimed Soul Brother No. 1. Despite his reputation as the foremost practitioner of black music, Brown appreciated white musicians. He recorded for a white man, hired a white man named Bob Hobgood as his recording director, hired a white promotion chief, and scoured local clubs for white—and black—players.

Brown alone kept the King factory working steadily for years. It became the busiest pressing plant in our region. Once, we planned to ask King to release Wayne Perry's "Mr. Bus Driver," our first record, but we arrived at the company offices too late. I will never forget the night in 1970 when Bob "Mr. Movin'" Patton, a former Hamilton disc jockey who promoted records for Brown, escorted us through the bowels of the gothic factory. Neither Wayne nor I understood the company's cultural significance until we saw a hallway lined with garish album covers representing dozens of country, blues, jazz, bluegrass, and R&B artists, including Brown and the Famous Flames, Earl Bostic, Hawkshaw Hawkins, Hank Ballard and the Midnighters, Freddy King, Little Willie John, the Stanley Brothers, the Five Royales, and Cowboy Copas. To us, that narrow hallway was the Roots Music Hall of Fame. In the shadows that night, record presses loomed like grotesque sculptures and microphone stands like skeletons. The cold factory air heaved inside my lungs. Our leather heels click-clacked on concrete floors, and Patton's deep voice boomed down empty corridors: "Is anybody at home . . . ?" But nobody stirred in the labyrinths and dark offices; King's Cincinnati office was finished. Its 35 x 50-foot studio could have given the world another hit record, but Patton said its eight-track recorder and instruments would go to the new owners' Nashville studio. Standing in the control room—where dozens of hits, including Ballard's original version of "The Twist," were recorded—I could almost hear Doggett playing the Hammond B-3 that sat in a corner. My mind played Copas singing "The Tennessee Waltz" and the Famous Flames blowing hot riffs on "Cold Sweat." Unable to resist temptation, Wayne leaped to the microphone and yelled, "I feel good!"

But Nathan was not the only man who turned out hits in Cincinnati. He had friendly competition from Harry Carlson, a Nebraska native, a former big-band saxophone player, and the owner of Fraternity Records. Unlike Nathan, Carlson had no studio band, no pressing plant—at times not even an office. Carlson, who enjoyed Nathan's company despite their different approaches and personalities, was the antithesis of the hard-bitten independent record company owner. He paid royalties regularly and considered his artists the children that he and his wife had never had. He grew so fond of Dale Wright ("She's Neat") that he special-ordered the young man's dream car, a powder-blue Corvette. Fraternity's roster consisted of an eclectic blend of country, pop (crooner John Gary), rockabilly (cult singers Sparkle Moore and Robin Hood Brians), R&B, and garage-band rock. Regardless of race, Carlson promoted soul men, now obscure guys named

Beau Dollar and the Coins and Albert Washington, who cut Carlson's original blues song "Turn on the Bright Lights."

Carslon came to the record business by way of a split lower lip, which forced him to give up the saxophone and seek work as a clothing salesman in Chicago. In 1933 he moved to Cincinnati and opened a photography studio that catered to the rich. But through the years he preferred to write songs—the novelty "Cincinnati Ding-Dong" and "When I'm Alone" by Nat "King" Cole. He started Fraternity in 1954 to promote a song he had written and recorded, "The Dream Girl of Phi Kappa Alpha," by WLW singer Dick Noel. Encouraged by the response, he continued to release singles on the new label. Nothing happened until early 1956, when club singer Cathy Carr cut "Ivory Tower." Carlson called her to propose the pop song, which he had discovered. He sang it to her on the telephone. She told him, "If it sounds that good with you singing it, it has to be a hit." On the day of Carlson's four-song session at Universal Recording in Chicago, arranger Lew Douglas forgot to write charts for "Ivory Tower." With only fifteen minutes of recording time left, Douglas distributed sheet music to the musicians and recorded the song in one swift take. It went to No. 2 on *Billboard*'s Top 100 and put Fraternity in business.

Working first from his photography studio, and later from a small mahogany desk in his suite-office in the Sheraton-Gibson Hotel on Fountain Square, Carlson would call the nation's top disc jockeys and influential trade magazine editors, who respected him for his intelligence, honesty, and kindness. Once he proposed an unusual deal: "Please listen to 'Memphis.' If you don't like it, Harry Carlson will never pester you again." They knew he meant it. The record was a hit. Yet Carlson didn't understand rock 'n' roll any better than he had before. He preferred big bands, double-breasted navy blue suits, and starched white collars. He and his wife, Louise, slept until noon and earned a living selling mostly 45s. At night the couple sipped martinis from crystal glasses, and Carlson talked on the telephone to record business contacts, sealing deals and careers with each click of his heavy black receiver. To these sophisticated people in their late fifties, "Memphis" might as well been called "Timbuktu," but they trusted Lonnie's talent. They knew the record sounded unlike anything Fraternity had released in its nine-year history. Until "Memphis," disc jockeys recognized the label primarily for its 1950s pop hits—"Ivory Tower," "So Rare" by Jimmy Dorsey, and the novelty rocker "All-American Boy" by Bill Parsons (really Bobby Bare). Carlson's last big hit was "Then You Can Tell Me Goodbye" by the Casinos in 1966. It sold more than 500,000 copies and kept Fraternity afloat until 1975, when

Carlson sold the label name and retired to Florida. He died there in 1986.

I met Carlson—always Mr. Carlson to me—in early 1970, when I wanted to be a record producer and he wanted another hit. Nervously clutching a reel-to-reel tape box, I walked into the downtown hotel, dialed his number, and boldly asked to see him. He told me to come up to his suite, a sparsely furnished place that somehow managed to feel like home. Carlson took my tape and moved slowly to a small, older reel-to-reel recorder on his desk. As he threaded the tape, I noticed his ruddy complexion, the bags under his blue eyes, and the face that drooped like a hound's. Nevertheless, he was a strikingly regal man of about six feet, with a moderately protruding stomach and slicked-down hair that made him look like a refugee from 1955. He held his cigarette for effect, like an actor in an old movie. With that long, expressionless face, I wasn't sure when he was joking until he welled up in laughter.

"Louise, pour the boy a drink," he said.

"Harry!" she scolded. "The boy's too young."

He looked at me, smiled, and winked.

Carlson was like the aging hotel: big, charming, resilient. Like everyone else, I came to love him and his stories. At his zenith, he was offered the presidency of MGM Records, but he rejected the offer because he preferred to live in Cincinnati—and he enjoyed his independence. Although he never did fit the image of a hip record mogul, Carlson was always a shrewd and convincing salesman. He talked like a 45 playing at 33$^1/_3$ rpm, saying to me, "Fabulous, simply fabulous. This record will be No. 1 in America in six weeks." Of course, his records seldom reached that high. "Harry couldn't tell a hit from a flop," Wright said. "He did a lot of things right, though." He befriended people, and they responded to his kindness. "Harry was really tickled when I named my son after him," Lonnie Mack said. "Little Harry Carlson Murphy McIntosh."

Carlson was a character in an era of record-business characters. "He sold masters when he needed money, which was often," said Rusty York, owner of Jewel Recording. "He owed me money for studio time, and offered the master to 'So Rare' as payment. I accepted. Years later, I ran into a guy who claimed he owned the master. We went back and forth about it until I realized Harry had sold the master to different people. He never did say he gave it to me exclusively. I couldn't be mad at him, though. He was just being Harry."

At night Carlson would sit at his small desk, next to a table with the older reel-to-reel recorder on top. He'd carefully thread demo tapes and listen to potential masters, looking as though he were in a trance. Every five minutes he'd say, "Fabulous."

Because I grew up listening to Fraternity hits, I decided to offer Carlson—what a deal!—our first master, "Mr. Bus Driver." The song was written by Wayne Carson Thompson, another writer hero who worked for a small publisher in Springfield, Missouri. We didn't have to look far for a studio band. We hired Wayne's group, the Young Breed, and two horn players who backed James Brown. We recorded our soulful rocker in Cincinnati on a January night when the temperature fell to five degrees below zero. The next morning, I lugged my old mono tape machine into the Mosler office to play our new track for the boss's middle-aged secretary. She provided my first review: "That's nice, honey. Now, where's the purchase orders?"

Carlson liked it much better. He wrote out a purchase order to a pressing plant and signed us to his Buckeye Music Inc. Then one day he called, dejected and determined to drop the project. Somebody named Neal Dover had just entered the bottom of the *Record World* charts with the same song. Carlson couldn't afford to wage an advertising war. But we didn't give up. In 1971, we finally leased our single to Avco-Embassy Records in New York, and I received a check for $2,000. When I showed it to my dad, his jaw dropped. He didn't have that much money in the bank.

Coincidentally, that night Harry Carlson called me at home from the office of his friend Aubrey Mayhew, president of the new Certron Records in Nashville. The men had just signed a contract to record the Casinos. "I haven't forgotten you boys," Carlson told me. "I made a deal for you, too, so your record will come out."

My heart sank. When I broke the news to him, I sensed his embarrassment. "Fabulous," Harry Carlson said. "Simply fabulous."

On a brisk October night in the late 1990s, I arrived at the Music Hall Ballroom in Cincinnati for a concert called "Legends of Cincinnati Rock 'n' Roll." Every two years, the Kiwanis Club sponsors it to raise money for charity and honor local disc jockeys and musicians. I wanted to talk to independent producer Carl Edmondson, who made a number of national and regional hit records in Cincinnati in the 1960s—and in the process influenced my early record-buying habits.

I found Edmondson sitting with some guys from the Casinos. He claimed that he played their hit for a year before they discovered it, but he didn't get around to producing the song for somebody, and the Casinos finally went into the studio with it. Edmondson found plenty of other action, though. Starting as a guitarist with the Emblems, he played R&B at the best gigs in town. At the Guys and Dolls, a major club in northern Kentucky, owner Ben Craft changed the band's name to the Driving Winds in the early 1960s. "All the motels down that way used to fill up with people going to the club," Edmondson said. "They'd pour into the club's huge parking lot and another one at a school a quarter of a mile away. This was at the height of the regional music era. Cincinnati was a dancing town then. Music was booming from all corners of the city. My ears would ring till Tuesday."

When his band cut their first record, "The Thrust," for their own Oh My Records, the guitarist was captivated by the studio. Immediately he knew what he wanted to do—produce records. He believed he was destined to make recordings, for he was a song collector who enjoyed listening to obscure records and demos in hopes of finding gems among the losers. He found a country song, "Sweet Violets," and recorded it with Cincinnati television celebrity Bob Braun. It became a local hit for Fraternity. Harry Carlson arranged a deal with Edmondson—$130 to produce a session, and half the publishing rights on original songs.

"I did the production thing just to mess around," Edmondson said. "Then things started happening locally with the records. I purposely stayed away from the road so that I could produce independently. Cincinnati was a happening place then. King Records was going strong, and Fraternity was coming in with hits, too, and a lot of them were doing well regionally. I think I was helped by playing on the bandstand for so many years. I knew good material. One night I went over at the Olympia Club, where Lonnie Mack was playing, and I heard them do 'Memphis.' I went to Harry Carlson and told him that the song would be a hit; it might sell 50,000 copies. He agreed to let me cut it with Lonnie sometime. Well, I already knew I'd cut an R&B girl group, the Charmaines, over in the King studio soon, and I decided to hire Lonnie on the session so that I could also cut 'Memphis' with him. To get him, though, I had to pay him double session fees and let him bring his band. They were getting ready to break up. He needed the money."

The Charmaines' record never took off nationally, but Mack's did. Edmondson produced three Fraternity chart singles for him, including the hit "Wham!" Then Edmondson helped form a new band, the Dolphins, and wrote "Hey-Da-Da-Dow," a pleasing up-tempo song. The band members each contributed $100 to record it, and Edmondson placed the master with Fraternity. The single reached No. 69 nationally in *Billboard* and became a regional hit for Fraternity. Edmondson couldn't believe what was happening: he was earning a living by producing records, and he didn't even have to leave his hometown.

In 1967 he found "Heart," the B side of a Petula Clark single, which he recorded with the popular 2 of Clubs. Members Linda Parrish, whom Carl later married, and partner Patti Valentine remain vividly in my mind for their hip blonde hairdos, trendy miniskirts, and soaring, soulful voices. (Seeing them at the "Legends" concert—without minis—was not disappointing, either.) The women met at the Guys and Dolls, where they were singing separately. One night in 1964 they decided to sing together. Edmondson thought their pop-rock sound would appeal to record buyers, so he produced "Heart," which echoed down the Ohio to Louisville as a large regional hit. Then the 2 of Clubs recorded "Walk Tall," a Paul Vance and Lee Pockriss song featured in the film *Doctor, You've Got to Be Kidding*. It bounced onto the bottom of the national charts for three weeks but still sold 100,000 copies and solidified the 2 of Clubs as a popular attraction in Ohio, Kentucky, and Indiana.

These days, Edmondson looks back in amazement at what happened in Cincinnati. "You have to give a lot of credit to Harry Carlson and Syd Nathan," he said. "They knew what they were doing. They never ran off to New York or Los Angeles. They were Cincinnati's reigning hit kings, and there couldn't have been two men more different. I'm so lucky to have known and worked with them. Syd, you hear all kinds of stories about him. He could be tough, but he was always a gentleman to me. He took nothing but an idea, found people to invest money in it, and built the label from the bottom up. His studio gave Cincinnati a professional recording outlet. Give Syd credit; he hired top-notch engineers, such as Dave Harrison, who went on to create the MCI console, an industry standard, and Chuck Seitz, who went on to work for RCA in Nashville and earn a Grammy, and Eddie Smith, who went to Bell Studios and became one of the better engineers in New York. Truthfully, when Syd died in 1968, the music died in Cincinnati. The man was sitting on top of the Lois Music catalog, with what—thirty million-sellers? All those country and R&B hits. The Delmore Brothers and James Brown. On the opposite side of things, Harry was always charming; everybody liked him. His label was never as big as Syd's, but it was respected. While Syd did everything himself, from pressing to production, Harry farmed nearly everything out. For years he didn't even have an office. He loved Jimmy Dorsey's music. Harry's high point was signing Dorsey and hitting with 'So Rare' in 1957, when the big bands were on the decline. Harry always could promote. If only there had been somebody in between Harry and Syd. I mean, Harry believed in promotion; Syd, in production. But Harry had a great feel for people. He could call a disc jockey and talk for hours. When 'Memphis' came out, Harry wrote a letter to a San Francisco station and said how sad he was that they had played the record for only two weeks, and that their decision to drop it was the biggest disappointment of his career. The station manager decided to jump on the record after all, just to please Harry! Of course, Harry was a good friend of Bill Gavin, and I'm sure that had a little something to do with it. To this day, I don't know if Harry really liked 'Memphis' and some other stuff I produced for him. If Harry would have had thirty percent more production, and Syd thirty percent more promotion, they both would have been monsters. Harry was unbelievable. He could do about anything, because people loved him so much. Syd, now, he *had* to have a real hit to get airplay, because nobody liked him. What did in Harry was his large number of returns. Had he been more production-oriented, taking more time to make better records, he could have overcome this to a degree."

Edmondson thrived as a producer and song publisher. He was unusual in that he recorded mostly for one label, Fraternity. He produced Braun, Mack, the Dolphins, the 2 of Clubs, Kenny Smith, and other acts. He published and produced Mack's instrumental hit "Wham!," but sold the publishing rights to Syd Nathan for $500. Two decades later, Stevie Ray Vaughan recorded the song.

By the time the disco craze arrived in 1974, Edmondson's production career had already declined, along with Cincinnati's reputation as a hit-making center. By then things had changed, musically and socially. Pop writers no longer adhered strictly to the simple hook-line pattern; Edmondson and the Driving Winds had lost their audience; and the record industry had moved on. Still, the producer continued to record.

"In New York, Los Angeles, and Nashville, they had great studios and other music interests," he said. "Cincinnati has lacked these things. The city didn't do movies and commercials. You've got to have more going for you than recordings. If you don't, you're in trouble when your writers go dry, and that's bound to happen. Chicago had a long run, but finally slipped. Muscle Shoals didn't stay hot. Neither did Memphis. When the hot local labels faltered, that was the end.

"I don't worry about trying to duplicate my success, though. I had a good run. I had a half-dozen national chart records. Some big hits, too. I'm teaching music now, raising a young son, and getting back into music. I'm reviving my publishing company. Publishing is where it's at now. I had my chances to leave Cincinnati, and when I realized I needed to leave, it was too late."

In what seemed another life, I returned to 1540 Brewster to write a magazine story about an unsuccessful effort to turn the former King factory into a museum. Many things had happened since my last visit: "Mr. Bus Driver" was lost on the office shelves in New York; Wayne Perry moved to Nashville and wrote hits for the Backstreet Boys and Lorrie Morgan; I found a newspaper job in Cincinnati and continued to work in the studio; and corporate ownership forever changed the record business. On arrival at King this time, I noticed that a convenience store chain—ironically, the one that had helped put my father's old dairy out of business—now occupied the building as a maintenance headquarters. A twenty-foot plastic cow guarded the parking lot. Inside the plant, the only trace of King was a faded color photograph of James Brown tacked to an office bulletin board, next to a delivery schedule. Pushing deeper, I saw heavy red and blue plastic milk crates everywhere. On the second floor, Nathan's old office was empty. To get there, we had to step over boxes of junk stacked on wooden stairs. The lights didn't work; I felt as if we were spelunking. Slowly we walked to the west side of the plant, where in 1948 Nathan built a concrete-block studio. By then, he claimed that King was the nation's sixth-largest record label. But as competition intensified in the 1950s, King slumped, and Nathan developed heart disease. After his death on March 5, 1968, the company couldn't survive without its founder's vision. The studio became a storage room, and the factory a dilapidated monument to the many hit-making independent labels that had flourished at mid-century. King's closing cost Cincinnati important music history, heritage, and a sense of community—all things my father taught me to appreciate.

Standing in the parking lot that day, I wondered why the King complex lacked a plaque to identify it as a historic site. The longer I stood there, the more songs I remembered. They reminded me of my father, the balding troubadour whose sudden death in 1976 left our house devoid of singing. Staring at the weathered studio walls, I realized that Wayne and I had been every aspiring kid producer in every burg across America, and Cincinnati a microcosm of national talent. Its story is the story of every local music center.

Driving home, I tried to imagine the time when hometown entrepreneurs took chances on talented people in their communities, starting record labels and nightclubs, and local broadcasters played records with no chance of national sales. I tried to understand how so many musicians and singers—black and white, from all over the country—could work together during times of political and social upheaval. Suddenly, I felt hopeful about the future. If they could succeed then, why not now?

Appendix: Selected Hits from Regional Music Centers, 1945–1975

This list of selected hit singles—mostly from the U.S., and a few from England—includes records released in regional music centers, recorded in them, or both. Although additional hits came later, they happened after the regional center had passed its prime. Also listed are selected independent recording studios and labels. Most regional cities had strong independent labels, but some, such as Tyler, Texas, were strictly recording centers.

Atlanta

"Down in the Boondocks," "I Knew You When," and "Cherry Hill Park," Billy Joe Royal
"Games People Play" and "Walk a Mile in My Shoes," Joe South
"Double Shot (of My Baby's Love)," the Swingin' Medallions
"No Love at All," B.J. Thomas
"People World," Jim and Jean
"Spooky," "Traces," "Stormy," and "Everyday with You Girl," the Classics IV
"Tell Me a Lie," Sami Jo
"Moonlight Feels Right," Starbuck
"So into You" and "Imaginary Lover," Atlanta Rhythm Section
"Cool Night" and "'65 Love Affair," Paul Davis

Studios: Master Sound; Studio One; Web IV Recording; Kin-Tel Recording
Labels: 1-2-3; GRC

Bakersfield

"Too Old to Cut the Mustard," Buddy Alan (with Buck Owens)

"My Heart Has a Mind of Its Own" and "Wheel of Fortune," Susan Raye
"The Key's in the Mailbox" and "Lonesome 7-7203," Tony Booth

STUDIOS: BUCK OWENS RECORDING
LABELS: NO LARGE INDEPENDENTS

Baton Rouge

"I'm Leaving It Up to You," "Stop and Think It Over," and "The Loneliest
    Night," Dale and Grace

STUDIOS: NO SIGNIFICANT STUDIOS
LABELS: MONTEL

Birmingham

"I've Been Lonely for So Long," Frederick Knight

STUDIOS: SOUNDS OF BIRMINGHAM
LABELS: NO LARGE INDEPENDENTS

Charlotte

"A Rose and a Baby Ruth," George Hamilton IV
"Sittin' in the Balcony," Johnny Dee
"Girl Watcher," the Okaysions (ABC Records)

STUDIOS: ARTHUR SMITH'S RECORDING
LABELS: COLONIAL RECORDS (CHAPEL HILL)

Chicago

"Maybellene," "School Day," and "Sweet Little Sixteen," Chuck Berry
"The Duke of Earl," Gene Chandler
"Kind of a Drag," the Buckinghams
"Gloria," Shadows of Knight
"Things I'd Like to Say," New Colony Six
"Julia," Ramsey Lewis
"Love Makes a Woman," Barbara Acklin
"Oh, What a Night," the Dells

"Superfly" and "Freddie's Dead," Curtis Mayfield

STUDIOS: CHESS RECORDS STUDIOS; UNIVERSAL RECORDING; STREETER-
VILLE RECORDING; PARAGON RECORDING
LABELS: CHESS; U.S.A.; SENTAR; BRUNSWICK; WOODEN NICKEL; OVATION;
CURTOM

Cincinnati

"Work with Me Annie," "Teardrops on Your Letter," and "Finger Poppin'
Time," Hank Ballard
"Dog House Boogie," "Slow Poke," and "Lonesome 7-7203," Hawkshaw
Hawkins
"Why Don't You Haul Off and Love Me," Wayne Raney
"Daddy-O," Bonnie Lou
"Cold Sweat (Part 1)," "I Got You (I Feel Good)," "It's a Man's Man's Man's
World," "Papa's Got a Brand New Bag," "Please, Please, Please," "I Got the
Feelin'," and "Say It Loud—I'm Black and I'm Proud," James Brown
"Then You Can Tell Me Goodbye," the Casinos
"All American Boy," Bill Parsons (Bobby Bare)
"Memphis," Lonnie Mack
"So Rare," Jimmy Dorsey
"Ivory Tower," Cathy Carr

STUDIOS: KING RECORDS STUDIO; JEWEL RECORDING; COUNTERPART
CREATIVE STUDIOS
LABELS: KING; FRATERNITY; COUNTERPART

Cleveland

"Time Won't Let Me," the Outsiders
"Nobody but Me," Human Beinz
"Closer to Home," Grand Funk Railroad
"Play That Funky Music," Wild Cherry
"The Morning After," Maureen McGovern
"My Pledge of Love," the Joe Jeffrey Group

STUDIOS: CLEVELAND RECORDING; SUMA RECORDING; AUDIO RECORDING
LABELS: CLEVELAND INTERNATIONAL

Clovis, New Mexico

"Party Doll," Buddy Knox
"I'm Sticking with You," Jimmy Bowen and the Rhythm Orchids
"Sugar Shack" and "Bottle of Wine," Jimmy Gilmer and the Fireballs
"That'll Be the Day," "Oh, Boy," and "Maybe Baby," the Crickets
"Peggy Sue," Buddy Holly

STUDIOS: NORMAN PETTY STUDIOS
LABELS: NO LARGE INDEPENDENTS

Dallas

"Do It Again (Just a Little Bit Slower)," Jon and Robin and the In Crowd
"Western Union" and "Sound of Love," the Five Americans
"If You've Got the Money I've Got the Time" and "I Love You a Thousand
  Ways," Lefty Frizzell

STUDIOS: JIM BECK STUDIO; DALLASONIC STUDIOS; CLIFF HERRING SOUND
  (FORT WORTH)
LABELS: ABNAK; POMPEII

Detroit

"Shop Around," "You've Really Got a Hold on Me," and "Mickey's Monkey,"
  the Miracles
"My Girl" and "Since I Lost My Baby," the Temptations
"The One Who Really Loves You," "Two Lovers," and "My Guy," Mary Wells
"Where Did Our Love Go," "Baby Love," and "Stop! In the Name of Love,"
  the Supremes
"Ramblin' Gamblin' Man," Bob Seger System

STUDIOS: MOTOWN RECORDS STUDIO; UNITED RECORDING
LABELS: MOTOWN; FORTUNE; ANNA; THE DETROIT SOUND

Hialeah, Florida

"Get Down Tonight," "That's the Way (I Like It)," and "(Shake, Shake, Shake)
  Your Booty," KC and the Sunshine Band
"Do You Wanna Get Funky with Me?" and "Dance with Me," Peter Brown

"Rock Your Baby," George McCrae

STUDIOS: T.K. STUDIOS; SUNSHINE SOUND
LABELS: T.K. AND SUBSIDIARIES

Houston

"Treat Her Right," Roy Head and the Traits
"I'm So Lonesome I Could Cry," B.J. Thomas
"Funny," Joe Hinton
"Hey, Baby," Bruce Channel
"I'm a Fool to Care," Joe Barry
"The Rains Came" and "She's about a Mover," Sir Douglas Quintet
"Hound Dog," Big Mama Thornton
"Mary Is Fine"/"My Time Is Expensive," Gatemouth Brown

STUDIOS: GOLD STAR; PASADENA SOUND
LABELS: DUKE-PEACOCK; GOLD STAR; CRAZY CAJUN; TRIBE RECORDS

Jackson

"Misty Blue," Dorothy Moore
"Mr. Big Stuff" and "Helping Hand," Jean Knight
"Groove Me," King Floyd
"Ring My Bell," Anita Ward
"Just a Dream," "Venus in Blue Jeans," and "Go, Jimmy, Go," Jimmy Clanton

STUDIOS: MALACO RECORDS STUDIOS; TRUMPET RECORDS STUDIO
LABELS: ACE; MALACO; TRUMPET

Lake Charles, Louisiana

"Sea of Love," Phil Phillips

STUDIOS: GOLDBAND RECORDING
LABELS: FOLK-STAR; GOLDBAND RECORDS

Memphis

"Rocket 88," Jackie Brenston
"Blue Suede Shoes," Carl Perkins

"Whole Lotta Shakin' Goin' On" and "Great Balls of Fire," Jerry Lee Lewis
"I Walk the Line," Johnny Cash
"Tragedy," Thomas Wayne
"Raunchy," Bill Justice
"Mohair Sam," Charlie Rich
"Walkin' the Dog," Rufus Thomas
"Green Onions," Booker T. & the M.G.'s
"Soul Man," Sam and Dave
"Kentucky Rain," "In the Ghetto," and "Suspicious Minds," Elvis Presley
"Keep On Dancing," the Gentrys
"The Letter," "Neon Rainbow," "Cry Like a Baby," and "Soul Deep," the Box
    Tops
"Let's Stay Together," Al Green
"I Just Can't Help Believing" and "Hooked on a Feeling," B.J. Thomas
"You've Lost That Lovin' Feelin'," Dionne Warwick
"Angel of the Morning," Merrilee Rush
"Brother Love's Traveling Salvation Show," "Sweet Caroline (Good Times
    Never Seemed So Good)," and "Holly Holy," Neil Diamond
"Son of a Preacher Man," Dusty Springfield
"Single Girl" and "I Take It Back," Sandy Posey

STUDIOS: ARDENT RECORDING; MEMPHIS RECORDING SERVICE; ROYAL
    RECORDING (HI RECORDS); AMERICAN RECORDING; FERNWOOD
    RECORDS STUDIO; LYN-LOU RECORDING
LABELS: SUN; HI; METEOR; FERNWOOD

Miami

"I Feel Good (I Got You)," James Brown (King Records)
"Rainy Night in Georgia," Brook Benton
"Rumors," Fleetwood Mac
"How Deep Is Your Love?" the Bee Gees
"Too Late to Turn Back Now," "Don't Ever Be Lonely," and "Treat Her Like a
    Lady," Cornelius Brothers and Sister Rose

STUDIOS: CRITERIA STUDIOS; THE MUSIC FACTORY
LABELS: PLATINUM

Minneapolis

"Mule Skinner Blues," the Trashmen
"Six Days on the Road," Dave Dudley
"Liar, Liar," the Castaways
"Don't Try to Lay No Boogie-Woogie (on the King of Rock 'n' Roll)," Crow

STUDIOS: KAY BANK STUDIOS
LABELS: SOMA; GARRETT

Muscle Shoals, Alabama

"Steal Away," Jimmy Hughes
"You Better Move On," Arthur Alexander
"Take a Letter, Maria" and "There's Always Something There to Remind
    Me," R.B. Greaves
"I Never Loved a Man (the Way I Love You)" and "Respect," Aretha Franklin
"Mustang Sally" and "Funky Broadway," Wilson Pickett
"Patches," Clarence Carter
"One Bad Apple," the Osmonds

STUDIOS: MUSCLE SHOALS SOUND STUDIOS; FAME STUDIOS
LABELS: MUSCLE SHOALS SOUND; FAME; TUNE

New Orleans

"Good Rockin' Tonight," Roy Brown
"Lawdy Miss Clawdy," Lloyd Price
"Tutti Frutti" and "Long Tall Sally," Little Richard
"The Fat Man," "Ain't That a Shame," and "Blueberry Hill," Fats Domino
"You Talk Too Much," Joe Jones
"I Like It Like That" and "Land of 1000 Dances," Chris Kenner
"I Know (You Don't Love Me No More)," Barbara George
"Mother-in-Law," Ernie K-Doe
"Chapel of Love," the Dixie Cups
"Ya Ya" and "Working in the Coal Mine," Lee Dorsey
"Sea Cruise," Frankie Ford
"Don't You Just Know It," Huey "Piano" Smith and the Clowns

"I Don't Know Why but I Do" and "You Always Hurt the One You Love,"
  Clarence "Frogman" Henry
"Barefootin'," Robert Parker
"Tell It Like It Is," Aaron Neville

STUDIOS: J&M RECORDING; COSIMO'S RECORDING
LABELS: NOLA; DOVER; MINIT

Norfolk, Virginia

"New Orleans," "Quarter to Three," "School Is Out," "School Is In," "Dear
  Lady Twist," and "Twist, Twist Senora," Gary U.S. Bonds
"If You Wanna Be Happy" and "Twistin' Matilda," Jimmy Soul

STUDIOS: NORFOLK SOUND RECORDING
LABELS: LEGRAND; S.P.Q.R.

Philadelphia

"The Wah-Watusi," "Don't Hang Up," and "South Street," the Orlons
"Wild One" and "Volare," Bobby Rydell
"The Twist," Chubby Checker
"La La Means I Love You," the Delphonics
"Me And Mrs. Jones," Billy Paul
"When Will I See You Again?" the Three Degrees
"The Love I Lost," Harold Melvin and the Blue Notes
"Back Stabbers" and "Love Train," the O'Jays
"Armed and Extremely Dangerous," First Choice
"Expressway to Your Heart," Soul Survivors

STUDIOS: CAMEO RECORDS STUDIOS; SIGMA SOUND STUDIOS; VIRTUE
  RECORDING
LABELS: CAMEO-PARKWAY; CRIMSON; GAMBLE; JAMIE; PHILLY GROOVE;
  TSOP (THE SOUND OF PHILADELPHIA)

Pittsburgh

"Come Go with Me," the Dell Vikings
"Since I Don't Have You" and "This I Swear," the Skyliners
"You're the One" and "Five O'Clock World," the Vogues

"Yesterday's Gone," "A Summer Song," "Willow Weep for Me," and "If You Loved Me," Chad and Jeremy

STUDIOS: GEORGE HYDE RECORDING; GATEWAY RECORDING
LABELS: CO & CE; WORLD ARTISTS; CALICO

St. Louis

"The Cheater," Bob Kuban and the In-Men
"A Fool in Love," Ike and Tina Turner

STUDIOS: TECHNISONIC STUDIOS
LABELS: MUSICLAND

San Francisco

"Suzie Q (Part One)," "Proud Mary," "Bad Moon Rising," "Green River," "Travelin' Band," "Sweet Hitch-Hiker," and "Lookin' Out My Back Door," Creedence Clearwater Revival
"Mendocino," Sir Douglas Quintet
"You Got Me Hummin'," Cold Blood

STUDIOS: WALLY HEIDER STUDIOS; HARRY MCCUNE SOUND SERVICE; GOLDEN STATE RECORDERS; PACIFIC HIGH RECORDERS
LABELS: FANTASY; SAN FRANCISCO

Shreveport

"Sweet Thing," Nat Stuckey
"Judy in Disguise (with Glasses)" and "Hey Hey Bunny," John Fred and His Playboy Band

STUDIOS: NO SIGNIFICANT STUDIOS
LABELS: JEWEL; PAULA; RONN

Tyler, Texas

"Tush," ZZ Top
"Keep On," Bruce Channel

STUDIOS: BRIANS RECORDING STUDIO
LABELS: NO LARGE INDEPENDENTS

Bibliography

1. Hamilton, Ohio

Gross, Mike. "'Backyard Studios: New-Sound Frontier." *Billboard,* April 27, 1968.

Stirling, Sally. "A Hit Record Cut in Hamilton, Ohio?" *Journal-News,* September 2, 1974.

Whitburn, Joel. *Top Pop: 1955–1982.* Menomonee Falls, Wis.: Record Research, 1983.

2. New Orleans

Berry, Jason, Jonathan Foose, and Tad Jones. *Up from the Cradle of Jazz: New Orleans Music since World War II.* New York: Da Capo Press, 1992.

Briltman, Bethany Ewald. *New Orleans.* New York: Fodor's.

Broven, John. *Rhythm and Blues in New Orleans.* Gretna, La.: Pelican Publishing, 1974.

Callahan, Mike. "New Orleans Rock and Roll." *Goldmine,* February 1981.

Collier, James Lincoln. *Louis Armstrong: An American Genius.* New York: Oxford University Press, 1983.

Dawson, Jim, and Steve Propes. *What Was the First Rock 'n' Roll Record?* Boston: Faber and Faber, 1992.

Dr. John (Mac Rebennack). *Under a Hoodoo Moon: The Life of the Night Tripper.* New York: St. Martin's Griffin, 1994.

Griggs, Bill. "Spotlight on New Orleans Featuring Ernie K-Doe." *Rockin' Fifties,* December 1991.

Hannusch, Jeff. *I Hear You Knockin': The Sound of New Orleans Rhythm and Blues.* Ville Platte, La.: Swallow Publications, 1985.

Hughes, Mike. "Little Richard, the Movie." *The Cincinnati Enquirer TV Week,* February 20, 2000.

Jeske, Lee. "Running the Hoodoo Down with Dr. John, in a Sentimental Mood." *Cashbox,* November 11, 1989.

Lichenstein, Grace, and Laura Dankner. *Musical Gumbo.* New York: W.W. Norton, 1993.

McGarvey, Seamus. "Charles Connor: That New Orleans Rhythm Man! Part One." *Now Dig This,* January 1989.

McNutt, Randy. *Too Hot to Handle: An Illustrated Encyclopedia of American Recording Studios of the 20th Century.* Hamilton, Ohio: HHP Books, 2001.

Nager, Larry. *Memphis Beat: The Lives and Times of America's Musical Crossroads.* New York: St. Martin's Press, 1998.

Robinson, Lura. *It's an Old New Orleans Custom.* New York: Bonanza Books, 1963.

Salaam, Kalamu Ya. "Music Legend: Dave Bartholomew." *Offbeat,* June 1990.

White, Charles. *The Life and Times of Little Richard, the Quasar of Rock.* New York: Harmony Books, 1984.

Wolfe, Charles K., and Kip Lornell. *The Life and Legend of Leadbelly.* New York: HarperCollins, 1993.

3. Jackson, Mississippi

Bowman, Rob. *The Last Soul Company.* Malaco Records, 1999.

Callahan, Mike. "New Orleans Rock and Roll." *Goldmine,* February 1981.

Dr. John (Mac Rebennack). *Under a Hoodoo Moon: The Life of the Night Tripper.* New York: St. Martin's Griffin, 1994.

Mabry, Donald. "The Rise and Fall of Ace Records: A Case Study in the Independent Record Business." *Business History Review,* Autumn 1990.

Ryan, Marc. *Trumpet Records: An Illustrated History with Discography.* Milford, N.H.: Big Nickel Press, 1992.

Vera, Billy. *The Best of Ace Records: The R&B Hits.* CD booklet. Rock 'n' Roll/Scotti Brothers Records, 1993.

Whitburn, Joel. *Top R&B Singles, 1955–1988.* Menomonee Falls, Wis.: Record Research, 1983.

4. Thibodaux, Louisiana

Griggs, Bill. "Guitar Slim." *Rockin' Fifties,* October 1991.

———. "Spotlight on New Orleans Featuring Ernie K-Doe." *Rockin' Fifties,* December 1991.

Guitar Slim: The Things that I Used to Do. Liner notes, Specialty Records, 1986.

Hannusch, Jeff. *I Hear You Knockin': The Sound of New Orleans Rhythm and Blues.* Ville Platte, La.: Swallow Publications, 1985.

Mabry, Donald J. "The Rise and Fall of Ace Records: A Case Study in the Independent Record Business." *Business History Review,* Autumn 1990.

Obrecht, James, ed. *Blues Guitar: The Men Who Made the Music.* San Francisco: Miller-Freeman Books, 1993.

Wexler, Jerry. *Guitar Slim: Sufferin' Mind.* CD booklet, Specialty Records, 1991.

5. Shreveport

Abel, Keith E. "Alabama Bound: A Leadbelly Retrospective Part Three." *Bluesville, U.S.A.,* March 1995.

Broven, John. *South to Louisiana: The Music of the Cajun Bayous.* Gretna, La.: Pelican Publishing, 1983.

Burton, Larry. "Legendary Bass Player Has His Day Thursday." *Shreveport Times,* June 14, 1991.

Foster, Mary. "Tillman Franks—He's Country to the Core." *The Fort Wayne Journal Gazette,* August 1, 1999.

Griffin, Bob. "Prime Time: Hayride Has Potential." *Shreveport Journal,* June 26, 1987.

Haig, Diana. *The Jewel/Paula Records Story.* CD booklet, Capricorn Records, 1993.

———. *The Cobra Records Story.* CD booklet, Capricorn Records, 1993.

"Jewel . . . Paula Ronn Catalog." 1995.

Logan, Horace, and Bill Sloan. *Elvis, Hank, and Me: Making Musical History on the Louisiana Hayride.* New York: St. Martin's Press, 1998.

"Music Hayride Turns Fifty." *The Cincinnati Enquirer,* April 5, 1999.

Prime, John Andrew. "Dale Hawkins Is Alive and Well in Little Rock." *One Shot,* Summer 1986.

———. "How the Hayride Fares Only Time, TV Can Tell." *The Times,* n.d.

Rosen, Steven. "John Fred: The Long Career of a One-Hit Wonder." *One Shot,* Fall 1987/Winter 1988.

Sandin, Erik. "Sheriff's Auction May Decide Future of Louisiana Hayride." *Shreveport Journal,* September 8, 1988.

Weill, Gus. *You Are My Sunshine: The Jimmie Davis Story.* Gretna, La.: Pelican Publishing, 1991.

6. Houston

Gart, Galen. *First Pressings: The History of Rhythm & Blues.* Vol. 6: *1956.* Milford, N.H.: Big Nickel Press, 1991.

Gart, Galen, and Roy C. Ames. *Duke/Peacock Records: An Illustrated Discography.* Milford, N.H.: Big Nickel Press, 1990.

Govenar, Alan. *Meeting the Blues: The Rise of the Texas Sound.* Dallas: Taylor Publishing Co., 1998.

Treat Her Right: The Best of Roy Head. CD booklet, Varese Sarabande Records, 1995.

7. Memphis

Barrera, Sandra. "Pompadours and Circumstance." *Los Angeles Daily News,* September 25, 2000.

Escott, Colin, with Martin Hawkins. *Good Rockin' Tonight: Sun Records and the Birth of Rock 'n' Roll.* New York: St. Martin's Press, 1991.

Leigh, Spencer. "Dan Penn and Spooner Oldham." *Country Music People,* January 2000.

McClain, Larry. "Allen Reynolds: One of the 'Four Runners' of Jack's Tracks." *Country Chart Analyst,* August 1990.

Patterson, Jim. "Crystal Gayle Sings Hoagy Carmichael." The Associated Press, February 9, 2000.

Williams, Bill. "The Memphis Sound: Home of Blues and Soul." *Billboard,* March 29, 1969.

8. Memphis Redux

Bowman, Rob. *Soulsville, U.S.A.* New York: Schirmer Books, 1997.

Cain, Robert. *Whole Lotta Shakin' Goin' On.* New York: The Dial Press, 1981.

Dawson, Jim, and Steve Propes. *What Was the First Rock 'n' Roll Record?* New York: Faber & Faber, 1992.

Dickerson, James. *Goin' Back to Memphis: A Century of Blues, Rock 'n' Roll, and Glorious Soul.* New York: Schirmer, 1996.

Escott, Colin, with Martin Hawkins. *Good Rockin' Tonight.* New York: St. Martin's Press, 1991.

Gordon, Gregg. *Dewey Phillips: Red, Hot & Blue.* CD booklet, Memphis Music Archives, 1995.

Gray, Michael, and Roger Osborne. *The Elvis Atlas: A Journey through Elvis Presley's America.* New York: Henry Holt, 1996.

Guralnick, Peter. *Last Train to Memphis: The Rise of Elvis Presley.* New York: Little, Brown, 1994.

McNutt, Randy. *Too Hot to Handle: An Illustrated Encyclopedia of American Recording Studios of the 20th Century.* Hamilton, Ohio: HHP Books, 2001.

———. *We Wanna Boogie: An Illustrated History of the American Rockabilly Movement.* Hamilton, Ohio: HHP Books, 1989.

Morse, Steve. "Sun Rhythm." *Boston Globe,* February 4, 1987.

Nix, Don. *Road Stories and Recipes.* New York: Schirmer, 1996.

Perkins, Carl, and David McGee. *Go, Cat, Go.* New York: Hyperion, 1996.

Point, Michael. "Sun Rhythm Section Gets Together to Make Music Shine." *American-Statesman,* n.d.

"Sun Rhythm Section: Pioneers of Rock 'n' Roll." Group promotion sheet, 1989.

Travis, Dave. *Fernwood Rockabillies.* CD booklet, Stomper Records, 1998.

"William Bell, Keepin' Busy." *Soul Sounds,* May 11, 1969.

9. Muscle Shoals

Barnett, Margie. "FAME Studio's Rick Hall Remembers When." *Record World,* May 19, 1979.

Campbell, Walter, and Sam Sutherland. "MSS Ensemble: 13 Years of Enthusiasm and Success." *Record World,* May 19, 1979.

Hinckley, David. "Re-emergence of Song Finds Sledge Neglected." *The Cincinnati Enquirer,* June 1, 1994.

Osmond, Donny, and Patricia Romanowski. *Life Is Just What You Make It.* New York: Hyperion Books, 1999.

Pace, Terry, and Robert Palmer. "Rhythm of the River." *The Times Daily,* n.d.

Poe, Randy. *The Muscle Shoals Sound.* CD booklet, Rhino Records, 1993.

"Time Machine." *Mojo,* February 1996.

Wessel, John. "Muscle Shoals Heritage Is Music and More Music." *The Huntsville Times,* December 14, 1999.

Wexler, Jerry. Liner notes to Tony Orlando self-titled album, 1978.

Whitman, Arthur. "The Big News." *South,* April 19, 1970.

Whitman, Victor. "Music Pioneers Gather to Tell of Muscle Shoals Scene." *Times Daily,* November 14, 1999.
Williams, Bill. "Music in Muscle Shoals: People Come Here to Work." *Billboard,* December 5, 1970.

10. Norfolk, Virginia

Cullinan, James F. "The Quarter Till Three Story." *The Norfolk Echo,* Summer 1991.
Guida, Frank. *Gary U.S. Bonds: Twist Up Calypso.* Liner notes, Legrand LP 3002: Twist Up Calypso.
Holloway, Lin. "Norfolk's No. 3 World Wonder is 'The Sound.'" *Norfolk Journal and Guide,* May 18, 1963.
Hurwitz, Sol. "Historic Norfolk, Va., Blooms with Arts." *The Cincinnati Enquirer,* April 12, 1998.
If You Wanna Be Happy: The Best of the Norfolk Sound. CD booklet, Varese Sarabande, 1999.
Kemme, Steve. "Jimmy Soul Couldn't Be Happy." *One Shot,* Fall 1991.
Walsh, Brian. "The Calypso Connection." *The Norfolk Echo,* Spring 1990.

11. Bakersfield

Grossi, Mark. "A Sound Born in Bakersfield." *The Bakersfield Californian,* August 10, 1981.
Haslam, Gerald. *The Other California: The Great Central Valley in Life and Letters.* Reno: University of Nevada Press, 1994.
Hunter, Glenn. "The Bakersfield Sound." *Westways,* July 1979.
Jacks, Jamie. "B.A.D. Bars." *The Bakersfield Californian,* July 21, 1989.
Knight, Kay. "Buck Owens: Still the Same Ole Buckaroo." Publication unknown. December 2, 1989.
McNutt, Randy. *Too Hot to Handle: An Illustrated Encyclopedia of American Recording Studios of the 20th Century.* Hamilton, Ohio: HHP Books, 2001.
Pace, Robert. "The Blackboard." *The Bakersfield Californian,* n.d.
Price, Robert. "Everyone's Favorite Cousin Didn't Have Much Talent—Unless Making Folks Smile Counts." *The Bakersfield Californian,* June 29, 1997.
Sheehan, Dale. "Gene Moles: Guitar Man." *Country Star News,* May 1978.
Woods, Bill. "Our Favorite Red-Head, Red Simpson." *Country Star News,* April 1976.

12. McGonigle, Ohio

Balfour, Brad. "Lonnie Mack: His Pride and His Guitar Are Back." *The Cincinnati Post,* November 19, 1977.
Best, Kenneth. "Legendary Guitarist Lonnie Mack Still Plays from the Guts." *The Stamford Advocate,* April 6, 1990.
Campbell, Mary. "Lonnie Mack Thinks It's His Time Again." Associated Press, August 21, 1985.
Forte, Dan. "That 'Memphis' Man Is Back." *Guitar Player,* March 1978.

Gettleman, Parry. "Guitar Hero Lonnie Mack a Tristate Legend." *The Cincinnati Enquirer,* July 25, 1993.

Guralnick, Peter. "Lonnie Mack: Fiery Rock Picker Goes Country." *Country Music,* n.d.

McNutt, Randy. "Mack's Back." *The Cincinnati Enquirer,* January 7, 1983.

———. "Dumpy." *Ohio Magazine,* January 1984.

Nager, Larry. "Comeback for Mack." *The Cincinnati Post,* April 18, 1985.

13. Cincinnati

Brown, James, and Bruce Tucker. *James Brown: The Godfather of Soul.* New York: Macmillan, 1986.

Carlson, Harry. "Portraits and Music Interest Harry Carlson—the Story of 'So Rare.'" *The Cincinnati Enquirer,* September 20, 1959.

Gillett, Charlie. *The Sound of the City: The Rise of Rock and Roll.* New York: Pantheon Books, 1983.

Hoffman, Steve. "In Search of Lost Hayriders." *The Cincinnati Enquirer,* April 30, 1978.

Kennedy, Rick, and Randy McNutt. *Little Labels—Big Sound: Small Record Companies and the Rise of American Music.* Bloomington: Indiana University Press, 1999.

"King-Federal-Deluxe Catalog." 1959.

McElfresh, Tom. "Carlson's Fraternity." *The Cincinnati Enquirer,* February 7, 1971.

McNutt, Randy. "A Spinner of Dreams Remembered." *The Cincinnati Enquirer,* March 22, 1986.

Ramey, Jack. "Jukebox Operator." *The Cincinnati Enquirer,* February 6, 1949.

Appendix

Link, Geoffrey. "San Francisco Today: Groups Seek $ Not Love." *Billboard,* November 29, 1969.

McNutt, Randy. *Too Hot to Handle: An Illustrated Encyclopedia of American Recording Studios of the 20th Century.* Hamilton, Ohio: HHP Books, 2001.

"Spotlight on Atlanta." *Billboard,* August 8, 1970.

Whitburn, Joel. *Top Country Singles, 1944–1988.* Menomonee Falls, Wis.: Record Research, 1989.

———. *Top Pop, 1955–1982.* Menomonee Falls, Wis.: Record Research, 1983.

———. *Top R&B Singles, 1942–1988.* Menomonee Falls, Wis.: Record Research, 1989.

Williams, Bill. "Chicago Gains as Studio Center." *Billboard,* April 16, 1975.

———. "The Memphis Sound: Home of Blues and Soul." *Billboard,* March 29, 1969.

———. "Music in Muscle Shoals: 'People Come Here to Work.'" *Billboard,* December 5, 1970.

INDEX

Index

Randy McNutt is an award-winning newspaper and magazine journalist, freelance writer, and independent record producer, and the author of *Little Labels—Big Sound: Small Record Companies and the Rise of American Music* (with Rick Kennedy, published by Indiana University Press). He can be reached at randymcnutt.com.